PREPARING
FOR THE FUTURE

PREPARING
FOR THE FUTURE

Strategic Planning in the U.S. Air Force

Michael Barzelay

Colin Campbell

BROOKINGS INSTITUTION PRESS
Washington, D.C.

ABOUT BROOKINGS

The Brookings Institution is a private nonprofit organization devoted to research, education, and publication on important issues of domestic and foreign policy. Its principal purpose is to bring knowledge to bear on current and emerging policy problems. The Institution maintains a position of neutrality on issues of public policy. Interpretations or conclusions in Brookings publications should be understood to be solely those of the authors.

Library of Congress Cataloging-in-Publication data
Barzelay, Michael.
  Preparing for the future : strategic planning in the U.S. Air Force /
Michael Barzelay and Colin Campbell.
       p.   cm.
Includes bibliographical references and index.
  ISBN 0-8157-0844-0 (cloth : alk. paper)—
  ISBN 0-8157-0845-9 (pbk. : alk. paper)
  1. Military planning—United States. 2. United States. Air
Force—Reorganization. 3. Strategic planning—United States.
I. Campbell, Colin, 1943– II. Title.
  UG633.B37 2003
  358.4'03'0973—dc21   2003011345

9 8 7 6 5 4 3 2 1

The paper used in this publication meets minimum requirements of the American
National Standard for Information Sciences—Permanence of Paper for
Printed Library Materials: ANSI Z39.48-1992.

Typeset in Sabon

Composition by OSP
Arlington, Virginia

Printed by R. R. Donnelley
Harrisonburg, Virginia

To our wives
Catherine Moukheibir
and
Moya J. Langtry

Contents

Preface

Insofar as the story recounted in this book begins at a specific moment, it is when Gen. Ronald Fogleman, the Air Force Chief of Staff, decided to embark on a major effort to reconsider the organization's strategic vision. In 1995, Fogleman challenged handpicked military and foreign affairs intellectuals, along with a group of emerging senior leaders, to prepare an extraordinary five-day conference attended by every four-star general in the service and their civilian equivalents. Preparing for what became a legendary Corona conference boiled down to answering two questions: how might the Air Force contribute to accomplishing national security goals twenty-five years or more in the future, and what steps should be taken nearer to the present in order to make such a contribution? In laying down this charter, General Fogleman challenged the institution to design and improvise a radically different approach to strategic planning than it had known. The Air Force met the challenge. By the time Fogleman retired in 1997, the senior leadership had gone public with an internally supported strategic vision, and it had come to agreement on the outlines of a long-range plan for developing its capacity to contribute to national security goals. The interplay between Fogleman and his followers was a seminal step in developing a novel managerial practice in government, which we call the preparing-for-the-future approach.

Every major research project has its own story. The story of this book begins in March 1997, about five months after the pivotal Corona conference and two months after Fogleman reorganized the Air Force headquarters with a view to institutionalizing strategic planning. The reorganization established a new directorate for strategic planning under a new deputy chief of staff role. On settling into his assignment, the first Deputy Chief of Staff for Plans and Programs, Lt. Gen. Lawrence P. Farrell Jr., decided to seek an outside perspective on the process and products of the strategic visioning and long-range planning effort that was winding down. The Strategic Planning Directorate engaged two teams of experts, including Synergy, Inc. One of the authors of this book (Barzelay) was invited to join the intensive six-week effort led by Dr. Terrence Colvin, chairman of Synergy, Inc.

After the effort was complete, Barzelay mentioned to Farrell that the Air Force experience would definitely merit a case study and perhaps one day a book. From the vantage point of mid-1997, the prospects for a continuation of long-range strategic planning beyond the Fogleman era were highly uncertain. As Barzelay wanted to write a book about strategic planning, rather than a case study of a talented executive, the idea was kept on the back burner. One year later, however, Fogleman retired unexpectedly, and his successor, General Michael Ryan, soon created a climate in which strategic planning efforts continued with great vitality. The idea of a book-length case study moved to the front burner.

With Farrell's support, the Strategic Planning Directorate, led by Maj. Gen. David McIlvoy and Dr. Clark Murdock, made arrangements in 1998 to fund the interview and archival research that ultimately led to this book. A contract was awarded to Synergy, Inc. Campbell, who at the time was University Professor of Public Policy at Georgetown University, joined the project as a coauthor. As a long-time researcher of governmentwide strategic planning, Campbell welcomed the opportunity to pursue his scholarly interest through an intense examination of preparing for the future in a government department. The Air Force allowed us unfettered access to its leaders, including General Fogleman, General Ryan, and Secretary F. Whitten Peters. Significantly, no provision was made for official Air Force review of the book manuscript, although it was agreed that it would be good practice for a professional staff historian to read and comment on it.

Interviewing for this project began in 1998, with the formal support of the Strategic Planning Directorate. At this stage, Dr. Colvin volunteered his time to share with us his deep understanding of both the Air Force as an institution and the substantive issues with which its strategic planning was concerned. He participated fully in the first round of interviews. Along the way, he helped us identify issues that we otherwise might have missed owing to a lack of direct acquaintance with the Air Force culture.

In the midst of the interview process, we learned that the Air Force leadership would formally revisit the Fogleman-era strategic vision in 1999, following a similar process as before. Thanks to this move, the Air Force conveniently made it possible for us to pursue a study with a pair of cases— a rare opportunity in a project such as this book. The comparison between the Fogleman and Ryan-Peters rounds functioned as a pivotal point in our attempt to understand how process and context influence the outcome of efforts to define strategic intent in a governmental organization.

In the interview process, we met respondents in active service and retirement. Within the Air Force, respondents were selected from Air Force headquarters, Air Combat Command, Air Education and Training Command, Air Force Materiel Command, Air Force Space Command, and Air Mobility Command. Additional interviews were conducted with strategically placed observers of the Air Force in the Washington community. The final interviews were conducted in mid-2001, before the September 11 attacks and the subsequent military conflicts. A brief methodological appendix is provided at the end of this book.

Case studies, in the words of political scientist Charles Ragin, result from a dialogue between theoretical interests and case evidence. In this instance, our theoretical interests differed almost as much as they converged. The case experience was sufficiently rich to accommodate the diversity. We therefore present case-based discussions of political-bureaucratic relations, linkages between planning and budgeting, the dynamics of organizational and technological innovation, and smart practices analysis of the strategic visioning function. In all these respects, our aim is to offer an instrumental case study that provides insight into important general questions about public management and executive governance.

In completing the manuscript, Michael Barzelay benefited from opportunities to present seminars on the book at the American University of Beirut, the Centre for Analysis and Regulation of Risk at the London School of Economics, the Imperial College Management School, the Luiz Eduardo Magalhães Foundation (Salvador, Brazil), the National School of Public Administration (Brasília), the School of Integrated Prevention and Security (Barcelona), the University of Michigan, and the Yale School of Management. Colin Campbell presented preliminary results at the National Defense University, the University of Oklahoma, and the University of Melbourne and also derived great benefit from his tenure as a guest scholar at the Brookings Institution during the first phases of this study.

We wish to acknowledge helpful comments on drafts of the book from numerous colleagues, especially Joel D. Aberbach, Mark A. Abramson, Alberto Asquer, Marshall Bailey, Eugene Bardach, John Bryson, Terrence Colvin, Anne Corbett, Graham Corbett, Robert Denhardt, Martha Feldman, Francisco Gaetani, Gerry Gingrich, Rafael Gomez, Christopher Hood, Larry Jones, Donald Kettl, Tom Mahler, James G. March, Donald Moynihan, Nancy Roberts, Jonathan Rosenhead, Martin Shubik, Rogers Smith, Fred Thompson, Juan Carlos Cortázar Velarde, Patrick Wolf, and anonymous referees appointed by the Brookings Institution Press. Nancy Farley, Campbell's assistant while he was at Georgetown, ringmastered the arduous process of transcribing interviews. In addition, we received valuable editorial advice from Dr. Helen Perry during many stages of the drafting process. Nancy Davidson, former acquisitions editor at the Brookings Institution, and her successor, Christopher Kelaher, gave us immense encouragement as we developed this book. Jennifer Hoover performed superbly as the Brookings copy editor for this project.

Individuals associated with the Air Force were equally generous with commenting on particular chapters, including Maj. Gen. Ronald Bath, Lt. Gen. Lawrence P. Farrell Jr. (Ret.), Maj. Gen. Michael Hamel, Maj. Gen. Charles Link (Ret.), Lt. Col. Paul McVinney (Ret.), Gen. Thomas Moorman (Ret.), Dr. Wayne Thompson (Air Force Historian's Office), and Lt. Gen. Joseph Wehrle. Two individuals—Gen. John W. Handy and James B. Engle—were kind enough to review multiple drafts of most of the chapters, provide detailed comments, and encourage us to go forward. We would like to thank them all immensely.

PREPARING
FOR THE
FUTURE

CHAPTER 1

Visioning, Strategic Planning, and Corporate Evolution

Since the mid-1990s, the United States Air Force has systematically engaged in a range of activities intended to shape its strategic planning to reflect its envisioned future. Two long-range planning processes stemmed from these activities. The most salient outputs of the first of these exercises included a 1996 vision document entitled *Global Engagement* and a 1997 Long-Range Plan, which outlined in detail the future Air Force envisioned for 2025. These documents communicated commitments on the part of the Air Force's senior leaders toward their service's emerging institutional identity and intended future technological capabilities. Together they specified the broad contours of thoroughgoing adjustment of the Air Force's strategic intent.

Soon after the first exercises were completed, nagging doubts arose that long-range visioning and planning would have little effect on the Air Force's actual matching of resources to programmatic commitments. These reservations subsided considerably, however, when the focus on visioning and planning survived the transition in leadership from Air Force Chief of Staff Gen. Ronald Fogleman—the program's initial champion—to his successor, Gen. Michael Ryan. In the fall of 1998, General Ryan launched a second complete strategic review that resulted in the publication of the vision document *Global Vigilance, Reach, and Power* in June 2000. The U.S. Air Force has thus twice deployed considerable efforts toward corporate strategic planning within a six-year period. By so doing, it appears to have

1

established robust visioning and planning as the basis for a stable, if evolving, pattern of decisionmaking. The Air Force has produced two successive waves of corporate strategic planning, both of which were exceptionally intense and sustained.

The long-range planning activities pursued since the mid-1990s represent a departure from the Air Force's routines for visioning and planning in two major respects. First, earlier planning usually focused on the development of technical systems, mostly connected with military operational issues and research and development, and downplayed other dimensions of the organization's technological capability, such as human knowledge and skills, managerial systems, and norms and values.[1] Second, the recent long-range planning activities have opened up issues that were previously regarded as settled matters, in particular whether the core technological capability of the Air Force should continue to be the application of military force by land-based fixed-wing aircraft flown by Air Force pilots.[2] Raising this question brought into open discussion what some participants called gut issues. These struck at the heart of how the Air Force defines itself and its core activities, and they prompted myriad questions associated with long-range adaptation to new opportunities and challenges.

A central facet of these gut issues was whether the Air Force would be abandoning its birthright if it broadened its core technological capability to include greater use of unmanned aerial vehicles (UAVs) or space-based platforms for weapons and command-and-control systems. Taking the focus off the application of military force by fixed-wing piloted aircraft could conceivably intensify interservice rivalries over what has been the Air Force's turf since 1947. It might also weaken conventional arguments for maintaining four military services, including the Air Force, if space emerges as a separate domain of national defense.

Just as a shift in core technological capabilities could unsettle the division of labor among military services, so too could it upset the status quo within the Air Force itself. Since its creation, the Air Force has construed its core technological capability as applying military force using aircraft flown by highly trained pilots selected from the crème de la crème of a large pool of prospective candidates. The resulting bias toward aeronautical acuity reached the highest ranks in the service, such that few "nonrated" airmen become generals, much less gain four stars. Even among pilots, a pecking order operates on the basis of the type of aircraft flown. This reflects the old saw that brain surgeons are the fighter pilots of medicine. That is, pilots who fly fighter jets advance to the upper echelons of the Air Force's leadership much more frequently than do those who fly bombers or transports. In light of these realities, redefining the core technological capabilities of the Air Force could easily transform career expectations and the internal power structure of the institution.

After deliberating on these matters in the initial round under General Fogleman's guidance, senior leaders agreed to alter the Air Force's technological capabilities. The ratification of this commitment took the form of a "vision" entitled *Global Engagement*. The document identified an array of core competencies, namely, air and space superiority, global attack, rapid global mobility, precision engagement, information superiority, and agile combat support. It also directly addressed the question of institutional identity: specifically, the document stated the intention to become an Air and Space Force en route to becoming a Space and Air Force.

The subsequent visioning process under General Ryan wrestled with three persistent issues: how to go about reconfiguring programmatic commitments and resources to coincide with intent; how to garner the resources for future programs while keeping personnel and equipment from breaking down as a result of the punishing tempo of activity necessary to meet demand for real-world operations; and whether the terminology of space and air, whatever the order of the words, simply perpetuates separatist views of the two domains.

The sections that follow in this chapter introduce five issues of central importance to this book. Does the Air Force approach to corporate strategic planning since the mid-1990s constitute a dramatic departure from previous efforts? To what degree did the Air Force investment stem from organizational characteristics peculiar to the culture of "bluesuiters"? Granted that other agencies might want to undertake a similar process, what might the case tell us about attempts at innovation in the seriously constricting framework of the U.S. policy arena? How do an agency's leaders go about expanding the horizons for strategic planning to encompass visioning? Finally, once an agency has stretched its planning ambitions toward futuristic projection, what are the steps for implementing strategic visioning in such a way that it actually brings about significant innovation within an organization?

The Degree of Departure from Previous Approaches

Corporate strategic planning, as pursued by the Air Force since the mid-1990s, fits broadly within the spectrum of executive entrepreneurship.[3] It emerged at a time in which leaders in government agencies—both political appointees and career officials—had come under the influence of a spirit of reinvention. This movement, which originated in the private sector and was expanded to encompass public service management, sought to foster organizational excellence by encouraging innovation.[4] It received exceptionally strong backing during the Clinton administration through the leadership of the vice president, Al Gore. He masterminded and guided the National Performance Review (NPR) that became the umbrella for the administrative reform movement in the federal government.[5]

Notwithstanding its kinship with the reinvention movement, the Air Force approach clearly went beyond entrepreneurship in a strictly managerial sense. Joel D. Aberbach and Bert A. Rockman assert that NPR focused on efficiency to the almost total exclusion of questions regarding programmatic effectiveness.[6] The distinction boils down to whether government entrepreneurship is limited to producing better goods and services more cheaply or whether it should consider how such goods and services contribute to public goals such as national security. The Air Force woke up one morning in the mid-1990s to the realization that it maintained a lot of programs that contributed little to national security, that things would get worse unless it dramatically shifted resources from activities with poor marginal utility to those showing great promise, and that in any case, it needed a bigger share of the federal budget to fulfill its growing obligations toward national security. This realization led to a process of reinvention that exploded the boundaries of managerial entrepreneurship and took the form of a very robust variant of policy entrepreneurship.[7]

Some readers might find themselves conjecturing that this book seeks primarily to tell the story of policy entrepreneurship on the part of General Fogleman and, perhaps, General Ryan. To be sure, General Fogleman led the ranks in the innovative movement of the mid-1990s. As chief, he enjoyed an excellent position from which to refine and advocate his view of the future. General Ryan is less a futurist by temperament than Fogleman, but he still considered the process of adaptation initiated by Fogleman as a key Air Force commitment. When he took over as chief of staff, he made a point of stating that he—along with the other four-star generals—had embraced the visioning process that resulted in the Air Force's new vision of its future. However, styling this case study as an examination of individual entrepreneurship—Fogleman's and Ryan's—would miss the point.

The case represents an instance in which an initiative pressed forcefully by a key player took on an organizational reality that transcended the vagaries of personalities. One well-placed and highly regarded respondent whom we interviewed maintains that survival of strategic visioning through the Ryan years provides prima facie evidence of institutionalization on the grounds that "two points define a line."[8] That statement might seem a bit facile, but we provide abundant evidence in this book that the Air Force's approach to strategic planning embodies a cultural shift that bespeaks a commitment to vision-based organizational entrepreneurship, rather than just compliance with an order handed down by the person filling the top job at the time.

The Fogleman-led visioning process that culminated in the fall 1996 Corona conference—a session of the tri-annual meeting of all Air Force four-star generals—was based on having first conceptualized important questions of identity and technological capabilities. The process of strategic planning began with the identification of issues. The explicit subject matter even at this early stage was the future of the Air Force, not the future of its technical systems, which stood in marked contrast to past planning efforts. That the focus concerned broad service capabilities rather than narrow technical systems became clear when the sixteen issues were released: they included contentious and potentially intractable matters such as integrating air and space, future space operations, battle management and command-and-control operations, unmanned aerial vehicles, and career patterns. With respect to the latter issue, for example, the 1997 Long-Range Plan affirmed that in the future, "any military or civilian member experienced in the employment and doctrine of air and space power will be considered an operator," whereas previously only pilots were considered "operators" and all others "support."

Strictly speaking, the outcome of the Fogleman strategy-formulation process was a declaration of intent, rather than a plan. The 1997 Long-Range Plan defined the desired future in terms of forty-two "end states" to be attained within the time frame of the 2000–25 planning horizon. For instance, integrating air and space involved four end states: education and training in exploitation of air and space assets in an integrated manner, organization of the Air Force for integrated operations, harmonizing air and space assets in a seamless manner, and establishing the Air Force as the leader in stewardship of the space domain. The Long-Range Plan stopped short, however, of specifying the exact paths for reaching these end states.

Clark Murdock, a key civilian player in the planning process, pressed the view that an end state would prove "sufficiently granular to be actionable." That is, it would make it possible to delineate more or less preferred actions in the near and mid-term. It would also exert normative force in decision-making processes (such as programming and budgeting) that have a more direct impact on the evolution of the Air Force's technical systems than does long-range planning. Murdock frequently incanted the mantra of Air Force programmers regarding planning: "If it ain't in the program, it ain't." This pithy one-liner became very long-winded indeed in the implementation of the plan—growing more into a book than a single sentence. At the time, however, it captured the determination of many key players to improve the connection between planning and programming.

If one thinks of a plan in terms of a point of origin, a path, and a destination, the 1997 product proved more precise than most plans in its specification of destinations. It was relatively vague, however, on the paths to be traveled from the point of origin to those destinations, especially considering that it was developed by the armed services. Military planners typically thrive on laying out the details of a journey from point A to point B.

The issue of whether the 1997 document actually constitutes a plan may be debatable, but the interviews conducted for this project strongly suggest that the participants in the process believed that they were planning strategically. Rather than engage in a lengthy semantic diversion, we choose here to briefly outline a few of the terms that credibly describe what participants in the Air Force's corporate process thought they were doing. To begin, adjoining *strategic* to *planning* adds to the latter's difficulty. According to Webster's, a plan is "a detailed formulation of a program of action." The same source characterizes a strategy (and, by extension, strategic) as "an adaptation or complex of adaptations . . . that serves or appears to serve an important function in achieving evolutionary success." Striving for evolutionary success undoubtedly motivated the Air Force's substantial investment in long-range planning. We therefore see little room to contest the issue of whether the Air Force has been engaged in strategic planning.

A futuristic projection to the year 2025 served as the preamble for the first Long-Range Plan; this was an express departure from the service's convention for such exercises. Visioning, which is what the participants were encouraged to undertake, required vision. Webster's defines *vision* as "unusual discernment or foresight." These definitional bearings reveal a huge difference between visioning and vision. The former gazes boldly into the future, but the latter is ascribed only when events prove the futurist right. Strategic planning as pursued by the Air Force during both the Fogleman and Ryan eras involved quintessentially a pooling of the senior leadership's perceptions of the future. These participants devised agreed visions of the opportunities and challenges that the Air Force would face over a long horizon. Only then did the Air Force leadership "backcast" from the visions to their current competencies and capabilities in order to assess the necessary adjustments for the service to prepare for the envisioned future. Third, the Air Force leadership then attempted to distill and gain consensus on the programmatic commitments required for achieving desired adaptations in a timely fashion.

We view this approach, above all, as positioning for opportunities. Writers such as Martha Derthick and Theda Skocpol identify a fairly robust specimen of the same practice in domestic agencies. They identify it most clearly in the maneuvers of the Social Security Administration (SSA) during the gradual expansion of the contributory social security system from its inception in 1935 to the inclusion of medical provision for the aged in 1965 and the indexation of Social Security pensions in 1972. Skocpol characterizes the SSA leadership as a spearhead for ending poverty among the aged; in particular, program coordinators seized auspicious contexts such as President Lyndon Johnson's War on Poverty as occasions "to institute long-planned extensions of universal provision for the elderly."[9] Derthick attributes the SSA's success over the years to a mix of restrained specificity in communicating its vision and pragmatism:

> In explaining and appraising the executive planners' success . . . it is important to keep the scope of their goals in perspective. They defined their objectives largely in instrumental terms. . . . They were successful in this. A big program exists today that conforms to the first principles laid down in the founding years. Had goals been defined in terms that stipulated ultimate social outcomes with some precision, success would surely have been much harder to achieve.[10]

The SSA track record stands in opposition to the permanent officials of an organization becoming so strongly associated with specific options that other players in the policy arena immediately discount the agency's contribution to discourse.[11] At the same time, the agency's permanent officials must have already done the internal spadework if they are to influence deliberations once an issue comes to the fore.[12]

Major adaptations in political systems and governmental organizations often stem from an intuitive grasp of epochal shifts in challenges and opportunities. When such renderings of epochal shifts gain currency, leaders find fertile ground for relatively substantial policy innovation. Their actual progress will depend on their persuasive powers, the cogency of their case, and, crucially, the degree to which unfolding events sustain or call into question their lines of argument. Fogleman's persuasive powers far exceeded Ryan's, but Ryan compensated through his reputation as a pragmatist—if he made the case, the Air Force leaders would more readily suspend their disbelief. Finally, events in Bosnia, Kosovo, and Afghanistan added credibility to the Air Force's view of its future. For instance, the tremendous success of drones in the Afghanistan campaign certainly made a visionary out of General Fogleman, who had pressed the case for unmanned aerial vehicles (UAVs) against some opposition during his stewardship of the Air Force.

In the mid-1980s Colin Campbell and Bert A. Rockman independently employed the term *metacycles* to describe epochal shifts that seem to call for departures from business as usual.[13] Both authors apply the term to the plight of chief executives in advanced democracies at that time. It seems, however, to pertain as readily to executives within government organizations—be they political appointees or career officials—who conclude that incremental approaches to evolutionary adaptation will fail to rise to new challenges and exploit new opportunities.

The political context for the U.S. Air Force in the mid-1990s similarly evoked a period of grappling with inchoate metacycles. These took the form of challenges that went far beyond the usual temporal horizons of Air Force planners. They spun off from a host of emergent issues. What was the role of the U.S. military going to be in the post–cold war era? How were the services going to adapt to the related expectation that they now contribute toward deficit reduction? And, most critically for the Air Force, what would happen if the U.S. military did considerably less of its fighting from fixed-wing aircraft with human pilots? The Air Force elected to address new challenges and canvass new opportunities by pursuing its future through strategic visioning. This evolved under General Fogleman into an effort to radically realign operations and programs on the basis of bold projections of what an envisioned Space and Air Force might look like in 2025. General Ryan's retreat to the more integrative concept of an Aerospace Force did not diminish the degree to which the Air Force engaged in strategic visioning of significantly stretched horizons.

As noted, we employ the term *positioning for opportunities* to describe the Air Force's investment in visioning. This nomenclature deliberately differentiates between what we have observed and opportunism. We agree with John Kingdon that the policy entrepreneur's connection to events often parallels the surfer in relation to the perfect wave. Surfers are "ready to paddle, and their readiness combined with their sense for riding the wave and using the forces beyond their control contribute to success."[14] However, two factors play heavily on the degree to which opportunities are successfully exploited. The first of these concerns the cogency of the policy entrepreneur's case in relation to those of other claimants to resources. Theda Skocpol notes that one underpinning of the Social Security Administration's success in gradually expanding its services was that the agency's proposals would fit with what was "actuarially sound."[15] An armed service can similarly trump other contenders by invoking the potential contribution of a proposed program to national security.

The second factor rests on the degree to which policy entrepreneurs in an organization extrapolate from experience to press their case and realize that garnering such evidence often requires up-front investments. Surfers do not have the time to discuss with their colleagues whether a wave presents a perfect opportunity (and challenge) and if so why. The policy entrepreneur, however, must justify the timeliness of committing. Furthermore, arguments extrapolated from agreed renderings of experience often tip the scale toward one programmatic investment over others. Consider, for example, the extra funds the second Bush administration sought for drones and satellite surveillance in the aftermath of their demonstrated effectiveness in Afghanistan. Marshalling such cases, to be sure, involves luck, but it also requires that an agency has adequately prepared the evidence in order to be able to present a plausible story line. The agency must also maintain links to others in the policy arena so that they will allow it to repeat and refine its case each time an opportunity presents itself.

More fundamentally, positioning for the wave often requires up-front commitments such as research and development and preliminary investments in hardware or infrastructure. We certainly can imagine policy sectors in which entrepreneurship remains cerebral. This condition, however, rarely pertains in an armed service. Such contexts confront us with the fact that even surfers require a state-of-the-art surfboard if they are to ride that perfect wave with optimal results.

Because this book covers two iterations of strategic visioning in the Air Force, namely, the 1996–97 and 1999–2000 exercises, it can assess the downstream effects of the long-range planning process. That is, the case considered in this book offers an exceptional opportunity to examine how visioning connects to the strategy-formulation phase and ultimately effects changes in programming and budgeting.[16] The focus is primarily on the way the Air Force created and used formalized processes to identify strategic issues (including the so-called gut issues) and to work toward their resolution. The key policy events were authoritative declarations of strategic intent, including the 1996 vision, the 1997 Long-Range Plan, and the updated vision published in June 2000.

The Role of Organizational Characteristics

We have personally met General Fogleman, who launched the Air Force on its prolonged episode of strategic visioning, and he did not strike us as being a Don Quixote. This raises the question of whether there is something peculiar about the Air Force that made it amenable to the process that we chronicle and analyze here. Alternatively, are there lessons that might apply to other organizations in the U.S. federal government? Are they missing something that the Air Force grasped?

In some respects, the Air Force is not a typical federal agency. One finds relatively few political appointees in its top positions, and Air Force personnel, rather than civilians, occupy most of the top positions in the service's executive leadership. To be sure, the generals who masterminded much of the process do not fit the image of a government of strangers—that is, the split in many agencies between political appointees and career officials—that Hugh Heclo evoked in his famous characterization of the divisions among key executives in most federal agencies.[17]

The so-called bluesuiters ultimately did have to contend with civilian supervision of their quest for evolutionary success. Indeed, civilian engagement seemed to rise exponentially as the blue-suit strategic visioning began to raise issues of major political significance, such as whether the weaponization of space was inevitable.

Even apart from such dynamics, the Air Force operates within the same political-governmental system as other federal agencies and, therefore, faces similar institutional constraints. Within the executive branch, bluesuiters must first win over the secretary of the Air Force, along with other political appointees vying for influence within the department. They must then make their case with the Joint Chiefs of Staff, the other services, the secretary of defense, and the White House and the Executive Office of the President. The latter two include officials in the National Security Council and the Office of Management and Budget. These players ostensibly should take an interest in long-range issues, but in fact they tend to get caught up in fighting brush fires for the administration, to the extent that they can devote little time to strategic visioning—especially if it concerns matters far in the future.

As the bluesuiters work through this maze, they often find it difficult to get other players' attention. Paradoxically, when they do get a response, they often encounter deep antagonism both from close competitors who have followed their maneuvers too keenly and from relatively distant parties who are convinced that the bluesuiters' agenda clashes with their own.

The web of interconnections between parts of the executive branch and supporters and opponents in Congress further exacerbates the difficulty of devising and pressing a coherent strategic vision for any organization in the U.S. government, much less a highly visible one such as the Air Force. Issues such as how many C-130s a state's Air National Guard maintains, whether the Air Force should have more F-22s and fewer Joint Strike Fighters, and whether it can reduce the number of B-1s in service generate passionate debate in Congress.

Bluesuiters aspiring to bring a strategic vision to the national agenda must first learn how to keep their eye on the big picture. They must also develop ways of using specific instances of tension in Congress as opportunities to educate players about the costs of deferring investments in the future in order to serve interests vested in the status quo. The "uniformed patriot" culture of a military service perhaps explains why the Air Force remains persistent in bringing its perception of future needs to the public forum. After all, members of the military see not only matters of life and death embedded in responses to the future, but also questions of national survival.

Nonetheless, we can certainly conceive of civilian agencies—operating entirely in the realm of domestic policy—in which officials similarly see themselves as responsible for plotting the long-term consequences of the status quo and recommending changes in course on the grounds of public and national interest. However, they have to play much more of an inside game than do bluesuiters. Joel D. Aberbach and Bert A. Rockman, who compare executive-bureaucratic political gamesmanship during the Nixon, Reagan, and Bush Sr. administrations, find sharp drops in career officials' interactions with congressmen and Hill staffers from the former to the latter two administrations.[18] They attribute these to the Reagan administration's strategy of severely constricting direct contact between senior career officials and those outside the executive branch as a means of curtailing the policy entrepreneurship of the former. The study raises the question of whether closing career officials out of direct participation in decisionmaking might prove a self-denying ordinance: "Why staff a public service with highly qualified individuals if they will not be given some latitude in figuring out how to do things and advising superiors as to the options?"[19] However, one of the respondents, whom the authors quote to support their claim that career officials view themselves as motivated by issues of public good, conveys a deep appreciation of the ambiguity surrounding such an assertion from the standpoint of executive-bureaucratic politics: "The one thing that keeps us still here . . . is that we do have a hell of a dedication to the mission of whatever it is that we are doing, and we seem to be willing to cope with all of these frustrations. We do it because we believe so deeply in these bigger things."[20]

The respondent's phraseology suggests an underlying skepticism about ultimately making a difference, which we did not encounter with our Air Force respondents. Aberbach and Rockman argue that the nation cannot expect creativity from its standing bureaucracy until it checks the competition between the political executive, Congress, and the federal judiciary over policy, which, in turn, has led to micromanagement of career officials. The scope of this problematic suggests the need to look more closely at just how encumbered agencies have become and what types of strategies they might pursue, in collaboration with their political leaders, to function more creatively with regard to evolutionary adaptation.

Contending with Constricted Latitude

Institutional constraints have become increasingly important for federal agencies in the past thirty years. In the mid-1960s, conventional wisdom among political scientists accepted that changes under American-style "polyarchy" would occur almost exclusively in "incremental" forms.[21] In other words, the system—with, for instance, separation of powers, federalism, and the malleability of the state apparatus to special interests—would usually serve up relatively modest responses to policy challenges. The past thirty years have seen a deterioration even of the system's capacity for incremental change. As described by Mancur Olson in the early 1980s, institutional stances have ossified to the point where change becomes ponderous, at best.[22] For example, deadlock between the White House and Congress used to be ascribed to divided government, that is, control of the former by one party and one or both chambers of the latter by another. However, the Herculean struggles faced by Jimmy Carter (1977–81) and Bill Clinton (1993–95) under a united government suggest that the separation of powers combined with the ossification of special-interest perspectives has transformed deadlock into gridlock, recurrent even when the same party controls both the executive and legislative branches.[23]

If we move away from Olson's ossification image into a different realm of anatomy, it would appear that the system has developed fairly significant arterial sclerosis. No matter how deeply committed they may be, those trying to pursue policies with greater strategic cogency will still face very constricted parameters. In cardiology, surgeons can achieve revascularization of blocked arteries through bypass surgery or, less invasively but potentially less successfully, angioplasty. The intractability faced by any reform-oriented federal agency usually precludes anything as dramatic and definitive as the institutional equivalent of bypass surgery. The Air Force's corporate strategic planning process might thus comport with revascularization through angioplasty. Alternatively, cardiorevascularization can also occur naturally through the formation of collateral vessels that give blood an alternate route to the heart. In the case at hand, this would mean that the Air Force, despite its institutional constraints, reinvented itself through internal resourcefulness and ingenuity. If so, any positive lessons learned from this study will find a ready audience among similarly limited federal agencies.

This book constitutes a case study of strategic planning in the federal government. All federal agencies are now required to undertake some form of strategic planning under the 1993 Government Performance and Results Act (GPRA). What constitutes strategic planning in the federal government has thus taken on new meaning.[24] The Air Force presents itself as an especially appealing research site for a case study in this emerging approach to achieving greater direction and coherence in federal agencies. The Air Force's strategic planning activities since the mid-1990s appear to be an exceptionally robust specimen of the generic practice.[25] This owes to the energy with which the Air Force based its approach to strategic planning on futuristic visioning about how it might best pursue evolutionary adaptation.

More important, perhaps, the type of visioning pursued in the Air Force takes us beyond the objectives of GPRA. It is one thing for the National Park Service to work more rigorously at establishing its medium-term objectives and then tracking performance toward fulfilling them. It is quite another for it to fast-forward to the year 2025, gaze at what National Parks will look like if current policies remain fundamentally unchanged, envision desirable alternatives to the status quo projected twenty-five years into the future, and then backcast to the present to see which course corrections suggest themselves as desirable and feasible.

This book therefore seeks primarily to explore a specific approach to strategic planning that evolved in the U.S. Air Force beginning in the mid-1990s. We also aim, however, to improve understanding and debate about the practice of strategic planning generally in federal agencies. Roughly speaking, we classify this work as an instance of best practice research, even while recognizing that many in the academic community use this term as an expression of disapproval rather than as a neutral concept. We hope that the scope of this study—limited to one case, to be sure, but one with exceptionally broad potential implications—will expand the boundaries of best practice research. In this way, our effort comports more with what Eugene Bardach styles as smart practice analysis.[26] This approach, in comparison with best practice research, attempts to identify the causal mechanisms and processes that allow particular practices to counteract the tendency of political, technical, and organizational systems in the public sector to perform unsatisfactorily with respect to evolutionary adaptation. We now turn to the parameters along which such a discussion might occur in connection with strategic visioning in the federal government.

Expanding the Horizons for Strategic Planning

Evolutionary adaptation proves exceptionally difficult for organizations within the U.S. federal government. When we look at other countries, we find higher capacities for longer-range thinking and action associated with evolutionary adaptation. Although significantly driven by the need to renew their mandates, governments in parliamentary systems frequently commit considerable energy to strategic thinking that goes beyond the current legislative calendar. In these systems, political appointees play only limited roles, so career civil servants often serve as the architects of innovative ways in which departments and agencies might face future challenges. Critically, two key elements of these systems are missing in the United States. First, the government-of-the-day often exerts sufficient control over the legislative branch to take initial steps toward a long-range strategic commitment once a consensus builds around it in the executive branch. This provides an incentive for career officials and a way for them to contribute to a legacy. Second, a strong, systemwide esprit de corps often prevails within these countries, which allows officials to detach themselves to some extent from the short-term interests within their units and departments.

Getting the innovative juices flowing among career officials within U.S. governmental organizations usually proves a much tougher sell. Officials seldom see that their political masters can deliver on commitments to take the first steps toward change. Moreover, units within agencies that float ideas for innovation can do a lot of damage to themselves by giving away hostages to opponents. In the fragmented U.S. bureaucracy, these might belong to the same organization—even wear the same uniform—yet maintain competing loyalties. In this regard, R. Kent Weaver and Bert A. Rockman's seminal inventory of the costs and benefits of the separation of powers offers pertinent guidance. Efforts to achieve innovation in the United States more frequently end in stalemate than is the case in other systems. However, in contrast to responsible party government as found in many parliamentary systems, the separation of powers can sometimes provide circumstances in which departments and agencies can play administration and congressional patrons off one another. Obviously, engaging key players in the policy domain requires promoting innovation as serving the national interest or fostering electoral approval. Under some circumstances, U.S. agencies can ride the crest of a bidding-up process to achieve relatively comprehensive policy change.[27]

Positioning for such opportunities—that is, being ready to spring forward with highly developed options when auspicious circumstances emerge—suggests itself here as a worthwhile strategy for innovators. In this regard, Martha Feldman's work on the crazy-quilt world of energy policymaking under Carter and Reagan demonstrates that while the process may not be coherent, it provides for myriad opportunities in which highly trained specialists can thoroughly examine their options. In particular, bureaucratic analysts develop and maintain inventories of "policy positions and reports that policymakers may request when needed."[28] In this regard, agencies play exceedingly important roles in what John Kingdon argues gets the innovative ball rolling—the predecisional process of alternative specification.[29]

The United States is not the only country in which engaging interest in corporate strategic planning faces serious difficulties; the conditions for the approach ebb and flow in other systems, as well. The United Kingdom, Canada, and Australia, for instance, all made considerable efforts at comprehensive strategic direction in the mid-1970s that ran afoul of departmental intransigence.[30] Broadly, the initiatives sought to prioritize demands for continued expansion of the welfare state, notwithstanding the exceedingly daunting fiscal pressures associated with the economics of decline. Fiscal realities won out in the end, and a politics of constraint emerged in which bold images of the future gave way to narrow-gauged concerns about the efficiency and effectiveness of existing government programs. The former focus spawned a very strong corporate—some call it managerial—mind-set in many non-American public services.

In the 1980s, many public sector organizations of English-speaking countries other than the United States guided themselves through management boards or direct contractual agreements between the heads of operational units and ministers. In both circumstances, the career executives of the principal "businesses" of government organizations would have to outline and justify their objectives and submit to reviews of their performance in terms of outputs and outcomes. Even with very substantial organizational commitments to such collective guidance, however, management boards and performance agreements inevitably encountered difficulty in installing and operating a feedback loop between corporate strategy and budgeting.[31]

The relation between the 1993 Government Performance and Results Act (GPRA) and what the Air Force has pursued proves somewhat tenuous. The Air Force effort has far exceeded the legal requirements of the act, and in many respects it reflects its own leaders' distillation of smart practices in the private sector. Despite its more limited scope, however, the GPRA has significantly increased discussion of strategic planning in the federal government. It attempts to graft onto the U.S. departments and agencies something roughly akin to the corporate approaches that emerged in the 1980s in other English-speaking systems.

Paul Light has correctly categorized GPRA as liberation management.[32] It seeks to improve performance through the carrot of increased managerial discretion over the use of resources and the stick of greater individual and organizational accountability to achieve specific goals. In this regard, GPRA fits within the general framework of new public management.[33] However, as Peter Aucoin pointed out very early on, new public management clashes with the overarching conception among politicians that government has grown too large and must be put under tighter scrutiny.[34] In 1997, the General Accounting Office (GAO) recognized the relevance of this dynamic for GPRA—especially given that departmental compliance with the act is a congressional mandate. The GAO noted that the legislative staffers who do the bulk of reviewing of GPRA reports concentrate on their "oversight roles and stress near-term performance," whereas agency officials emphasize "long-term goals, adaptability to changing needs, and flexibility in execution."[35]

In some respects, GPRA can trace its lineage to the Planning, Programming, and Budgeting System (PPBS) that emerged in the Department of Defense under Robert McNamara and ultimately won the imprimatur of Lyndon Johnson for implementation throughout the U.S. government. The fact that the Pentagon still follows a PPBS approach makes this point especially pertinent to our case. However, GPRA's architecture concerns itself much more with the need for coordination between agencies and Congress on corporate strategy than with the primary focus of PPBS—namely, prioritization of long-range objectives so that decisionmakers might align budgetary commitments more cogently.[36]

The Air Force strategic visioning commitment thus fits the PPBS template more closely than the GPRA one—with the important caveat that planning, programming, and budgeting will never link sufficiently unless Congress grasps and supports how a service seeks to connect the three. Indeed, our analysis suggests that the Air Force encountered a sharp learning curve in this area, at first attempting to run an in-house process and eventually recognizing that it had to work much more intensively in educating Congress about the long-range consequences of budgetary choices.

This comports with Aaron Wildavsky's view of how PPBS might have worked had the proper conditions prevailed in the 1960s. He saw a strong analytic culture as the sine qua non for PPBS and, in fact, viewed this as a strength of the Pentagon not often shared by domestic agencies.[37] Wildavsky held a very high standard for policy analysis. He viewed it as a capacity to transcend "the fire-house environment of day-to-day administration" and trace out "the consequences of innovative ideas" rather than "projecting the status quo" into the future. In words that could easily apply to the principal rationale behind the Fogleman and Ryan planning efforts, Wildavsky noted that the originators of PPBS wanted to close the gap between planning and budgeting: "They wanted to stop blue-sky planning and integrate planning and budgeting. . . . They wanted to use the program budget to bridge the gap between military planners, who cared about requirements but not about resources, and budget people, who were narrowly concerned with financial costs but not necessarily with effective policies."

Since GPRA does not encompass strategic visioning in this sense, we find ourselves looking beyond agencies' efforts to comply with the act in order to relate our case to dialogue about smart practices for corporate strategic planning in the federal government. While the literature still has a considerable way to go, it can provide some guidance for the case at hand. For instance, Sandford Borins aims to distill best practices for innovators in bureaucratic agencies at the federal, state, and local levels. In particular, he concedes that the best innovation in large organizations most frequently arises "through the efforts of mavericks at 'skunkworks' far from central offices, operating without a clear mandate from above and using bootlegged resources."[38]

Borins's characterization of innovation might strike the reader as the furthest thing conceivable from the situation of the U.S. Air Force. Not only does the Air Force run an exceedingly diverse and complex bureaucratic system, but it gobbles up nearly 4 percent of the annual budget of the federal government. The U.S. Air Force case thus presents a daunting challenge, as the magnitude of corporate strategic planning in an organization of this size far exceeds the scale of any existing benchmarks. However, it provides a unique and timely opportunity to establish a benchmark for exercises of similar scale that other sizable agencies have begun to pursue under GPRA and other auspices.

Steps for Effective Implementation

Notwithstanding the difference in scale between the Air Force's strategic visioning efforts and those undertaken in other public service organizations, the latter initiatives do bring important themes to the discussion. First, the agency must devise a feasible and convincing framework for visioning and planning that nonetheless establishes true "stretch goals" that challenge the organization profoundly. Second, processes focused on adaptation to possible events far in the future rely extensively on scenario building and war gaming. Third, the success of the process depends substantially on the personal qualities of the organization's leaders and the extent to which they involve themselves in the strategic visioning and planning. Fourth, collective processes will greatly enhance the cooperation of both the barons and the rank and file of an organization. Finally, factoring in the likely responses of stakeholders is crucial to both visioning and planning.

Devising stretch goals is one of the mechanisms through which strategic visioning takes an organization beyond planning in the classic sense. It can make the planning process even more difficult and elusive than it normally is. Public sector organizations must grapple with government's inherent limitations in reconciling the standards of a plan—namely, a detailed formulation of a program of action—with strategy. Bureaucratic strategy usually falls short of detailed prescription because of uncertainties in both the identification of the future public good and the degree to which stakeholders will support the stated goals. In this respect, our concept of strategic visioning perhaps fits government agencies even better than private sector organizations. Though difficult to pursue, it takes into account the degree to which corporate strategic planners in the public sector find themselves discerning and targeting inchoate futures whose value ultimately lies in the extent to which they wrench stakeholders from incremental adaptations to the status quo.

Advocacy of strategic visioning implies two things. First, while organizations cannot discern their future with certitude, they can improve their performance by anticipating environmental changes that will require them to draw on capabilities that they would not develop by following the status quo. Second, incremental change based on piecemeal modifications of the status quo will inevitably result in the organization falling short of requirements sometime in the future, and this failure to adapt will endanger its institutional viability. In the case of a government organization, the failure to adapt could appreciably harm the public good—for the Air Force, national security—just as a similar lapse in a key industrial concern could erode a country's competitiveness in the global economy.

The available literature suggests that more often than not, organizations that have succeeded in corporate strategic planning were able to wean themselves off incrementalism and establish stretch goals. For instance, Sandford Borins analyzes submissions from 217 semifinalists for the Ford Foundation's state and local Innovations in American Government Awards program between 1990 and 1994. He finds that only seven percent of the innovations emerged from organizationwide strategic planning.[39] However, 59 percent of the reforms that were developed by discrete units of an umbrella organization emerged from comprehensive efforts at redesign. Only 30 percent of the initiatives evolved from "groping" or incremental efforts to adapt to change.[40] Borins also finds that comprehensive planning occurs most frequently among organizations that require large capital investments, programs that involve the coordination of a large number of organizations, and theory-driven programs.[41]

Borins's findings comport with those of a 1997 Federal Benchmarking Consortium (FBC) study of best practices in the private and public sectors that might be appropriate for large federal government organizations. The study promotes a view of corporate strategic planning that assumes a high degree of visioning—and even asserts that corporate strategic planning stands at the intersection of art and science.[42] However, the study also emphasizes that visioning and planning far into the future most frequently occur in organizations with either complex processes or very long-range programs (or both).[43] The report highlights the importance of future thinking for devising stretch goals and for enabling the organization "to recognize and capitalize on the events transpiring outside its span of control."

As already noted, our analysis of the Air Force experience takes this concept a step further by employing the notion of positioning for opportunities. The Air Force's visioning acknowledges the profound bias toward incrementalism of its real-world context but anticipates circumstances in which it might, if adequately prepared, seize opportunities for substantial evolutionary adaptation. Its approach to unmanned aerial vehicles (UAVs) serves as an example of this phenomenon. Through what were initially relatively modest investments and deployments, the Air Force has, in just a few years, given life to a new concept—namely, that much of its work can be done with drones that do not endanger human resources. The increase in the role of UAVs from Kosovo (1999) to Iraq (2003) probably exceeds even General Fogleman's expectations for this approach to surveillance and attack, which in the mid-1990s prompted skepticism in the Air Force's pilot-dominated culture.

The FBC report also finds that scenario building and role playing can greatly assist an organization in identifying its desired path into the future.[44] Such approaches constitute the second key factor for connecting visioning and planning, as mentioned at the start of this section. The FBC study observes that private corporations use this approach extensively, often even employing the term *war games*. Obviously, the military brings to such a task immense experience with war games. Such exercises serve little purpose in visioning, however, if they consist in applying existing methods of operation to the status quo projected x years out. In other words, stretch goals will not emerge unless the game itself forces thinking beyond conventional parameters. In any case, role playing through scenarios that invite a realistic grasp of future challenges can have immense effects in organizations: the players develop an appreciation of the need to prepare for uncertain futures, and nonplayers similarly broaden their views of organizational challenges when the findings from the games are properly disseminated. War gaming not only adds cogency to organizational visions, but can also inject a sense of urgency into the process of planning for the future.

General Fogleman considered that visioning would be relevant only if the Air Force backcast, so that expectations for the future actually guided changes in current programmatic commitments. The FBC study finds that the private corporations that prove most successful at strategic planning have achieved a similar discipline: "After describing the vision of the future using standard techniques, the company leaders essentially move backward from the future state to identify how the company must look at a given point in time if the desired future is to materialize."[45]

The third key factor for strategic planning, leadership, depends on the personal qualities of those in charge and their full engagement in the process. Borins describes what he calls a trichotomy of innovation: politicians usually lead innovation when an organization faces a major crisis; agency heads normally assert themselves most clearly when they first assume their responsibilities; and middle-level and frontline officials most often probe creative options when faced with internal problems or technical opportunities.[46] In all three cases, the courage to lead agencies to innovation stems from the integrity of those in charge—meaning they have not allowed crises to arise or deepen through neglect of warning signs or paralysis in the face of gridlock. In Borins's words, they bring to their work "the ability to recognize problems or opportunities in a proactive manner."[47]

The FBC report highlights the important role of the chief executive in taking an active part in a strategic management group, together with the other top leaders of a corporation.[48] It also stresses the need for the chief executive to personally "explain and cascade" the resulting strategic vision throughout an organization. Public service organizations do present ambiguity, however, along the lines identified by Borins. Who is the chief executive? The former British prime minister Margaret Thatcher (1979–90), for instance, wanted her ministers to actively manage their departments. Some did. In fact, a few participated directly on their ministries' management boards. Most ministers, however, remained aloof from managerial activities, notwithstanding Thatcher's preferences. In such cases, either the head career civil servant was given or assumed the managerial mantle, or the department shunned the corporate approach completely. The best results with corporate approaches to management came from departments in which the ministers took a keen and direct interest in managing their departments.[49] The nature of these organizations' activities played a role, as well. If they broke down relatively neatly into comparatively free-standing "businesses," then the minister could gain a cogent view of each major unit's objectives and gauge its civil-service head's performance on the basis of whether the objectives were met. In other words, the department would operate as a conglomerate and the minister as chairman of the board and chief executive officer.

Ambiguity existed in the U.S. Air Force in three ways. In the first round, the political head of the Air Force—the secretary, Sheila Widnall—did not engage in the strategic planning process until issues with serious political dimensions emerged. General Fogleman was thus clear to act as a chief executive along the lines suggested by Borins and the FBC report. This fit the preference for having bluesuiters run the business end of the Air Force. Ambiguity entered the equation, however, because governmental corporate strategic planning, by nature, takes an organization into a stratum of policy commitments that ultimately require authoritative sanction by the political leaders. As we discuss in chapter 4, Dr. Widnall's successor, F. Whitten Peters, assumed an active role in the second round, led by General Ryan. This introduced a dynamic whereby the private sector model of principal executive authority being clearly vested in one individual did not pertain. Although Peters essentially functioned as chief executive officer and Ryan as chief operating officer, the two often worked in tandem over matters pertaining to the former role. Even so, role ambiguity played a more important part during the first rather than second round. Restrained political leadership allowed General Fogleman to follow the prevailing stylistic preference of bluesuiters at the time, whereby secretaries played mainly symbolic and legitimizing roles while chiefs got on with the business of running the Air Force.

The second ambiguity lies in the entrenched cultural tensions of the U.S. executive-bureaucratic system, and it is amplified by the high stakes connected with what the Air Force does and the perpetual disputes over the resources it receives. The separation of powers makes it hard for federal government organizations to plan like private corporations. For the purposes of institutional survival, chief operating officers must weigh issues such as their departmental secretary's standing in the administration and the ability of the administration to get its positions through Congress. Even in a symbiotic arrangement such as that enjoyed by Peters and Ryan, the relationship between a secretary and a chief of staff proves much less hierarchical than that between a chairman of the board and a chief operating officer or even a British cabinet minister and the permanent civil servant who heads the department. If departmental secretaries in the United States choose to engage in corporate strategic planning, they must enter a dialogue with permanent officials. Officials will thus find it hard to bring about authoritative corporate change if their political appointees have not participated in the process. Similarly, political appointees, who can change policies against the will of their permanent officials so long as the president and Congress approve, cannot change the corporate ethos of their organizations unless they have worked through the dialogue.

The third ambiguity stems from the fact that the Air Force's core businesses do not lend themselves to the tidy divisions found in a conglomerate. Two large operations—the so-called shooting commands of Air Combat and Space—differ in that the latter draws on considerably fewer resources than the former and faces huge political obstacles to developing space-based attack capabilities. In addition, much of its surveillance role operates in support of Air Combat operations. A much smaller shooting command, Special Operations, participates extensively in joint operations with other services. The Air Mobility, Air Force Materiel, and Air Education and Training commands support the shooters, and Air Mobility also performs substantial functions for other services, especially the Army and the Marines. Furthermore, Air Force Materiel and Air Education operate largely with pass-through funds expended in the service of other commands. Finally, the Air Force ultimately operates at the behest of five regional combatant commanders who are mandated to prepare for and preside over military operations in the European, Northern, Southern, Central, and Pacific geographic divisions established by the Pentagon. Coordinating plans and operations with combatant commanders greatly compounds the difficulty of corporate approaches to leadership in all of the services.

These three ambiguities make it exceedingly difficult to delineate businesses and their objectives within the Air Force or to achieve horizontal resolution of conflicts between the major corporate units. These and similar circumstances are commonplace in the federal bureaucracy. One might therefore expect to find a keen interest in collective mechanisms for developing strategies and coordinating units, but in fact convincing participants of the utility of such devices is a hard sell in the U.S. federal bureaucracy. The separation of powers sustains an incentive system that encourages units to work alone in the search for political mandates and budget resources. Likewise, experience teaches them that corporate strategic approaches often fail even to gain the attention of the political leaders, much less negotiate the treacherous waters of executive-legislative relations.

Notwithstanding these counterindications, the literature suggests that collective processes are key to obtaining a consensus among leaders regarding future directions and ensuring that the rank and file understand and support the objectives. The FBC report states emphatically that without a consensus, there is no plan.[50] Moreover, chief executives cannot devise visions and plans on their own, but rather must work closely with other corporate leaders.[51] Borins also makes a strong, empirically based case that holistic innovation in organizations most frequently takes place when the process has been supported by the central staff and the agency's leaders have interacted regularly through formal coordinative mechanisms.[52] Borins concludes that "collaboration across organizational boundaries does not happen naturally; it must be made to happen."[53]

General Fogleman did not stumble on this concept. He believed that the Air Force had functioned in a consultative way in other difficult phases of its development and that it should do so again when he became chief in 1994. It took some time to formalize the exact contours of the process, but they were eventually clarified through the critical roles of Corona—the council of four-star generals who developed the 1996 vision—and the board of directors—the group of three-star generals who prepared issues for the Corona conference. Fogleman subsequently created an Air Force Staff unit, XP, whose three-star head assumed responsibility for the integration of planning and programming. The two disciplines continued to operate independently, however, because XP served two separate sets of deliberative machinery, one for planning and another for programming. Moreover, the Corona council and, in particular, the board of directors did not function in the same way under General Ryan's visioning round as they had under Fogleman's. These considerations present a number of issues surrounding the question of where exactly the Air Force's corporate persona is lodged. For instance, should the Staff control the programming process despite inroads made by the major commands in the visioning and planning processes? The debate spawned an initiative focused on revamping the planning, programming, and budgeting systems along more inclusive corporate lines—namely, the Air Force Resource Allocation Process (AFRAP).

Finally, the literature strongly prescribes external consultation with stakeholders as a key ingredient to successful corporate strategic planning. While this presents problems for any federal government agency, the secrecy surrounding many of the weapons systems and concepts of operations envisioned for the future seriously limits the Air Force's ability to pursue external consultations. Space, for example, was a central concern in General Fogleman's planning process, but most of the related issues were classified as top secret throughout the period in which he was chief.

The adversarial politics associated with the separation of powers discourages the planner from cooperating with congressmen, congressional staff, and contractors, who are likely to betray confidences if they feel that their agendas and priorities will not prevail. The FBC report makes a strong plea for external consultation, although it frequently refers to the marketplace and customers, which suggests that it is mainly oriented to agencies that provide goods and services to specific individuals and groups.[54] Such commercial analogies do not apply to the Air Force because the market, even including other military services, does not offer substitutes for much of what it provides. Furthermore, it generally cannot discriminate among the citizens who receive its benefits.

Liaison with Congress would certainly constitute the most important form of external consultation for the Air Force. The two organizations are not likely to work in tandem, however, as indicated by the General Accounting Office's assessment of the likely dynamics for dialogue between agencies and Congress on strategic plans produced in compliance with the Government Performance and Results Act. The cultural divide leaves agency heads "skeptical that consensus on strategic goals could be reached, especially given the often conflicting views among agencies' multiple congressional stakeholders."[55]

The Air Force ultimately developed a successful approach for bringing the results of its visioning and planning to bear on congressional budgeting decisions. Rather than pressing a comprehensive transformation package, the Air Force chose a more gradual approach of focusing on fork-in-the-road issues: if Congress made the wrong choice on one of these critical decisions, the chance that it would be able to purchase a critical capability within the desired time frame would shrink to dangerous proportions from the standpoint of national security.

Such smart practice fits recent research on historical institutional adaptation in the federal government. For instance, Patrick J. Wolf, who analyzes 170 cases of federal agency reform from 1890 to the present time, finds that organizations operating with a relatively high degree of autonomy from direct political control are the most innovative.[56] This suggests that the Air Force was wise to incorporate administration appointees in its visioning and planning processes and to become increasingly judicious in the types of pleas it makes to Congress. Daniel P. Carpenter's study of innovation in executive-branch agencies between 1862 and 1928 finds that the most effective organizations partook of state building by seizing opportunities to demonstrate to Congress and the public how they could make a difference in areas of great national concern.[57] They gained relevance not by articulating grand designs, but by establishing symbiosis with sympathetic parties in the policy marketplace.

This section has shown how the available literature reveals certain standards with which to assess how the Air Force has proceeded with relatively far-reaching efforts at corporate strategic visioning and planning. By the nature of its business, the Air Force's planning must go far into the future in order to evoke significant stretch goals. Scenario building and war gaming should position the leadership for realistic consideration of what will be required of the Air Force in the future. The chief must guide the process personally and cogently, despite the ambiguities in the division of corporate direction between himself and the secretary. A collective dynamic encompassing the rest of the senior leadership is crucial for garnering support and, perhaps most significantly, helping generalize the Air Force's grasp of likely challenges. External consultation, however, will most likely remain subdued as the nature of the Air Force's business exposes it to a type of stakeholder scrutiny whereby a dialogic approach might prove counterproductive.

The Plan for This Book

The rest of this book is divided into eight chapters. The first of these examines the circumstances faced by the Air Force in the early 1990s that set the stage for the Fogleman visioning and planning initiatives. Chapter 3 focuses on how the Fogleman round developed, while chapter 4 charts the continuation of the Fogleman approach under Secretary Peters and General Ryan and underscores ways in which the second round followed on or departed from the philosophy and rubrics of its predecessor. Chapter 5 assesses the operation of the two rounds from the standpoint of smart practices. Chapter 6 probes the consequences of the Air Force's investment in visioning and planning for its governance and programming and budgeting systems. Chapter 7 focuses on the case of unmanned aerial vehicles (UAVs) as a specific instance in which institutional commitments accelerated and coalesced as a result of the visioning and planning regimen. Chapter 8 analyzes three substantial initiatives that deeply engaged the Air Force in efforts to go beyond a linear implementation agenda to thoroughgoing reassessments of key elements of its vision. Finally, Chapter 9 distills the key findings of this book and examines their relevance for other public sector organizations attempting to prepare for the future.

CHAPTER 2

Precursors of Strategic Visioning: Discontinuous Change in the Early Post–Cold War Period

Context contributed to the development of a serious practice of strategic visioning during the Fogleman round and to the specific content of *Global Engagement*. Important elements of that context include shifting alliances among the military services, the unification of the Air Force as an institution, changes in the role of airpower in combat situations, and a growing appreciation of the role of space-based systems in the process of conducting war. These specific factors affected the defense policy subsystem as well as important aspects of the Air Force, including its constitution and accepted strategic thinking. The present chapter provides a historical understanding of the strategic visioning context, with an overview of the key discontinuous changes that swept the Air Force at the end of the cold war and the service's responses to them.

The Rice-McPeak Era: Supplying the Air Force with a Strategic Vision

At the outset of the 1990s, the Air Force published a strategic vision document entitled *Global Reach—Global Power*. The document was initially prepared in 1989–90, just as the cold war came to its abrupt end. The principal architect was Donald Rice, who had served as president of the RAND Corporation—a federally funded think-tank with close ties to the Air Force—before President George H. W. Bush appointed him as secretary of

the Air Force. Air Force Chief of Staff Gen. Merrill A. "Tony" McPeak
was also closely involved. As Fogleman later recalled,

> Rice put a group of people together in the fall of 1989 and said,
> "Look, the world's changing, and if the United States Air Force is
> going to make its maximum contribution to the nation, we've got to
> change, too. We have got to understand what the post–cold war envi-
> ronment is like, and we have got to structure ourselves to operate in
> that environment." The outgrowth of that initiative by Rice was the
> strategic vision for the Air Force, called *Global Reach—Global
> Power*.[1]

The document acknowledged that war with Russia on the plains of
Europe was no longer a likely scenario and that threats had become geo-
graphically dispersed and less predictable. The changed international
political scene was viewed as leading inexorably away from a garrison-type
Air Force, in which a large fraction of the service's forces remains stationed
outside the United States. Instead, the Air Force would gravitate toward an
expeditionary-type service, with its forces stationed predominately on U.S.
soil and deployed overseas as needed.

The assumptions underlying *Global Reach—Global Power* mirror the
conclusions that were being reached by the White House staff in the development of a post–cold war national security policy, to which Secretary Rice
was privy. The Air Force was unique among the services, however, in publishing its own post–cold war strategic vision document. As Fogleman
remarked, "There weren't a whole lot of visions floating around at that
time."

Global Reach—Global Power argued that the emerging national security
strategy placed a high premium on airpower's distinctive qualities: speed,
range, and flexibility. The document maintained that the Air Force was
capable of projecting dominating power to any point on Earth in hours,
rather than in the days, weeks, or months that would be required to move
ships or ground forces into position.[2] The implication was that the Air
Force would make a strategic contribution to future military campaigns.

Less than two months after the Air Force published *Global Reach—
Global Power*, Iraq invaded Kuwait. Attention in defense circles naturally
centered on defending Saudi Arabia against invasion and on the operation
to expel Iraqi forces from Kuwait and weaken the Iraqi military and political regime. By the time anyone noticed the Air Force's strategic vision
document, the military services were engaged in post–Gulf War policy man-

agement. These events colored outside perceptions of the Air Force's announced strategic vision, which many saw as an aggressive attempt to capitalize on the service's successes in the Persian Gulf War.

The development of a strategic vision under Secretary Rice had several important effects. First, *Global Reach—Global Power* set the standard for Air Force long-range planning: Fogleman and his fellow senior officers sought to improve on this strategic vision, rather than to supplant it. Second, Fogleman was determined to calm interservice tensions—an approach that counseled a different sort of rhetoric from that employed in the original document. Third, Fogleman's assessment of the service's experience with this approach to planning led him to rethink the process of developing a strategic vision:

> *Global Reach—Global Power* was a top inner-circle piece of paper. . . . Many people inside and outside the Air Force thought *Global Reach—Global Power* was a slogan rather than a strategic vision and blueprint. They didn't take the time to seriously read through it. A lot of people in the Air Force never understood that most of the changes that McPeak made were based on ideas developed in writing *Global Reach—Global Power*—for instance, the idea that there was no room for a Strategic Air Command that was just focused on nuclear war.

Global Reach—Global Power thus served as both a positive and negative model of strategic visioning. It anchored Fogleman's thinking about how to use his prerogatives and skills in leading a strategic planning effort while he served as chief.

The Gulf War: Changing the Air Force's Self-Conception

Air Force officers describe the Gulf War as a pivotal event in the service's development. The Gulf War was precipitated by Iraq's invasion of Kuwait on August 2, 1990. The task of presenting the president and secretary of defense with military options fell to the joint command responsible for Southwest Asia, known as the U.S. Central Command. The commander-in-chief of this joint command was Norman Schwartzkopf, a four-star Army general. Two days after the invasion of Kuwait, U.S. Central Command briefed President Bush on how to defend Saudi Arabia from a further Iraqi invasion. The options presented were based on operational plans prepared earlier. The defensive operation approved by the president was eventually designated Desert Shield. During the conduct of Desert Shield, plans for an offensive operation to expel the Iraqis from Kuwait (among other objectives) were developed. The eventual result was the offensive operation known as Desert Storm, which began with an air campaign in January 1991.[3]

Some insight into the Gulf War's impact on the Air Force can be gleaned from insider accounts. The following version was given by Charles Link, now a retired two-star general and former commandant of the Air War College, who played a major role in the development and dissemination of revised Air Force thinking about the use of airpower in conventional wars:

> Hussein is in Kuwait. We're building up forces in the south, but there is no plan. Plans are being developed. One of those plans is affectionately known now as hey diddle diddle, straight up the middle. [The reference is to a plan to launch a ground campaign at the outset of an offensive operation against Iraqi forces in Kuwait and southern Iraq.] Schwartzkopf realized that this war [Desert Storm] really was going to happen on his watch and hey diddle diddle, straight up the middle probably was not the best approach. . . . He called the Air Force. Mike Dugan was still in charge; he committed John Warden to plan some alternative.

Col. John Warden's Air Staff directorate quickly produced a design for what was termed an air campaign, reflecting recent theoretical developments within the Air Force. Two years earlier Warden had published a book entitled *The Air Campaign*, in which he laid out his then-unconventional views.[4] These ideas found their way into the specific air campaign developed at General Schwartzkopf's request. The directorate recommended that airpower be employed before the introduction of ground troops into actual combat. Normally, the U.S. employed airpower concurrently with a ground campaign. The military objective was to vastly degrade the opponent's capacity to defend itself in the face of an offensive by ground forces. To achieve this objective, the directorate called for using airpower to attack so-called centers of gravity within each of the several subsystems that collectively functioned as the opponent's military capability. These subsystems included command-and-control installations and transportation links crucial for resupply. The air campaign design showed how intelligence available to the U.S. government could be used to identify targets that, if destroyed, would unravel Iraq's war-making system; it also called for striking the selected targets with precision munitions.[5]

Airpower theory was translated into an actual air campaign executed under U.S. Central Command's Joint Force Air Component Commander, Air Force Lt. Gen. Charles Horner, who reported to Schwartzkopf. The outcome of the air campaign is well known. In the first twenty-four hours of the Desert Storm air war, coalition forces established air supremacy, decapitated Iraq's command-and-control system, shut down the country's electrical production, and seriously reduced the effectiveness of many of its surface-to-air missile sites and antiaircraft batteries. During the air war, coalition aircraft destroyed more than 1,000 tanks and nearly as many armored personnel carriers.[6] According to an Air Force chronicler,

> By the time the ground campaign began on February 24, 1991, many Iraqi units were at or below the 50 percent point in their nominal combat strength. With communications destroyed, reinforcement impossible, food and water scarce, and their major strengths—artillery and tanks—being plinked into oblivion day by day, morale fell rapidly. When morale was factored in, they were even less effective than the 50 percent figure indicated. . . . The most extensive and successful preparation of the battlefield in history had been accomplished by airpower.[7]

Within the Air Force, an important effect of Desert Storm was to prove that airpower could make a direct contribution to achieving high-level, strategic military objectives in a conventional war. According to Charles Link,

> The Gulf War gave some airmen a reason to think about an air campaign. An air campaign, by definition, would be the use of airpower directly to pursue strategic objectives or policy goals, as opposed to the way we had been doing it, [which] was to translate the policy goal into a land war and then organize land, air, and sea capabilities around the land war. In raising our airmen, we never asked them to relate what they did directly to a policy goal, particularly on the tactical [nonnuclear] side. Sure enough, after the Gulf War, airmen began thinking about how to relate airpower directly to policy goals.

This change in thinking was part of a move to separate Air Force doctrine from the joint Army-Air Force doctrine of an air-land battle, which was at odds with the concept of an air campaign. According to Link, the problem was not in the Army doctrine itself, but in how the Air Force "embraced it uncritically" without looking for ways to expand its role beyond supporting Army-directed campaigns:

> Throughout the cold war, we had two kinds of air power: strategic nuclear airpower and tactical conventional air power. Airmen divided into two camps. One, airmen who couldn't separate the term *strategic* from the term *nuclear*. And, two, airmen who got the leftovers after the strategic nuclear forces were appropriately postured. The latter—the tactical Air Force—gravitated to the service that loved them: the Army. . . . As late as 1990, the commander of Tactical Air Command [TAC] was known to say publicly that the only purpose of TAC is to support the U.S. Army on the ground.

One specific institutional mechanism by which the Air Force absorbed Army doctrine was the Air-Land Forces Application (ALFA) Directorate, which was set up jointly by the Army and the Air Force. ALFA strongly influenced the content of Air Force doctrine, which consequently did not entertain the possibility of the strategic use of conventional airpower. In Link's words, "The Air Force spent a long time imprisoned by somebody else's construct."

The new construct, in which the Air Force fulfilled a strategic role in conventional warfare, was becoming established within the Air Force when Fogleman became chief in 1994. It was strengthened during the Fogleman period, in part because Link was selected as the chief's point man on Air Force preparations for the Quadrennial Defense Review, which proceeded in concert with the strategic planning process.

Alliance Reversal:
The Impact of the Gulf War on the Defense Policy Subsystem

The Gulf War was a pivotal event in the Air Force's reconceptualization of its role in national security and defense strategy, but that reconceptualization was part of a larger event. A concomitant change occurred within the defense policy subsystem. According to Link, "The Gulf War was actually pivotal in two ways. It gave some airmen a reason to think about an air campaign. But it was also pivotal in organizing the other services in opposition to any Air Force initiative in ways that they might not otherwise have done."

The realignment of services within the defense policy subsystem was marked by the formation of an Army-Navy Board in 1992. The Air Force was deliberately excluded from the first meeting of that board, even though the agenda included topics that clearly affected the service. The coalition between the Army and the tactical Air Force thus fell apart after the Gulf War.[8] As a result, the Air Force's strategic visioning efforts during the Fogleman period (and subsequently under General Ryan) were conducted in an awkward policy environment. This difficult situation was exacerbated by the Air Force's increasing advocacy of significant change in national military strategy. Such advocacy was initially set forth in *Global Reach—Global Power;* it was also a factor in many of General McPeak's encounters with his fellow members of the Joint Chiefs of Staff. As Link explained, "The way McPeak went about that, some people say, aroused a great deal of bad feelings on the part of the Army, Navy, and Marine Corps." Fogleman later calmed those feelings somewhat by pursuing a different style, but relations among the services remained awkward from the Air Force point of view.

Space-Based Provision of Military Intelligence

As mentioned in chapter 1, the 1996 *Global Engagement* vision document states that within a couple of decades, the Air Force would have evolved into the nation's Space and Air Force. Among its various effects, the Gulf War shifted the emphasis onto space by drawing attention to the way space can be integrated into the conduct of warfare, as we later discuss. The integration of space and combat was the result of a long-term process of technological innovation. Thomas Moorman, who headed the Air Force Space Command during the Gulf War, recalled how space-based assets had been integrated into air operations for the first time:

> The first time that a space system was used for combat purposes was a weather satellite in Vietnam. For a long while, we sent airplanes across a battle zone—a place we intended to bomb, North Vietnam. Guys looked out, saying, "Clouds at 30,000 feet" or whatever, and they'd radio it back, and we would write it up on a piece of acetate and brief it in the morning. That's the way we did it in World War II—why not in Vietnam? At the same time, we were developing a weather reconnaissance capability, where we could take the entire Indochina littoral and see the weather pattern from space. This occurred in the 1966–67 time frame. It was fundamental. We stopped flying airplanes across there. Thenceforth, every morning briefing for air operations began with a satellite weather photo.

In the intervening years, space-based assets contributed increasingly to performing such military functions as navigation, missile defense alarm, communications, and surveillance, as well as meteorology. They were also employed in intelligence gathering beginning in the 1960s, when flying over the Soviet Union in manned aircraft—namely, the infamous U-2—had become too risky.[9] However, space-based assets were not used to meet the *military's* needs for intelligence until the end of the cold war. Instead, a top-secret agency called the National Reconnaissance Office (NRO) operated intelligence satellites to satisfy the needs of high-level national security decisionmakers. The NRO simply did not play the role of providing military intelligence. This situation changed as the Gulf War approached. According to Moorman,

> Desert Storm was the first time the full spectrum of space systems was available to combat forces. . . . As a result, during Desert Storm many aviators felt that, "All of a sudden I get a chance to see this stuff which heretofore has been black" [that is, classified secret and compartmentalized and, hence, off-limits even to those with top-secret security clearances, unless they had a specific need to know]. Over time, those products had been decompartmentalized. They had been available [before the Gulf War], but not as broadly. Because of the access to previously highly classified reconnaissance products and because of the vital importance of missile warning, weather forecasting, communications, and navigation from space, for the *flying* Air Force, Desert Storm was a Eureka.

This Eureka effect can be traced to an increase in both the demand for and supply of information collected and relayed by satellites, including military intelligence. The ratcheting up of demand was tied to the Desert Storm air campaign. As mentioned earlier, this campaign targeted so-called centers of gravity within the Iraqi military system, which were to be destroyed with precision munitions. Intelligence collected from satellites operated by the NRO was valuable in identifying targets and pinpointing their location for the purposes of programming smart munitions. The increased demand for operationally relevant information provided by space-based assets is thus related to the story traced in the previous section, namely, the birth and application of contemporary airpower theory.

The increase in the supply of satellite-based military intelligence was of a different origin. Moorman believes that the NRO had to redefine its role to remain relevant following the end of the cold war: "In the cold war, the

NRO had bipartisan support for its relevance and priority. When the [Berlin] Wall came down, there was an erosion of that unanimity, and they became more broadly customer focused."

When the NRO shifted its focus to include military customers, operational planners gained access. Air Force aviators began to consider space a medium in which technologies could enhance their combat capabilities—in the vernacular, to put steel on targets. The Eureka effect noted by Tom Moorman gave the whole question of space a prominent position on the Air Force planning agenda, whereas it was not a main topic of *Global Reach—Global Power*.

Origins of the Fogleman-Era Strategic Vision

The Air Force experienced overlapping discontinuous changes just before Fogleman took charge. First, the doctrines underpinning the so-called tactical Air Force were utterly transformed. The Air Force mission had expanded beyond supporting the Army on the ground, to include directly achieving strategic military objectives through the systematic deployment of airpower in well-devised air campaigns as part of joint and coalition operations. This discontinuous change in doctrinal beliefs had yet to be codified in Air Force doctrine or expressed in the institution's strategic vision; nonetheless, the main lines of airpower theory presented in John Warden's book, *The Air Campaign*, no longer represented a minority view. The cultural significance of this transformation included a growing belief among senior officers that the Air Force as a whole could contribute directly to the pursuit of national military objectives.

Second, the relationship between airpower and space-based assets had suddenly become a subject of keen interest to aviators. Space became more broadly recognized as a critical medium for the success of air campaigns, and interest in space was no longer limited to the space community within the Air Force.

Third, the Air Force found its positions regularly opposed by the other military services. The Air Force was even excluded from some interservice dialogues, such as those of the Army-Navy Board, even when the discussion affected the Air Force. Gone were the days when the Air Force—specifically, the Tactical Air Command—could easily make common cause with the Army, as was the case in the heyday of the air-land battle. The change struck some in the Air Force as a realignment among the military services.

These discontinuous changes were interrelated, with a common link to the Gulf War. Within the Air Force, the Gulf War proved the value of emergent airpower theory. It also left the air-land battle doctrine in tatters: the Air Force no longer considered it militarily rational or politically convenient to pledge itself to the Army's strategic-level doctrines of conventional war. The realignment of interservice relations was also sparked by the Gulf War, which emboldened Air Force leaders to advocate changes in defense policy that the other services found wanting.

These changes also share a link to the end of the cold war. First, with the Soviet Union unraveling, the Air Force's nuclear mission was no longer preeminent. The Air Force thus had an incentive to gain recognition for its contribution to conventional combat. While this incentive does not explain why airpower theory was recast or why it came to be applied to the Gulf War, it does help explain why the Air Force leadership sought to capitalize on its successes in that conflict. Second, the spike in aviators' interest in space grew out of the Eureka effect, which was linked to the increased supply of military intelligence provided by the NRO. That increased supply, in turn, was the result of the expansion of the NRO's mission to include providing military intelligence for operational purposes, which reflected the domestic political and fiscal ramifications of the end of the cold war. The potential for realignment was apparently accentuated by Air Force policy management, including the *Global Reach—Global Power* vision, which was itself a self-conscious response to the end of the cold war.[10]

These events—or, more specifically, their intersection—were to have a profound effect on strategic visioning in the Air Force. In some respects, the task of the Fogleman round was to enshrine the institution's emerging strategic vision in a way that would ensure it was acceptable to internal and external constituencies alike. The task was also to decide how to handle the whole question of space, which was already an issue on the informal Air Force planning agenda—albeit one weakly structured as an area for internal debate. Finally, the Air Force was presented with an opportunity to move toward thinking strategically and collectively about the institution's longer-range future and engage in efforts, both internal and external, to act on that collective point of view. How this task was performed during the Fogleman period is the subject of the following chapter.

CHAPTER 3

Planning with Dialogue and Passion: The Fogleman Round

The story of Air Force strategic planning during the 1994–97 period is intimately related to how Gen. Ronald Fogleman led the Air Force as chief of staff. Having been nominated by President Clinton and confirmed by the U.S. Senate, Ronald Fogleman became chief on October 24, 1994. Fogleman entered office intending to improve on the existing Air Force strategic vision; to press the Air Force's case for an enhanced role in national defense while smoothing relations with sister military services; and to institutionalize a long-term planning capability for the Air Force as a whole. What linked these related intentions was Fogleman's sense of his responsibilities of office. As he stated in our interview with him, "A person that heads an institution must consider, how does one posture such an institution to contribute what it's supposed to do for the country?"[1]

During his first year in office, neither strategic visioning nor long-range planning was uppermost in his mind. He was more concerned with allowing the Air Force to settle down after a period of painful change.[2] The turbulence was the result of a proactive response to a combination of events: first, the emergence of the post–cold war national security strategy and, second, decreases in defense spending that implied proportional cuts in funding for the Air Force. The Air Force responded by downsizing and reorganizing under Secretary Rice and Chief of Staff McPeak. In the ten-year period from 1986 to 1995, Air Force funding dropped 34 percent, active personnel strength declined 27 percent, and base installations fell 24 percent.[3]

The reorganization, which took effect in 1992, included the historic disestablishment of both the Tactical Air Command and the Strategic Air Command. Their respective mission areas were initially assigned to the newly formed Air Combat Command; a year later, the mission area involving intercontinental ballistic missiles was reassigned to Air Force Space Command. The reorganization of major commands also included disestablishing the Military Airlift Command and establishing the Air Mobility Command, with some of the former's responsibilities moving to the Air Combat Command while the bulk was transferred to the Air Mobility Command. Another change at the major command level was the establishment of the Air Force Materiel Command, which absorbed the mission areas of the disestablished Air Force Systems Command and Air Force Logistics Command.

The Rice-McPeak period was thus highly stressful for Air Force personnel. Career prospects—even the prospect of continued service—had been placed in jeopardy, while the work patterns of personnel both within and far below the major command headquarters level were significantly affected by the various reorganizations. Fogleman believed that the Air Force now required a period in which to digest these changes. Accordingly, he wanted the outset of his term to be marked by stability:

> The day before I became the chief, I asked to meet with all the four-stars, who had come to Washington for the outgoing chief's retirement ceremony. I sat down with them and said, "First of all, we have just been through an awful lot of turbulence in the Air Force." We talked through the fact that the first priority that we wanted to take on in the opening months of my tenure as chief was to provide some stability to the Air Force. Instability comes from both external and internal forces. We agreed it would be extremely valuable if we could give the Air Force some [relief] from internal turbulence for a period of time.

However, while the initial phase of the Fogleman period emphasized a return to normalcy, the new chief's attention was fastened on the possibility of significant change over the long run. The specific objects of his attention were issues on the defense policy agenda:

> When I returned to Washington as the chief, all the buzzwords in town had to do with information warfare and the revolution in military affairs. I had been a little out of the loop on the literature about these subjects when I was at Scott Air Force Base, Illinois, as Com-

mander of both U.S. Transportation Command and Air Force Mobility Command. I was so wrapped up in the day-to-day business that I had allowed myself to get out of the habit of reading the latest professional journals with any care. At a staff meeting not long after I became chief, I just said, "I'd like the smartest people on the Staff in information warfare to come see me so I can learn more about it." Two people showed up, one from Intelligence and the other from Operations. For lack of a better term, they gave dueling briefings about what information warfare was about. So right away I knew we had a problem.

Strategic Visioning and Long-Range Planning as Policy Management

It became apparent to Fogleman that the Air Force was ill prepared to participate in a major review of national military strategy any time soon. There was no immediate prospect of such a review, however: the Clinton Administration's bottom-up review of defense was over and the Roles and Missions Commission would soon complete its work. By Fogleman's calculations, the Air Force had about two years before the next major defense review. A Quadrennial Defense Review (QDR) had been mandated by the Goldwater-Nichols Department of Defense Reorganization Act of 1986, but no such event had yet occurred. Fogleman thought that the QDR provision in Goldwater-Nichols would finally be implemented during his term: "John White made it a specific recommendation in his Roles and Missions report, and it was not a contentious recommendation like [moving] the artillery from the Army to the Marines." Fogleman anticipated that the QDR would commence in late 1996 and culminate in early 1997.

In the run-up to the expected QDR, Fogleman wanted to encourage debate within the Air Force in order to arrive at internal consensus on a range of matters, including issues currently high on the defense policy agenda. This inclination was strengthened as Fogleman learned more about information technology and its applications in warfare:

The dueling briefings on information warfare caused me to do a tremendous amount of reading in that area. The more I read about what was happening with information technology and thought about how that melded with the traditional Air Force strengths of speed, range, and flexibility, [the more I began to question] whether we were really postured for what was very likely to happen in the opening decade of the twenty-first century.

Fogleman's doubts were coupled with a conviction that the nation—not just the Air Force—needed to have an informed, searching debate about national defense strategy. The chief hoped that participants in the Quadrennial Defense Review would rise to the occasion. The aspiration was fueled by his own intellectual and professional engagement with the substantive issues that he believed should be dealt with in defense policymaking forums. Fogleman discussed his initial hopes for the QDR in an interview with former Air Force historian Richard Kohn, conducted soon after his retirement:

> Viewing the Air Force from the outside as a military historian, as someone who has tried to stay involved in academic affairs as well as national security affairs, I sincerely believed that the nation was at a unique crossroads, that the country had a tremendous number of internal needs, that the external threats were lower than we had faced in half a century, and that we had an opportunity—if we could have a serious discussion about national security strategy and defense issues—to restructure our military into a smaller, better focused institution to respond to the kinds of challenges coming in the next ten to fifteen years. It was not a military that was going to be shaped by some force-structure slogan like two MRCs [major regional conflicts], and it had to include a fundamental understanding of whether there really was a 'revolution in military affairs' and how we could and should fight future wars.[4]

This aspiration, combined with his role and statutory responsibilities, led Fogleman to dedicate much of his energy as chief to forging an internal consensus on national security and defense issues, especially as they pertained to the Air Force. A significant amount of this energy was channeled through the interrelated activities of strategic visioning and long-range planning. The activity of strategic planning was bound up with externally oriented policy management. As much as Fogleman wanted to facilitate change within the Air Force, the overriding idea was to build a foundation for more informed and effective Air Force participation in the external defense policymaking process. Fogleman described it as follows:

> It became clear to me that there was going to be a Quadrennial Defense Review and that it was going to kick off in the fall of 1996,

with the full review in play in the Spring of 1997. . . . We wanted to have the institution of the Air Force on one piece of paper when we went into that QDR, so that . . . the guys at Langley [the headquarters of Air Combat Command] weren't off in one direction and the guys at Colorado Springs [headquarters of Space Command] off in another.

In a way, the function of strategic planning was to shape internal beliefs, so that the Air Force as an institution operated as an effective policy entrepreneur in the channels through which national defense policy is made. Fogleman believed that to achieve this, he had to interact differently with his fellow chiefs than his predecessor had done:

> I had come out of the joint arena and had seen that it's really counterproductive to be confrontational. . . . I wanted to lower the interservice rivalry rhetoric, if you will, when I became the chief. I took a very deliberate approach that said, "I don't want to be the lightning rod." But I recognized that in interservice rivalries, you cannot leave the field of battle. Somebody's got to be out there stating your position. And so Chuck Link, a two-star general, picked up that role to a great extent. He could go make a speech and if it turned out that it really offended somebody and if they came to me, I could always say, "Well, you know Link, he needs a little adult guidance. I'll talk to him; we'll see what we can do about that." I'd call Link in and say, "I think you're getting close to the heart on this one. Keep pressing; this is pretty good."

Equally deliberate was the development of a strategic vision and long-range plan to serve as the basis for how the Air Force would participate in the Quadrennial Defense Review, which Fogleman envisaged would take place some two years into his term as chief.

The Strategic Planning Agenda

A specific design for rethinking the Air Force strategic vision and writing a long-range plan took shape during the ensuing year, as did Fogleman's own views about the direction in which the Air Force should evolve. It was during this period that Fogleman became absolutely convinced that the Air Force's strategic planning process was weak, confirming suspicions first formed during his time as the Air Force programmer. In that role, Fogleman had seen first-hand that long-range considerations exerted scant influence over resource allocation decisions, not only because of the politics of defense spending, but also because of how the Air Staff operated. Planning activities were separated from the action channels through which funding decisions were made and were thus frequently overridden. Fogleman's observations were consistent with the well-worn Pentagon adage that planning was the silent *P* in PPBS, the acronym for the Defense Department's forty-year-old Planning, Programming, and Budgeting System.

When Fogleman became chief, the major commands rather than the Air Staff in Washington generated long-range plans. His review of the major commands' long-range Mission Area Plans suggested that mission area planning was not especially strategic, however. Planning meant forecasting the need to replace current systems, rather than considering how missions might be performed completely differently in the future. A legendary incident drove this point home. In the course of a briefing on the mission area plan of the Air Combat Command, Fogleman asked about plans for a successor to the current Airborne Warning and Control System (AWACS). The components of this twenty-year old system included a Boeing 707 airframe, sensors housed in a dome mounted prominently above the fuselage, data processing equipment, and a sizable on-board crew. In response to Fogleman's unanticipated question, the briefer volunteered that the next-generation system would presumably use a more recent model Boeing as a platform, equipped with a dome mounted on top. The chief, in turn, suggested the possibility of performing the AWACS mission using space-based sensors that transmitted data to crews situated on the ground and thereby out of harm's way. The incident reportedly confirmed Fogleman's growing suspicion that the Air Force's legendary innovative spirit had somehow been sapped, at least in the modernization planning process.

Buy-in and Backcasting

By late 1995, Fogleman was ready to launch—and lead—an intensive effort to rework the Air Force strategic vision, write an Air Force long-range plan, and prepare the service for the anticipated Quadrennial Defense Review. Some of the spadework had already been done, since Fogleman had been thinking about and preparing for long-range planning since his early days in office.

Fogleman wanted to improve on the process followed by Secretary Rice in writing *Global Reach—Global Power* by involving a broader segment of the Air Force. As he explains, "There were things I wanted to do differently—trying to get the buy-in of the institution, trying to get a bottom-up process, and trying to get very respected external folks to come in and be part of the process."

Two principles were employed in designing the machinery and analytical constructs of the strategic visioning and long-range planning effort. The first principle dictated that Fogleman would need to secure collective support for the resulting strategic vision, which he called buy-in. No such collective support had resulted from the relatively invisible process through which Secretary Rice and General McPeak had developed *Global Reach— Global Power*. For Fogleman, buy-in meant that the strategic vision would represent an Air Force view, not just the chief's personal opinion: "I had observed the institution for many years and recognized that the life span of a chief's decision can be very short if it's one that the institution does not understand."

The benefits of buy-in were thought to be generated by connecting the strategic vision to long-range plans, overcoming cultural divides within the Air Force, strengthening the Air Force's hand in the defense policymaking process, and institutionalizing long-range planning as an Air Force process. All of these outcomes were thought to require the support of senior leadership. In Fogleman's words, "Before you can get your senior leadership to sell anything, they've got to believe in it."

The second principle was to formulate the Air Force's strategic vision and long-range plan by what Fogleman called backcasting from the future, rather than by what he characterized as forecasting from the present. The latter method was reflected in Air Force planning routines, epitomized by the Extended Planning Annex to the Air Force program. This perennial planning product answered the question of what would be the spending implications of current policy commitments and objectives for the period after the end of the official medium-term programming horizon. When Fogleman initially gave the long-standing Directorate of Plans the task of supporting the long-range planning effort, the eventual response was to provide an answer to *that* question. This disappointing response led Fogleman to coin the phrase backcasting from the future, conceived as the antithesis of forecasting from the present. Rather than project the long-range spending consequences of the current planning direction, the backcasting principle called for formulating a point of view about the future, which would then provide a basis for making nearer-term decisions. As Fogleman recalled, participants in the planning process were charged to think along the following lines:

I want you to go into low earth orbit in a satellite and you sit up there at 2025, and you look down at the world as it is in 2025 and then you try to figure out what the Air Force should be contributing to national defense. And then look back from that point and see where the pivotal events occur—when we shift from air-breathing to spaced-based AWACS; when we go through a divestiture program and get rid of something we're doing today.

The buy-in and backcasting principles shaped the planning process, the blueprint of which emerged by the end of 1995. The buy-in principle implied that the strategic vision and long-range plan needed to be invested with the authority of the senior leadership as a whole, including all of Fogleman's four-star colleagues (a group of about a dozen), plus top civilian Air Force officials. This group, known as the Corona council, met three times a year, normally for a three-day conference. Fogleman decided that the long-range planning efforts were to culminate in the fall 1996 Corona meeting, at that time about a year away. He intended for this event to result in a meeting of minds. Accordingly, Fogleman ruled out discussion of any subject apart from long-range planning, and he extended the conference's duration from the usual three days to five.

The buy-in principle was also the source of another key feature of the process, namely the establishment of the Long-Range Planning Board of Directors. This high-level working group was charged with preparing the fall 1996 Corona conference. Members of the board included three-star generals currently serving outside Washington in the major commands, as well as their peers in key staff positions under the chief at Air Force headquarters. Also appointed to the board were equivalently ranked civilians working for the secretary of the Air Force. The chairman's role was assigned to the four-star vice chief of staff.

Fogleman settled on the idea of forming the board of directors for several reasons, all related to the principle of buy-in. First, three-star vice commanders in the major commands were conduits to their four-star commanders, who needed to be connected to the process if the fall 1996 Corona meeting were to succeed, but who were too busy to participate regularly before that stage. Second, the board of directors was intended to demonstrate that strategic visioning and long-range planning was an institutionwide activity, rather than an exercise limited to the Air Force headquarters at the Pentagon. Third, Fogleman wanted strategic planning to outlive his term as chief, and he knew full well that the next cohort of top-ranked officers were currently three-star generals.

A designated time horizon of 2025 emerged from applying the principle of backcasting from the future. Fogleman initially settled on a thirty-year horizon when he commissioned an Air University study of so-called alternative futures, and he did not revise the time frame when tasking the board of directors. But after a period of time, he began to have second thoughts: "The first time I knew I was in trouble on the horizon issue was when somebody started talking to me about light sabers; that was probably a step further than I wanted to be," he said.

The organizational logic of a thirty-year planning horizon was nonetheless clear. If the horizon had been just beyond that of the Air Force program, which extended up to seven years in the future, then participants would have applied what they already knew from their own past experience. Furthermore, they might have identified with their own institutional loyalties within the Air Force, rather than acting as senior general officers planning the future of the Service as a whole. As a practical matter, the shorter the designated time horizon, the greater the likelihood that backcasting from the future would give way to forecasting from the present. It was for that reason that the board of directors, meeting in 1995, was requested to "look down at the world as it is in 2025," although the planning horizon was eventually brought forward to 2015.

Casting Key Roles

Protocol called for a group such as the board of directors to be chaired by an officer of higher rank than the rest of its members. Fogleman thus designated his four-star vice chief of staff, Tom Moorman, as the board's chairman. Moorman's career was centered in the Air Force's space community, in contrast with most who reach the pinnacle of status in the service. In Moorman's words, "I'm the first career four-star space guy." He had been selected to serve as vice chief by Tony McPeak, Fogleman's predecessor.

The vice chief was acutely aware of the elephant in the room—the issue of space. One of his objectives was to help the board of directors to fully appreciate that space was coming of age in the national security consciousness. Moorman believed, "There will be a time when we have weapons in space, which are infinitely more efficient than a ground-based solution in terms of capabilities and [global reach]." He feared that when that time came, decisionmakers would say that space was too important to put in a service that has an air orientation:

Space in the Air Force has had a very checkered history. Dominated by the black [secret] programs, dominated by civilians, lukewarm support, x number of people believe Space threatens airplanes in a budget sense, et cetera. All those things are not good if you are going to want to claim that you're the space service and want to continue to have this mission.

Establishing the board of directors went hand-in-hand with forming a staff group to support long-range planning. This unit, known as the Special Assistant to the Chief for Long-Range Planning (AF/LR), was organized in early 1995. At first, the unit was beset with turnover at the top. The first director, John Gordon, a two-star general, was soon detailed to a top position at the Central Intelligence Agency. Some months later, his replacement, Bob Linhardt, suffered a fatal heart attack. Linhardt's successor was David McIlvoy, a two-star general whose career had once before intersected with the long-range planning function. Throughout this critical period, the civilian deputy director, Clark Murdock, provided continuity.

Murdock, whose imprint on Air Force strategic planning was to grow over time, came to Fogleman's attention after the chief read an article he had written on the subject of long-range defense planning. Fogleman sent Murdock a complimentary note on the piece. A former professor of political science, Central Intelligence Agency official, National Security Council staff member, and aide to Les Aspin during his tenure as chairman of the House Armed Services Committee and later as secretary of defense, Murdock responded by seeking an appointment with Fogleman, which he was granted. The two quickly established an intellectual rapport, which led to Murdock's selection as the civilian deputy in the staff group known as AF/LR.

Socializing the Long-Range Planning Board of Directors

From the outset, Moorman told board members that their scheduled two- to three-day meetings were "mandatory formations," meaning no substitutes would be allowed. He feared that participants would increasingly send deputies to take part in their stead, leaving him surrounded by two- or even one-star subordinates rather than by the three-star principals. Moorman specifically requested that the major command vice commanders keep their four-star commanders engaged in the long-range planning process: "With Fogleman's okay, I charged every vice commander, after every board of directors meeting, to go back and . . . deliver their commander. I said, 'That's your job, and I'm going to know whether you are doing it well.'"

The first board of directors sessions were held in conference centers away from the Pentagon. Moorman recalled: "We had futurists come in and talk about trends and then what wild cards might do. Fogleman brought in movie directors to talk about how [to] think about technology. RAND analyst Carl Bilder, a noted critic of Air Force culture, introduced the board to things they didn't want to hear about." The board of directors was also given status reports on projects that Fogleman had earlier commissioned. For instance, Jay Kelly, from Air University, presented a methodology that his organization was developing to evaluate what Fogleman called alternative future Air Forces.

According to Moorman, the purpose of the early board meetings was socialization. The chairman was in no rush to focus the group on the specific task of preparing the fall 1996 Corona meeting. Rather, his intention was to allow the board of directors to evolve through the first three stages of group development, the full sequence of which is classically described as forming, storming, norming, and performing.[5] "The overall purpose," recalls Moorman, "was getting people's minds away from the day-to-day functioning of [say] Materiel Command or Mobility Command, [to get them] focused on this effort." The process, according to one civilian participant, "allowed people to step outside their part of the Air Force and to think about what the whole organization needed."

Nonetheless, some ambivalence was felt by at least a few of the mandatory participants who had not set the agenda. One participant recalled, "They brought in facilitators. They brought in futurologists. Guys that believed in UFOs and guys that talked about the wild card in history and how the course of history could have been changed. It was kind of a mind stretching exercise, but we sometimes wondered where the hell this thing was going." Moorman sensed the ambivalence of some board members, but he remained committed to working through the socialization process: "Some members sitting around the table were thinking, 'What a big political-science bunch of crap this is.' I could see it on their faces. But by the third meeting, they're all into it. Later, the biggest cynics turned out to be some of the greatest contributors."

During the long socialization process, however, even those participants sympathetic to the cause experienced ambivalence about spending precious time discussing the future of the world and of the Air Force. In the words of the head of logistics on the Air Staff at the time,

> We'd go to these board of directors meetings, and my emotions would go up and down. Sometimes I'd think it was really going to lead someplace, and other times I'd think it was a real waste of time, and I wouldn't choose to participate any more. I went through many of those cycles. . . . It's not that the meetings weren't interesting; there

were some good discussions. But I got the sense that after we sat there and had all of these discussions, nobody would know much more about what to do next than they did when they came in. I was really worried at the time that it was not going to produce any usable results.

One source of ambivalence was the principle of backcasting from the future. A key participant felt that "the notion of being able to fast-forward yourself to some perch out there in 2015 or 2025 and then, with perfect clarity, cast back to the present is terribly difficult." The demands of applying the backcasting principle were compounded by Fogleman's initial framing of a thirty-year planning horizon. As a result, the board members sometimes felt they had been asked to do the impossible. According to Tom Moorman, "We used to debate how far out we can really look before the giggle factor sets in."

Not all the board's work was structured by the principle of backcasting from the future. The board of directors became a forum for discussing the latest strategic thinking about airpower, developed by the specialized Air Force community that concerned itself with military theory and doctrine. According to one board member, "It seemed to me that all of a sudden there was this awakening. People in the Air Force [realized] there are some things that we can say that are pretty persuasive and logical, and we can talk about it in a doctrinal way, and it could very well influence how people think about warfare."

Whether the Air Force was giving a wide enough berth to the space community was a major recurring theme in board proceedings. As mentioned earlier, the participants, especially Moorman, were well aware of the cultural divide between aviation- and space-oriented personnel in the Air Force. Some worried that the institutional loyalty of personnel in space-oriented career fields would eventually be tested. Future champions of the space mission could be foreseen joining with external constituencies to seek the establishment of a space force separate from the Air Force. A recent precedent involved the U.S. Special Operations Command. In the 1980s, partly in response to the botched mission to rescue the American hostages held in Tehran, Congress determined that the services were not giving adequate focus to special operations. One observer of the board of directors remarked, "The U.S. Special Operations Command was given special authorization to do those same Title X organize, train, and equip [statutory] functions that services have—and they didn't want that to happen with space." The Air Force itself had come into existence some forty years earlier in much the same way, when aviation-oriented leaders in the Army advocated a separate service.

Getting down to the Task

Once the forming, storming, and norming phases of the group development process had run their course, the board of directors increasingly felt the pressure to perform. Yet board members still felt at sea, faced with the unbounded task they had been assigned and with only six months before the fall 1996 Corona conference. One participant described this stage of the board's evolution as follows:

> They let us kind of stumble around for a while. Then they brought Fogleman in to focus us down a bit. . . . He talked about the trends that were affecting how we do business right now and how we will do business in the future. He talked for about an hour and a half. A lot of people asked him questions, and in that way we kind of got a sense of where he wanted to go. He didn't come out and tell us to do certain things; he just kind of tried to focus us a little bit. That was a very useful exercise.

Thus oriented, the board of directors began to identify the issues on which to focus, using nominal group techniques of the sort they had practiced in the days when total quality management had swept through the Air Force. The vice commander of the Air Force Materiel Command, Larry Farrell, recalled:

> We went through these exercises where we just threw out a lot of ideas, like integrating air and space, infrastructure, and logistics. The recorders collected 200 ideas. Then they sent these 200 ideas out to guys like me and said, "Okay, group them into logical piles and send them back to the board of directors." . . . I think I sent in five groupings, but other guys sent in as many as thirteen. Then we went through another exercise as a group trying to rationalize that. Then we went through it *again* as a group. And then we sent Fogleman a list with about two dozen issues on it.

Fogleman circled fifteen issues from the board's list, and he added one of his own. Once Fogleman had signed off on what became known as the sixteen Corona issues, the board's days of working on an extremely unstructured task were over. The list of issues structured the board's agenda and also became the basis of Corona's week-long conference several months later. In the meantime, the board of directors had to organize itself to prepare the sixteen issues for discussion and resolution at the Corona conference.

The issues were assembled into functionally oriented groupings, such as operations, logistics, and personnel. Each grouping became the responsibility of a panel headed by an individual board member. This move turned out to be a major turning point. In the words of Larry Farrell, who was appointed chairman of the logistics panel, "It looked like a huge task to me. I knew I was going to be stuck with having to present to Corona. I had never been to a Corona [conference] in my life, but what I did know about it was that every four-star in the Air Force was there. I got real serious." George Babbitt, a three-star deputy chief of staff during the Corona issues process, noted that panel chairs, like Farrell, stepped up to the task: "I think it was the individuals, facing the prospect of embarrassing themselves in front of the group, who had to put a lot of personal time into trying to make this thing rational and logical."

Identifying Core Competencies

As the board's work continued, the idea that the Air Force's strategic vision should include a statement of the Service's core competencies began to take hold. The idea was picked up by the board of directors and the long-range planning staff after it had been developed elsewhere within the Air Staff. The impetus was to identify areas in which the Air Force might divest resources and activities, a thorny task that was regularly debated in the 1995–96 period. The concept of core competencies was suggested by a senior official working on the Air Force Board as a way to discriminate between sensible and unacceptable divestments. Several years later, John Handy recalled the session he had chaired:

> We were sitting down there as an Air Force Board saying, "Where do we focus our energy? Where do we put our dollars? There are certain things we are highly competent at, and there are other things we ought to just divest ourselves of." And a civil engineer said, "I've got an idea," and he put up a chart with some competencies that he had thought about. So we debated that idea, and we came up with a list of corporate competencies.

The initial list of core competencies developed for that purpose was closely related to the capabilities that had been key to the Air Force's contribution to the Gulf War: namely, rapid global mobility, air superiority, and precision engagement. The Air Force Board's list was refined by the Directorate of Programs and Evaluation and later briefed to the Air Force Council, a standing committee of senior leaders at Air Force headquarters chaired by the four-star vice chief of staff. The council took a favorable view, adding to the momentum of the idea.

The attractions of the core competencies construct for the strategic planning effort were several. First, the chosen competencies were collectively comprehensive, so all the Air Force's numerous professional communities would feel included. Second, core competencies provided a language in which to express the strategic vision that emerged during the Rice-McPeak period. The idea that the Air Force was transitioning from a garrison to an expeditionary force, which was a central issue in *Global Reach—Global Power,* was conveyed in the core competencies of rapid global mobility and global strike. Precision engagement and information superiority were tied to the idea that air campaigns would contribute directly to achieving national military objectives by using information and precision munitions to strike an opponent's centers of gravity and other targets. The insertion of the word *space* in the core competency of air and space superiority indicated that air campaigns depended on space-based assets performing the full spectrum of military functions, including intelligence. The core competencies were thus well suited for conveying the Air Force's strategic vision. The rhetoric of core competencies, it was thought, might also be less provocative than the language Rice and McPeak had used in their communications with the other services.

Third, the core competencies resonated with concepts that Fogleman and his planners anticipated would appear in *Joint Vision 2010,* the strategic vision being developed elsewhere in the Pentagon by the chairman of the Joint Chiefs of Staff. These concepts included dominant maneuver, information dominance, full-dimensional protection, and focused logistics. By including core competencies, such as global attack, information superiority, and agile combat support in its strategic vision, the Air Force could argue that its direction was consistent with *Joint Vision 2010.*

Fourth, core competencies comported well with a key aspect of Fogleman's overall approach to strategic planning, backcasting from the future. Whereas the long-practiced approach inferred long-term future spending on the basis of current programmatic directions, the chief ideally wanted to decide current programmatic directions on the basis of what the Air Force could contribute to national defense in the future. Strategic planners began to pick up on the idea that the Air Force would be able to decide what core competencies to cultivate as it backcasted from the future.

One advocate for interpreting backcasting from the future in terms of managing competencies was Tom Moorman, who chaired the Long-Range Planning Board of Directors. The vice chief's own agenda included discussing how to reconstitute the Air Force's community of space professionals, of which he was the highest-ranked member. Moorman wanted to restore the Air Force space community's ability to develop technologies to perform military functions from space-based platforms. A concern among space professionals was that key management decisions, including the McPeak-era major command reorganization, had damaged their increasingly fragmented community of 20,000. By placing the idea of backcasting in the same framework as managing competencies, Moorman was able to pursue this agenda in preparing the fall 1996 Corona conference, which would decide the Air Force's strategic vision and the outline of its long-range plan.

Once the stakes were raised, additional core competencies came to be identified. A perfect example is agile combat support. This core competency was advocated by George Babbitt, the deputy chief of staff for logistics and supply and also a board of directors member. Agile combat support had several attractions for those involved in preparing the fall 1996 Corona conference. One was that many of the nonaviator professional communities working in such career fields as supply, maintenance, acquisition, personnel, and civil engineering would see themselves more clearly in the strategic vision. A second was that the Air Force's core competencies would then include a counterpart to the concept of focused logistics put forth in *Joint Vision 2010*. Finally, Babbitt, a three-star general at the time, later conjectured that Clark Murdock, then the civilian deputy director of the chief's ad hoc long-range planning unit, saw an opportunity to win Babbitt's full support for the strategic planning process, and he pressed Babbitt's views among the full-time long-range planners. Thus agile combat support became an Air Force core competency for three reasons, each of which was political in the wide, neutral sense of the word.

Moving toward the Corona Conference

Under the direction of the panel chairs, the task of preparing the Corona issue papers was shared widely. Contributions were required of functional experts at both the headquarters and major command levels. For example, work on the future of issues assigned to the logistics panel was carried out by personnel in the functional staff organization at the Pentagon, as well as by personnel assigned to the Air Force Materiel Command's headquarters at Wright-Patterson Air Force Base, near Dayton, Ohio. The idea of involving so many people in the process was in some way prompted by the board of directors meeting in which Fogleman spent an hour and a half sharing his views of the future. The chief recalled that session, held in the Pentagon:

> I went into that room upstairs, 5C 1042, where I've spent about half my life, and there was the board of directors. They were all my contemporaries or older, so this is a crowd that was going to be gone in three or four years. Afterward, I met with the vice chief and said, "We really need to get some colonels and brigadiers in here to work as subcommittee members, because they're the people that will take this forward if they believe in it, but if we just drive it down on them they won't." So we tried to get some young blood into the process, and that became part of it.

Fogleman's request was carried out. A lieutenant colonel assigned to the long-range planning unit, remembered the process:

> It was really a wide, extensive network of people that worked on these issues. The major command vice commanders had their staffs work on these issues, and then each of the offices at headquarters had their staffs. I don't know anybody who wasn't touched in some way by the effort to make things happen prior to the Corona conference.

In the months leading up to the fall 1996 conference, strategic planning had become a more structured task—with an increasingly tight deadline. While narrowing the world down to sixteen issues focused attention, preparing a Corona issue paper was demanding work. In preparing the papers, panels were obliged to apply the principle of backcasting from the future. In the end, the panel chairs would have to go before the Corona council and discuss alternative ways the Air Force could position itself in 2025 with respect to the sixteen issues. The board of directors served as a forum for testing these alternatives, which came to be referred to as end states. The principals, together with some additional participants, met monthly during this period. A few were said to have had occasional private access to the chief to "see whether they were on track," in the words of one more peripheral principal.

Not long before the fall 1996 Corona conference, Fogleman decided how long a planning horizon he wanted to insist on. He instructed the board of directors and the long-range planners to shorten the horizon from 2025 to 2015, because "it was becoming too hard to make [the connection] from 2025 back to the late 1990s." The chief was also thinking about how the products of long-range planning would be viewed by those who had not participated in the process: "We said that this has to believable. It also has to be something that in their own minds the average airman, who's out there trying to make an airplane fly or computer work, can see will happen. We had put the horizon out a bit too far and decided to pull it back."

While the Board of Directors was organizing itself to write sixteen issue papers, Fogleman was paving the way for the fall 1996 Corona conference to be an important event. The task for the full complement of four-star generals and civilian counterparts was to settle on a new Air Force strategic vision and outline the written long-range plan. The chief wanted his colleagues to take this task as seriously as he did. Fogleman signaled his intent in comments delivered during the preceding Corona meeting, held in June:

> I made it known that I had blocked my schedule for two weeks prior to Corona to do nothing but review the material associated with long-range planning. No international travel, no hosting of anybody. All I was going to do was review the material. I told them, "Look guys, you've got to be on the step; you have to know what the issues are that we're talking about. We can't rehash everything for those of you who aren't up to speed, so that we can have meaningful discussions."

The chief's scheduling decision is considered to have contributed to the senior leadership's engagement with strategic planning in the period leading up to the fall 1996 Corona session. According to Tom Moorman,

> When Fogleman announced, "I'm going to spend two weeks getting ready for this—nothing else," all those other four-stars probably thought, "If the chief is going to spend this much time, I'm going to spend every bit as much time. I'm going to be equally prepared." It was a stroke of genius. His demonstrative commitment ensured that the primary actors knew how important this Corona was to the chief and reinforced the message that all the actors should be well versed in the issues and ready to participate.

Moorman's perception was echoed by David McIlvoy, the two-star general directing AF/LR. "I remember the four-stars all of a sudden getting really interested in doing their homework." With the prodigious output of the board of directors, the long-range planning unit, functional staffs at the Pentagon, consultants, and major command staffs supporting panel chairs, the four-star generals were given plenty to absorb in advance of the Corona session.

Finally, in October 1996, four-star generals, the department's civilian leadership department, the board of directors, and legions of Staff officers assembled at the Air Force Academy in Colorado Springs, Colorado. The only item on the agenda for the extraordinary five-day session called by Ronald Fogleman was long-range planning. The conference included two types of sessions. One was roundtable discussion on thematic issues that were to be addressed in the strategic vision document, prospectively entitled *Global Engagement.* These included the proposal to incorporate the core competencies of air and space superiority, rapid global mobility, global attack, information dominance, and agile combat support into the strategic vision. Another major thematic issue was space. The second type of session was oriented toward writing a long-range plan. These sessions focused on the sixteen Corona briefing papers, grouped together in functional categories. The specific task was to consider options that the panels had formulated and to achieve consensus on the future of the Air Force. The eventual consensus was to be expressed as a body of directive statements about the sixteen issues brought to the Corona conference.

The conference is reported to have been lively, compared with many previous ones. "Everybody engaged around the table," recalled Tom Moorman. "The guys talking about space were all the nonspace guys, who were really excited about the future of the Air Force as it relates to space. And it showed that they did their homework prior to the meeting." One board of directors member described the dynamics of the meeting as follows:

> At the Corona [conference], the briefer would stand up there and brief certain slides, but Fogleman controlled the discussion. And he was familiar enough with the issues. We could tell he was trying to lead to consensus, but from a perspective that he already had a gut feeling was the right perspective. He was open enough about it, so that when new information was presented, he was willing to listen to that and maybe change direction. He kind of had it in his mind where he wanted to go, but he wanted to get consensus.

The most significant issue on which Fogleman seemed to achieve consensus was space. The senior leadership endorsed the following statement, which was later incorporated into both the *Global Engagement* vision and the Long-Range Plan: "We are an Air Force today transitioning to an air and space force on an evolutionary path to a space and air force." The argument that seemed to bring about consensus on what some describe as the gut issue of the Air Force's commitment to the space mission involved the long-term dynamics of interservice competition in the context of American politics. Moorman put it as follows:

> In the future, space may be what makes the Air Force unique. Obviously, the Air Force is the only service that provides the full complement of airpower, but one could argue that every service has an air force. For example, the Army has more airplanes than the Air Force. However, the Air Force is without question the space service. Being a historian, Ron Fogleman had a broad perspective of the past and was a student of the lessons of history. He also had a strategic perspective. I think he clearly understood how space might evolve and how important space was likely to become to our national security. I think he perceived a risk that a predominantly air-oriented Air Force could well lose the space mission in a similar way that the Army lost much of its earlier role in aviation.

Some respondents held that the conspicuousness of space in *Global Engagement* was triggered by anticipatory fears of a schism. They were troubled by the possibility that the advocacy coalition for military space—linking certain Congressional leaders (such as Senator Robert Smith of New Hampshire), elements of the Office of the Secretary of Defense, some segments of industry, and the Air Force space community—could successfully push for the establishment of a separate space force. As already mentioned, Moorman was concerned that "the decisionmakers will say that space is too important to be put in a service that has an air orientation." Fogleman, however, flatly dismissed such a prospect in an interview in which he detailed his trajectory toward the "space and air force."

Another set of authoritative words to emerge from the Corona conference related to the sixteen issues. For each issue, consensus was expressed in terms of one or more end states for 2015. Overall, forty-two end states were identified. The theory behind this construct was to steer attention away from the present. By insisting on the end-state construct, the long-range planning staff sought to honor Fogleman's principle of backcasting from the future.

Each end state was characterized in a directive statement. Interestingly, the very concept of a directive statement was novel. It was developed because the available terms in the Air Force's bureaucratic lexicon were inappropriate. The usual term, *guidance,* did not work, since Fogleman and his long-range planners wanted to imbue the Corona outcome with more authority than implied in the term *guidance.* The alternative standard term, *policy,* did not suffice, either. Most statements coming out of the fall 1996 Corona conference were pitched at too general a level to be described as policy. Consequently, the term *directive statement* was coined to describe the outcomes of the Corona meeting.

One of the least abstract directive statements to emerge from the Corona conference dealt with unmanned aerial vehicles (UAVs). Typically, UAVs perform military functions of surveillance and reconnaissance. Unlike the manned platforms performing these functions, UAVs are remote-controlled: their "aviators" operate from stations on the ground. According to principals in the Corona issues process, UAVs stood as an object lesson in allowing the Air Force's culture—centered on manned aviation—to dictate technological choices. Fogleman chose to use the UAV issue, in part, to make the point that the Air Force needed to revitalize its culture of innovation if it were to succeed in the future.

In our interview, Fogleman described the outcome of the fall 1996 Corona conference in the following terms:

> I think the major conclusion was that we needed to put the Air Force on a path from being a predominantly air-breathing Air Force to one that was going toward more balance between air and space, to one that would eventually be dominated by space, with the air-breathing assets taking on less of a role. There was also our whole theme that the United States Air Force was in direct support of the national security strategy and had some core competencies that the nation could not afford to back away from.

Not all the principals at the Corona conference were satisfied with the outcome, however. One reason was that attention had focused on just a few of the vast range of subjects that deserved the same intensity of collective, senior-level engagement. Several principals were concerned that the directive statements specifying forty-two end states did not amount to a plan, since they were too numerous and yet did not deal with all subjects relevant to the future of the Air Force. Nonetheless, the strategic visioning process itself received high marks. Fogleman's own understated evaluation was that the Corona conference involved "meaningful discussions on the important points."

From Strategic Vision to Long-Range Plan

The task of documenting the Corona consensus and formulating a long-range plan fell to Fogleman's long-range planning group, led by Dave McIlvoy and Clark Murdock. Their deadline was February 1. One action officer recalled:

> It was like everybody looked around at the end of 1996 and said, "Geez, we've got to write this long-range plan. We don't have much time to do it. We have the holidays, too. Who's going to help us?" So this call went out, and Farrell said, "Come to Wright-Patt. I'll take your guys, and we'll do it." He activated his whole staff at Materiel Command to serve the creation of the long-range plan. He set conference rooms aside; he set up a command post for the thing. It was amazing.

While Farrell was deploying Materiel Command resources to write up the long-range plan at Wright-Patterson Air Force Base in Ohio, Fogleman moved forward to sell the *Global Engagement* vision inside the Air Force. "I remember when Fogleman brought all of the general officers from around the country into one room in Omaha and personally briefed them for three and a half hours on what took place at Corona," McIlvoy recalled. "He did the same overseas. He brought all guard and reserve senior leadership together, as well."

The process of transforming the output of the Corona conference into a long-range plan was to prove treacherous, however, as McIlvoy soon discovered. "When we built the first long-range plan, General Hawley, the commander down at Air Combat Command, told me he disapproved." McIlvoy called on Fogleman, who held the line. However, the static coming from Air Combat Command Headquarters at Langley Air Force Base foreshadowed a pattern of events that recurred frequently in the ensuing months. According to McIlvoy, a two-star general at the time, "I started getting personal calls from the four-star major commanders saying, 'Your plan is too damn specific; you're getting into our business.'"

Calling on the board of directors for cover was apparently not an option at the time. Asked about that period, one action officer surmised, "I think the board of directors said, 'Man, we're pooped.' So they let the staff handle the publication of the long-range plan and met some time later." A former principal of the group gave another explanation: "I think people felt they had already achieved what they were after."

Institutionalizing Long-Range Planning

An event that was to have significant repercussions for strategic planning was a major reorganization of Air Force headquarters. The reorganization was prefigured by Fogleman on establishing the Special Assistant to the Chief for Long-Range Planning in 1995. The chief imposed an informal sundown clause on AF/LR, due to expire sometime after the fall 1996 Corona conference. In mid-1996, Fogleman directed John Handy, the Air Force programmer, to formulate a reorganization plan. The effort's principal objective was to institutionalize the long-range planning function.

Long-range planning was traditionally the domain of the Directorate of Plans, which fell under the deputy chief of staff for operations (known as the XO). From Fogleman's perspective, the thought of reassigning AF/LR's responsibilities to the Directorate of Plans (known as AF/XOX) was unappealing for several reasons. First, AF/XOX's staple planning product, the Extended Planning Annex, epitomized forecasting from the present rather than backcasting from the future, the approach adopted during the Corona issues process. Second, the wider operations functional area—referred to colloquially as the XO world—was considered a bastion of combat-oriented aviators. Few XO leaders would have served in positions in which they might become immersed in space issues. Institutionalizing the new approach to long-range planning, as well as moving in the direction of a Space and Air Force, was expected to be an uphill battle in the XO community.

Consequently, a new Strategic Planning Directorate was established in January 1997, a few months after the Corona conference. AF/LR's responsibilities were transferred to the new directorate along with its assigned personnel, including David McIlvoy, the two-star director, and Clark Murdock, the civilian deputy director. As part of the reorganization, a new three-star role was created: the deputy chief of staff for plans and programs. The Strategic Planning Directorate (AF/XPX), together with directorates for programming dollars (AF/XPP) and manpower (AF/XPM), came under the new deputy chief, who came to be known as the XP.

The official rationale for establishing the XP organization was couched in the Defense Department's management language: PPBS. Handy argued that implementing strategic plans required a close connection between the strategic planning and programming processes. Historically, the planning-programming relationship did not involve reciprocal interdependence; rather, the work flow was sequential, with planners handing off their planning products to programmers based in a separate directorate. McIlvoy, who directed AF/LR before the reorganization, said of his days as an

AF/XOX planner during the cold war: "We produced great, beautiful plans, and the programmers simply ignored them." In a reorganized structure, however, strategic planners and dollar-oriented, nearer-term programmers would be part of a single community of planners and programmers, headed by the XP. A stated intention behind the organizational change, implemented in January 1997, was to link Air Force planning and resource allocation more closely than was normally the case.

The feeling inside the Strategic Planning Directorate in the months after its establishment was a combination of fatigue following the intense Corona issues process and a sense that the reorganization did not, in itself, institutionalize long-range planning. A telltale sign of institutionalization, its leaders felt, would be for the directorate's work to be visibly valued by Fogleman's eventual successor. The chief, by contrast, was confident that the structural change, combined with his choice of Larry Farrell as the first XP, would keep alive the practice of long-range strategic planning in the Air Force: "When we established the XP structure, . . . I began to feel that it would truly last, because we now had in place somebody that was a belly button for long-range planning and we'd actually laid out the groundwork about how we would do that."

Ending the Tour of Duty as Chief

By early 1997, Fogleman had become confident about the durability of corporate strategic planning within the Air Force. He was not so confident, however, that the Quadrennial Defense Review would occasion a serious discussion about national security strategy and defense issues, as he had earlier hoped. In an interview with former Air Force historian Richard Kohn, Fogleman recounted an incident during the early days of the QDR process that he found deeply disappointing. The chief was visited by a two-star Army general sent to deliver an informal message from his superior, the chairman of the Joint Chiefs of Staff. As described in the Kohn interview, the message was this: "In the QDR we want to work hard to try and maintain as close to the status quo as we can. In fact, the chairman says we don't need any Billy Mitchells during this process."[6] Billy Mitchell was an early advocate for the importance of airpower, who was court-martialed in 1925 for insubordination in criticizing the War Department for negligence in its provision of equipment for airmen, but who later rose to become assistant to the chief of the Army's Air Service. Recalling the incident, Fogleman reported: "From that point on, I really did not have much hope for the QDR. I guess I lost all hope when [Secretary of Defense] Bill Perry left, because he had the stature to have given the services the blueprint, and I think the services would have fallen in line."

Owing to increasingly severe conflicts with Clinton administration officials, including Secretary William Cohen, over important issues unrelated to strategic planning and the QDR, Ronald Fogleman decided to step aside a year before his appointment as chief was due to expire.[7] The announcement of his retirement came in August 1997, and his successor, General Michael Ryan, took office the following month. Fogleman recalled this period during our interview in 1999: "The guy I really wanted to see become the chief was Mike Ryan. . . . Farrell had already been brought in as the XP when I left, and I sincerely believed that the combination of Ryan and Farrell would take this process and move it to another step."

CHAPTER 4

The Ryan-Peters Round

As described in chapter 3, General Ronald Fogleman sought to lead the Air Force through a thorough reassessment of its future. Fogleman took a collegial approach to this enterprise with the aim of achieving consensus on the service's organizational coordinates. Collegiality, Fogleman believed, would increase the likelihood that the Air Force leadership would operate from a shared vision when requesting the resources needed for modernization. Fogleman's conviction that the Air Force would have to open up to the role of space in its mission functioned as a core motivation behind his effort, and it fueled an ambitious process that involved visioning far beyond the normal ken of planners. Fogleman also wanted to spark the institutionalization of changes in the way the Air Force planned for the future. He believed that the service should make a much greater investment in corporate strategic planning.

This chapter discusses the degree to which Fogleman's aspirations for Air Force modernization and institutionalization carried over into the regime of his successor, General Michael Ryan. The Ryan period entailed, as well, a greater involvement of the secretary of the Air Force in corporate strategic planning than was the case under Fogleman. This chapter thus also canvasses the vagaries of discourse between the political leadership and uniformed career officials in such dynamics.

Taking Stock of the Fogleman Round

General Fogleman set out not only to rehabilitate planning in the Air Force, but also to extend its horizons. He originally set thirty years as his time frame but retreated to twenty-five years when his four-star colleagues found that the former strained believability. General Ryan was openly skeptical of projecting even twenty-five years into the future, such that the 2000 vision contemplated twenty years. In any case, both chiefs went beyond giving greater profile to planning in the Air Force. They raised the bar, pushing the planning horizon far beyond the eight-year span of the Future Years Defense Program (FYDP), for which the Air Force produces its Program Objective Memorandum (POM) in even-numbered years. For instance, the POM developed in 2002 projected six years beyond the 2002 and 2003 fiscal years and went by the name "FY02–07 POM."

Some might argue that the period covered by a POM provides a more plausible time frame for planning than either the Fogleman or Ryan visioning exercises. A POM fixes on clearly specified programmatic objectives and defines in great detail how these will come to fruition within a precise number of years. Most of what it lays out, however, reflects the status quo. In contrast, Fogleman and Ryan pursued long-term strategic planning, in the belief that this would spur the Air Force to anticipate adaptations of its missions and capabilities to situations outside its current and projected programmatic commitments. Their efforts took the shape of a collegial engagement in visioning and a readiness to entertain the possibility that the Air Force might have to radically alter its core programmatic commitments to maintain its long-range viability.

Facing the Imperatives of Visioning Collegially

The nature of the Air Force's core activities requires that it look further into the future when planning than would most private and public sector organizations. The Air Force does not function monocratically, however, so it is not simply a matter of the chief of staff developing a strategic vision in splendid isolation. Even if that were possible, the chief would still have to reconcile the resulting vision with skeptical and, more important, powerful internal and external stakeholders.

Key players in the Air Force visioning and planning processes have become acutely aware that chiefs can only do so much to change their service. They wrestle with a need for clear guidance about the future but must deal with conditions of governance that limit the capacity of the chief or, for that matter, the secretary to fix the organization on a specific vision. As one respondent put it, neither is likely to say, "I've got it. I can see the future. I know this is the right answer."[1]

The question arises then, why bother with visioning at all? The answer rests in the culture of the service whereby the key players consider themselves patriots and in a vocational sense worry about the Air Force's future ability to sustain national security. As one civilian participant observed: "Joining the military is not a job, it's a vocation. There's a personal commitment to it. . . . The senior leadership of the Air Force is the custodian of their service's future."

Although the Air Force has a much shorter tradition than the Army, Navy, and Marines, it has tended to place relatively greater emphasis on strategic planning than the other services. This might owe to the tortuous metamorphosis of the Air Force from the Army Air Corps when strategic air warfare came of age during World War II.[2] The Air Force had to justify its development into a separate service each step of the way, and this pressure established a stronger planning culture than those prevailing in the other branches of the U.S. military.

Notwithstanding a fairly strong innovative culture, planning itself usually functioned incrementally and focused on, as one respondent noted, the replacement of old platforms with something that looked and functioned just the same. He went on to note that "the strategic investment streams that the Air Force had underway or was going to embark upon . . . weren't about the operational relevance of the Air Force in the future or about how to fight in the future. They weren't about fighting at all."

The development of the controversial F-22 fighter as a replacement of the aging F-15 serves as an example of such relatively long-term yet essentially incremental planning. A more revolutionary possibility would have been an examination of whether a space maneuvering system might prove technologically feasible in the lead time required to replace the F-15. One encounters a wide range of views about the efficacy of such deliberations, which, by definition, require taking a visionary view of capabilities and operations. In fact, stark propositions, such as that the function of the F-15 might be performed from space, provoked skepticism among the bulk of players who were plotting the Air Force's future over much of the period covered by this book. Conventional thinking tends to gravitate toward the status quo, with incremental steps toward change. One planner conveyed to us his understanding of the types of responses visionary propositions often provoke: "If I weren't in the planning world, I would say, 'I don't know what the hell those guys . . . have been smoking up there.'"

Many of the participants in the Fogleman and Ryan-Peters planning rounds believed that looking even fifteen years into the future amounts to gazing into a crystal ball. Alternatively, they suggested devising a range of futures so as not to overinvest in specific scenarios based upon assumptions about how reality will actually work out. As one key major command player argued, "[We have to] try to predict a range of futures, rather than one future that is most likely to confront us, and then make sure that we plan for an Air Force that can deal with that spectrum of possible futures." Such an approach would prove prohibitively expensive, however, if it translated into investments in a multiplicity of options.

Another issue emerges here. Because the Air Force consists of constituent organizations with substantial latitude for quasi-autonomous activity centered on the programs brigaded under each command, the interconnectedness of programs often escapes those entrenched in the day-to-day affairs of specific commands. Indeed, command-centric preoccupations can work varying effects on how the process of envisioning the future is perceived. For instance, the Air Mobility Command, which frequently faces operational requirements that exceed capacity and which has suffered from serious underinvestment in equipment, might be expected to take a reserved stance in strongly futuristic strategic planning. Devising ways of maximizing force under less-than-optimal circumstances and giving new life to aging aircraft would demand more immediate attention than long-range strategic views of the command's mission.

On the other hand, the Air Combat Command can readily envisage the future ten or fifteen years out. Its core mission revolves around shooting platforms flown by pilots—namely, fighters and bombers. Over the past several years, the Air Combat Command has found itself at the center of the debate over the relative merits of two fighters, the F-22 and the Joint Strike Fighter (JSF). The former is destined exclusively for the Air Force, while the latter is intended for use by the Navy and the Marines, as well as the Air Force. To be effective in the ongoing political struggle, the command must develop clear ideas about the optimal mix of F-22s and JSFs and how this might meet the operational challenges that the United States will face when these aircraft compose the bulk of the Air Force fighter capability.

The Space Command presents the clearest context in which long-range planning is relevant, and it is thus the most amenable of the commands to the visioning process. In that culture, the twenty-five- to thirty-year span

engaged by Fogleman would strike many as essential to any credible planning effort. As one respondent put it, developments in space come down to
pacing, rather than to setting specific time parameters. The central issue
that emerges under this rubric is not whether there should be a separate
space force, but when. Thus, much of the command would like to focus its
futuristic energies on theorizing about the environmental conditions that
would justify a separate force and examining how the new entity would
address them. Such conditions would presumably involve space becoming
an economic center of gravity, the need to protect space-based commercial,
communications, and military assets from hostile attack, and space serving
as a medium for mitigating threats defensively and offensively—including,
unspeakably, extraterrestrial ones. Many in the Space Command seem to
perceive General Fogleman's greatest fear—namely, that the Air Force would
fail to adapt quickly enough to keep space in its domain, much as the Army
had failed with regard to aviation—as the prologue to their destiny. As one
especially experienced respondent argued,

> It's naïve to think that the Air Force evolved because it couldn't get
> resources from the Army. What emerged was a global ability for avi-
> ation and that caused a military threat. . . . [It is] very much linked to
> economics. When will we get the ability to put huge investments in a
> speculative manner into space to make money? . . . [It is also] related
> to psychology.

Some Air Force planners look to a day when it will be easier to engage
such disparate cultures. Dramatic advances in futurist technology might
allow strategic visioning to more readily employ holistic principles that are
relevant to the entire Air Force, regardless of individual perspective. In this
respect, the Air Force has operated since 1996 under a "demand and supply" construct, which emphasizes a range of envisioned demands on
national security, rather than specific scenarios for identifying desirable
directions in which to develop force structure. In the meantime, the coun-
sel that stresses the need for continual revisiting of visions will probably
prove the wisest. Even a skeptic among our respondents allowed that the Air
Force needed "a living, responsive type of process" whereby the vision and
programmatic investments would eventually connect.

Despite the reserve, if not skepticism, about visioning and planning among
the Air Force's top leadership, we still found support for such processes from
the standpoint of positioning for opportunities. One well-placed four-star
general who registered concern that "long-range planners don't have to pay

bills today" still recognized the merit of setting goals and being prepared to invest in them should the opportunity arise. A planner believed that the Air Force was "capitalizing on opportunities and events as they unfold." At the end of the day, however, many respondents remained wary of investments in the future that would leave the Air Force shortchanged with respect to current capabilities. Some even registered the practical concern that many units lack the time and resources with which to satisfy seemingly insatiable demands for information provoked by some approaches to planning. One highly experienced insider put the issue especially starkly: "They have been given this task. They have produced these incredibly fancy charts. . . . Their goal is doing this job so that they can get back to their real job." Others worried about how solid the market is for visions and plans, as the Air Force's political leadership often focuses mainly on day-to-day issues. Further, some noted that the Office of the Secretary of Defense reveals little consistency in its demand for corporate strategic planning in the services.

Real Events Drive Home Urgency

As discussed earlier in the book, scenario building and war games can add cogency to voices among the top leadership exhorting greater concern for the future. During the period in which General Fogleman led the Air Force, however, reality itself seemed to be bearing down on the organization. Issues centering on the future role of space, as well as fundamental shifts in Air Force doctrine on war fighting, played key roles in this regard.

As already noted, the outside world had begun to debate openly the issue of whether the Air Force had neglected development of space-based capabilities—and if so, whether it warranted the creation of a separate Space Force. Such a challenge strikes a very deep cultural nerve in the Air Force. Here we run into the divide between "rated" officers who fly and "nonrated" officers who do not. Rated officers dominate the Air Force's corporate leadership. Indeed, until 2002, the practice whereby the commander of the Space Command also headed the North American Aerospace Defense Command (NORAD) preordained that the top officer in charge of space was, in fact, a pilot whose career has not centered on space. Young majors and lieutenant colonels in the Space Command found it especially grating that one of their own could not aspire to head their command. A retired nonrated four-star general with deep exposure to both the Space Community and the Air Force Staff asserted that it will become increasingly difficult for the Air Force to attract and retain top minds to space unless the rated/nonrated demarcation recedes considerably.

For their part, the lieutenant colonels and majors with whom we spoke at the Space Command headquarters appeared anxious for expanded roles. They fully expected that within the next twenty-five years or so the command will have weapons in space and that the individuals who actually fire them will be nonrated operators. They even raised the issue of whether noncommissioned officers could fulfill such roles. Contrast such speculation with a current debate in the Air Force over whether nonpilots could be trained to fly the Predator unmanned aerial vehicle.[3] Not only will pilots now receive flying hours for guiding the Predator, but the current Air Force secretary, James G. Roche, mused, "I want to have pilots fly the Predator. . . . If you try to stand up people who are not pilots, it is like an organ transplant, and I'm afraid the body might reject them."

Obviously, such speculation evokes strong reactions from the Air Force's top leadership—a response, however, that takes into account the need to redefine the role of space in its mission. As one major command commander granted, the perception that space advocates are second-class citizens in the Air Force provokes separatist sentiments both in the Space Command and among its constituencies. He thus held that the Air Force had to open up the debate over resources: "We are setting ourselves up for a repeat of the Army/Air Force divide by not giving an open forum to people advocating space power."

Quite apart from the issue of who will fire from space-based platforms in the future, many in the service had deep concerns that the integration of command and control in the Air Force has fallen way behind potential technological innovation. Command and control has become extremely space-dependent, raising a host of special challenges for integration. A four-star general highlighted how this had become an issue when General Fogleman contrasted modern command and control with the integrative approach that prevailed in the heyday of the Strategic Air Command: "He concluded that we understood nothing about it and that we had really lost a core competency."

Beyond the issues of technology and the role of space, Air Force doctrine was undergoing a major shift when Fogleman took office. In this case, actual engagement rather than war games provided the stimulus. Historically, Army doctrine governed the use of the Air Force in combat. In the view of one respondent, the doctrine held that the Air Force should bomb an opponent until the Army reached the theater in overwhelming numbers. Then, "the two opposing ground forces would meet as if there had not been any air warfare."

In 1991, Desert Storm put a wrench in this doctrine. By the time the Army engaged Iraqi troops, the latter had been sapped not only by air attacks on Iraqi battle lines, but also by highly effective assaults at the regime's command-and-control systems in Baghdad. This provoked Maj. Gen. Charles Link to press for a reconsideration of how the halt phase—the thwarting of enemy aggression—might be achieved in warfare. He championed the concept of a rapid halt, claiming that in some cases, airpower could stymie an opponent without waiting for the Army and Marines to get "boots on the ground" in substantial forces. Link left the Air Force early— some believe to advocate his views more freely. However, this did not take away the nettlesome problem. The other services became defensive about the Air Force challenging what one respondent called the little league definition of jointness, meaning that "everybody's here, everybody's on the team, and everybody plays." One key four-star general emphasized that discretion might prove the better part of valor as the Air Force promoted a doctrinal shift: "Right now, everything the Air Force says about itself appears threatening to everybody else. . . . When we talk about the ability to find, fix, target, and engage anything on the face of the earth, the reaction is, 'You guys think you can do it all!'"

Connecting Planning with Resource Allocation

Organizations' interest in corporate strategic planning waxes and wanes in relation to epochal shifts in their circumstances. In the case of the Air Force, a number of such factors came to the fore. First, a great deal of uncertainty about the Air Force's future in relation to other services—including the possibility of a separate Space Force—placed a premium on getting priorities straight and developing rationales for future capabilities. Second, substantial developments in thinking about warfare further justified a thoroughgoing reexamination of the Air Force's missions. Third, players generally recognized that visioning and planning would prove meaningless without the support and participation of the top leadership. Such considerations worked in favor of General Ryan continuing to employ the consultative mechanisms devised under General Fogleman. These circumstances gave planning in the Air Force not just a high profile, but also great legitimacy under both chiefs. Translating the plans into a redirection of resources proved difficult, however.

When we began our interviews in the fall of 1998, most respondents proved hesitant to draw strong connections between the visioning process, the long-range plan, and resource allocations. This owed partially to the compressed time frame between the development of the long-range plan (spring 1997) and the budgeting cycle: the Fogleman round had not been fully internalized before the jockeying began in connection with the 2000–05 Program Objective Memorandum (POM) as part of the Future Years Defense Program (FYDP). Further, General Fogleman's distraction by other issues and his eventual departure as chief in the summer of 1997 lengthened the time lag between the planning process and its effect on resource issues.

Many participants who affirmed a connection between the planning process and resource allocation did so with reserve or even embarrassment. One major command commander styled his own efforts to promote so-called agile combat support—a just-in-time approach to getting material to combat zones—as an exercise in "resource advocacy." A colonel who played a critical role in the process noted that the 1997 Long-Range Plan became a hot potato when the major commands realized that they could lose resources if the leadership became serious about implementing the plan: "If they would have begun knowing that they were in for an Air Force plan that included force structure decisions it would have been more difficult than say-ing, 'we need a vision to posture ourselves for the next [Quadrennial Defense Review].'"

An incisive three-star general stated that the connection between planning and resource allocation was usually tenuous, except when players engage in "malicious obedience" by pushing their projects because the plan prescribes them rather than because the projects merit it. We do not necessarily share this view. A substantial number of respondents believed that the rhetorical cues coming from the vision proved seminal with respect to the Air Force rethinking its fundamental commitments, even if in the first few years the connections between the long-range plan and resource decisions proved loose rather than tight. In particular, the core competencies articulated in the 1996 vision document became central to discourse. They evolved out of an integrative perspective of the different services with regard to the require-ments of the regional combatant commanders, who actually deploy forces in specific combat engagements. They also stressed the interconnectedness of capabilities serviced by the individual major commands. For instance, the vision construed quality people as a foundational core competency that must run through the organization. It considered air and space power as an overarching objective to which the Air Combat and Space commands con-tribute in partnership.

One four-star general who at the time of our interviews had reason not to be especially sympathetic to an enhanced role for the Space Command surprised us by presenting a transformed view of the role of space within the Air Force: "[It's] more than just an enabler. It's a true medium . . . operating and defending, and, someday, attacking—although we don't like to talk about that because of political issues." A three-star general who played a significant role in the 2000–05 POM process reported that the core competencies served as the subgroups for briefing on the POM. We found plenty of evidence of core-competency-oriented thinking outside the upper reaches of the Pentagon, notwithstanding frustrations with the gap between the plan and actual resource commitments. A young major heading up a requirements assessment for the Air Mobility Command provided a vivid testimony of the utility of the so-called parthenon—the chart in the 1996 *Global Engagement* that portrays the interconnectedness of core competencies:

> A new guy came in and asked what the value of global engagement is. . . . It's in the archway diagram. This is a major step from being bomber-centric or fighter-centric or nuclear-centric. This diagram shows what we have to be able to do as an Air Force, and what everybody's job is, and what core competencies they affect.

Several political appointees found great utility in the process, even though they shared reservations about the degree to which the strategic plan achieved tangible results in the allocation of resources. One such respondent argued that the vision was quietly working a paradigm shift:

> The process has been aided by lessons from Desert Storm and Kosovo. If there were future shares in parts of the defense budget, I'd buy Air Force. . . . It's clear that [the United States] wants to reach out and conduct wars without putting people on the ground. . . . Our current planning is useful since it drags people out of their day-to-day myopia. . . . The process creates mental images that shape day-to-day decisions.

The 1997 Long-Range Plan

The above discussion uncovers a split in respondents' views, whereby they were broadly favorable toward the 1996 vision document and, at best, reserved about the 1997 Long-Range Plan. Most participants expressed uncertainty about whether a long-range plan was desirable and, if so, how detailed it should be.

The 1997 Federal Benchmarking Consortium Study Report noted that many private sector organizations complete their vision and then leave development of long-range plans to individual business units, rather than working up an encompassing planning document.[4] General Fogleman clearly chose to produce a detailed long-range plan, and immense energy went into its preparation within a very compressed time frame. Yet the most negative observers felt that it was a dead letter the minute it went out the door. In the words of one respondent, "There was no coordination between the teams on the long-range plan. . . . The previous guy's section finished on page 9, and then the next guy would start on page 10. . . . It was a frantic effort to put this thing together at the end and kick it out the door. And that's where it stayed."

The horizons of the long-range plan apparently fell well short of those established for the vision. Even key players in the Air Force Staff's coordination of the long-range plan asserted that it scarcely stretched conventional horizons. A respondent who was deeply involved in developing the plan as a two-star general observed that "most of the stuff in the long-range plan was actually in the POM for 1998–2003, so Clark [Murdock, the top civilian Staff planner] and I would look at each other and say, 'Is this really long-range planning?'"

Moreover, many participants, even those from major commands, noted that the long-range plan was not specific enough to provide meaningful guidance for resource allocation. One four-star general observed that the long-range plan stopped short of providing requisite guidance on divestiture. He echoed the Federal Benchmarking Consortium report, however, in asserting that "long-range planning ought to focus on positive things, . . . [like] what is it we want to do, and then put some responsibility on people to try to drive that performance up and costs down. By [the] very nature [of the process], they're going to have to try to get rid of some things to try to make it all fit." The four-star general in charge of Air Combat Command, General Richard Hawley, received praise from his staff for doing precisely this, but his six-year plan essentially addressed tool-box issues connected with the Air Combat Command getting through the next Future Years Defense Program.

The long-range plan had thus encountered serious inertia, and many observers were fatalistic with regard to its actual consequences on resource allocation. An interview in 1998 with a recently retired official from the Office of Management and Budget, who had a long track record with the Air Force, reminded us that intractability can be a dominate feature of the governance of any bureaucratic organization under the separation of powers: "[It's] very tough for a chief to overlay his vision on the Air Force where investment programs are concerned . . . Hardware programs happen in the

[United States] in a very diffuse way, with contractors bringing new ideas to field generals like [Air Combat Command]." A crucially placed four-star general seemed to invoke the principle that a bird in the hand is worth two on the bush, "because what we have in the long-range plan is not going to sell right now." A frustrated Air Combat Command planner implicitly acknowledged that in the long run, paralysis about divestiture would not advance the cause of pilots with space looming as a real option: "The Air Force has lost control of pilots' destiny . . . [owing] to their inability to divest themselves of anything because of Capitol Hill."

The consistent references to contractors, field generals, and Congress sound like cries of "the devil made me do it." Whether the Air Force could close the gap between its aspirations to plan corporately and the rather meager first steps it took toward building programs that reflected the plan would depend on whether it could devise a way to increase the corporate character of programming.

Modest Tangible Progress

To be sure, both planning fatigue and Fogleman's distraction and eventual departure took their toll on the Air Force's follow-through on *Global Engagement*. Even so, the service did take significant, though modest steps toward integrating planning and programming and investing resources in fulfilling its new vision. Chapters 6 and 7 provide a detailed treatment of this process, but several developments deserve mention here.

With respect to the integration of planning and programming, the Air Force created a new unit in the Staff that, among other functions, brought planning and programming together under the same deputy chief of staff (see chapter 3). This institutional reform addressed the historic tendency for planners and programmers to circulate in different orbits.

The new Plans and Programs Directorate, known as XP, develops Annual Planning and Programming Guidance (APPG) to keep track of the resource commitments required to implement the Air Force vision. The APPG remains indicative rather than prescriptive, however, owing to continued disjunctions between planning, programming, and budgeting. That is, the APPG specifies planning coordinates without closing debate on actual resource commitments. The Air Force Planning Projection (AFPP), in turn, which was first issued in 2000, identifies critical decision points for getting resource commitments to programs that further the goals identified in the plans. Ostensibly, flagging these points helps the Air Force stage its claims for resources in order to optimize fulfillment of its vision. One respondent close to the nexus between planning and programming saw this as part of the effort to gradually tighten the relationship between the two disciplines: "The entire process over the past four years has laid the groundwork for a better audit trail between plans and programs." An outside consultant retained to examine the Air Force's resource allocation process echoed this assessment, adding that the AFPP, in particular, increases the Air Force's ability to sway the Office of the Secretary of Defense by demonstrating how a particular funding request supports the service's long-range goals.

The core competencies identified in the 1996 vision document began to shape the debate over capabilities and requirements at the outset. Even though different major commands would present conflicting interpretations of *Global Engagement*, they would use sections that had attained corporate legitimacy to gain sympathy to their cause. Lieutenant colonels and majors in major commands could cite passages favorable to their mission—and even identify the page numbers. A former participant who had kept tabs on the process characterized the effect of the 1996 vision document on space advocates this way: "All the space guys have *Global Engagement* trading cards, and the one they keep in their wallet is from page 7, where it says we're on an evolutionary path to a Space and Air Force. Those guys live and breathe that statement, and they really believe it." Unlike the vision document, the 1997 plan did not spawn such "trading cards" for reform. It had not been properly integrated and was overly complex.

However slowly, resources began to follow rhetoric in response to the 1996 vision document. More money was going into space research and development, unmanned aerial vehicles, and the training of young officers in aerospace concepts. Doctrine, too, was shifting. Agile combat support— a just-in-time concept that greatly reduces the front-end supply requirements for transporting combat units to theaters—became Air Force doctrine after having been embraced at the 1996 Corona meeting. Even before the Kosovo campaign, the debates surrounding capabilities during the visioning process had deepened acceptance in the Air Force of Major General Link's view that air power should play a dominant rather than supporting role in many engagements. Finally, on the organizational level, a new agency—led at the two-star level and lodged in the Air Combat Command—assumed responsibility for integrating the Air Force's highly fragmented intelligence, surveillance, and reconnaissance and command-and-control systems. This move addressed a concern that had operated at the core of Fogleman's unease about the Air Force's ability to develop and maintain command and control.

The Next Round: Unfinished Business

Despite such progress, General Ryan inherited an unfinished process. Those left with following through on the Fogleman initiative still sought to achieve a high degree of connectivity between the 1997 plan and Air Force programmatic commitments. This objective would have satisfied Fogleman's desire that the Air Force backcast from its vision to greatly enhance the adjustment of programmatic commitments to future challenges.

Backcasting continues to function as a driving force behind efforts to relate planning and programming. When we began interviewing in summer 1998, however, it appeared that the planning process had stalled dangerously. The difficulties partially stemmed from a natural reflex whereby key players bought into the vision but balked when they saw the extent of divestiture from existing programs necessary for it to come to fruition. A participant in the deliberations on divestiture held by the board of directors reached the conclusion that the leadership lacked the will to make tough choices:

> It was clear that we would have to divest ourselves of something to free up the money to do the types of activities that space was required to do because of the vision. The [board of directors] met to discuss divestment, but really spent a lot of time admiring the problem. . . . We could have [for instance] gotten rid of land-based ICBMs [intercontinental ballistic missiles]; that would have freed up a lot of money. But the policy was we couldn't have unilateral disarmament.

Key players concerned with this disjunction put an immense amount of effort into closing the gap. They devised the thrust area transformation plans (TATPs) to serve as bridges between the core competencies that the vision specified for the future and the programmatic investments necessary to reach those objectives. The clustering of programs that service requisite core competencies would put issues connected with integration, timing, and prioritization in bolder relief.

Thrust area transformation plans were developed under the stewardship of Lt. Gen. Lawrence P. Farrell Jr., who served as the first deputy chief of staff for plans and programs. Farrell had played an important ringmaster role in preparing the long-range planning issues for the Fall 1996 Corona meeting. The Long-Range Plan contained sixteen goals, each of which addressed one of the issues discussed at the Fall 1996 Corona conference. The published Long-Range Plan summary identified forty-one end states—

a forty-second end state addressing future space operations remained classified—which specified operational or support capabilities necessary for
fulfilling the goals of each of the directive statements.

The concept of thrust areas was derived from two concerns among those
trying to relate the Long-Range Plan to programming. Many viewed the
core competencies as static concepts that did not distinguish adequately
between the future and the present. On the other hand, the end states proved
too numerous and their interrelations too complex to galvanize the attention of the leadership both in the Staff and in the major commands. General
John Jumper—who at the time was the deputy chief of staff for operations
and currently is chief—pressed the view that adding verbs to the discourse
would capture what the Air Force sought to achieve by aligning itself toward
future goals. For instance, a thrust area under the heading "Be an Expeditionary Aerospace Force" would capture the Air Force's commitment to
"provide the ability to deploy rapidly, employ, and sustain aerospace power
anywhere in the world." It would thus dynamically unify efforts to address
four directive statements in the Long-Range Plan.

Thrust area transformation plans presented more of a challenge than
either Jumper or Farrell anticipated. First, some of the six thrust areas themselves came off as pretty complex, even when couched as verbs—for
instance, "conduct seamless operations to control the aerospace dimension." Second, no real consensus had congealed over the thrust areas that
the Staff had selected as priorities. Third, the process for building TATPs
involved six analytic steps that were mind-boggling to the major commands.

The major commands thus began to complain bitterly about thrust area
transformation plans. They believed that they could not provide meaningful inputs for TATPs both because the future could not be divined with the
requisite complexity and, even if it could, because they lacked the resources
to do the work. One well-placed Staff member with a deep experience in
programming suggested that TATPs perhaps tested the outer bounds of the
Air Force's appetite for analytic exercises:

> This is a culture of pretty basic human beings. We really are basic.
> There are no geniuses running around this business. They are dedi-
> cated people who are closer to farmers than they are nuclear
> physicists. . . . What do thrust area transformation plans mean to a
> farmer who needs to plow straight rows in his field, who is just wor-
> ried about erosion?

A Staff planner seemed to concur, highlighting as well the approach's failure to concentrate minds on the need for divestiture:

[It] was an attempt to move into the future without anybody giving anything up. The idea was that we would be able to so integrate one level below our core competencies that we would be able to say, "We'll buy this first and the other thing later. We'll still buy it, so nobody's losing anything. We'll all agree, and we'll live happily ever after." First, [it was so complex that] nobody could see how the parts related to each other. Then, the order for buying couldn't be agreed on. Transformation planning collapsed because thousands of people would be required. Knowing all of the details would have been a nightmare.

By fall 1998, a mini-revolution was erupting against the principle that programmatic commitments had to faithfully reflect the plan. One indispensable player expressed frustration that the dogmatic adherence to the doctrine interfered with the complex process of implementing the plan. He underscored the importance of participants setting realistic objectives given the separation of powers and, at the time, a Democratic president and a Republican Congress: "We need to set expectations in a rational way and not set the bar so high that it's unachievable because of the democratic process that occurs in this town. If we had a different form of government, there would be lots of opportunity for a different methodology."

In what was to prove a harbinger of General Ryan's approach to strategic planning in the 1999 process, the same respondent made a plea for selectivity in bringing detailed targets to bear on programs: "We have to go from an eight-inch howitzer to a sniper rifle, . . . focusing this thing down on issues that are of true consequence and of particular interest to leadership." Similarly, a key programmer made the case that he needed more specific guidance on the crunch issues associated with what had to be done in the next five to seven years to get a future capability on track:

Thrust areas? Great. Super. But to me as a programmer? Irrelevant. We have to establish a glide slope. . . . If we want, in 2025, to be able to do all our surveillance from space and have no more air-breathers [manned aircraft doing surveillance], what capability do we need in 2005 to be able to reach that?

Such thinking reflects a marked shift in emphasis in the relationship between planners and programmers from a comprehensive, rationalistic approach to what Amitai Etzioni terms *mixed scanning*.[5] Etzioni proposes this as a midpoint between rationalism and incrementalism. In the 1960s, public policy scholars were deeply divided into rationalists, who sought greater programmatic coherence, and incrementalists, who claimed that the nature of the American political system greatly limited anything even approaching comprehensive rationality. Mixed-scanning, Etzioni believes, would prevent decisional overload and concentrate effort along productive lines by differentiating between contextuating (or fundamental) decisions and bit (or item) ones:

> Contextuating decisions are made through an exploration of the main alternatives seen by the actor in view of his conception of his goals, but—unlike what comprehensive rationality would indicate—details and specifications are omitted so that overviews are feasible. Bit decisions are made "incrementally" but within the contexts set by fundamental decisions (and reviews).[6]

The implementation of the 1996 vision got bogged down by the sheer magnitude of trying to devise highly specific connections between plans and programs, along with the realization that the Air Force was still missing crucial decision points. The situation provided ample justification for General Ryan to pursue an approach to strategic planning that ultimately would more closely resemble mixed-scanning than comprehensive rationality.

New Challenges

In addition to serious difficulties in achieving the desired correlation between the plans and programs, the challenges faced by the Air Force changed sufficiently between 1996 and 1999 to warrant some adjustments to the vision itself. To begin, Fogleman's concept of the Air Force transforming itself first into an Air and Space Force and eventually into a Space and Air Force came across as bordering on sectional. Many participants believed that it needlessly injected a sense of winners and losers to what essentially consisted of cultural resocialization and organizational adjustment. General Ryan's creation of the Aerospace Integration Task Force (AITF) reflected the role of integration in his view of the Air Force's trajectory. He expressed to us in no uncertain terms his belief that the 1996 vision misunderstood the interrelationship of Air and Space:

> In our past vision, we had Air and Space. I think that's a bad construct. Space and air are places. They are not missions. . . . We want capa-

bilities that are produced in aerospace, and we don't care where the vehicle is, in the atmosphere or orbital. . . . [Nonetheless,] we have people out there who are medium-centered rather than effects-centered and are advocates for it for different reasons than the reason we are an institution. That is, we are an institution to fight and win America's wars.

Serious questions had also arisen about the cost of aggressive development of space capabilities. A key four-star general compared the Air Force's position concerning space to that of the Army in the 1930s, when "there was a movement to make sure that there were no expensive weapons on aircraft." A strong advocate of space during the Fogleman round asserted that serious reservations had developed purely in cost-benefit terms: "It became clear that the air-to-space migration paradigm was wrong. . . . First of all, you don't migrate things to space as an end in itself. Things go to space when it's a faster, cheaper way to do the mission." An important three-star general sympathetic to space noted that even Ryan's concept of air and space integration under the banner Aerospace might be ahead of what the nation wanted at that stage. Key here was the weaponization of space, especially setting up platforms with offensive missions: "We are still basically an Air Force; we are not an integrated Air and Space Force. . . . Until the country decides as a country that space is also offensive in nature, they will never be equal."

During this period, vociferous space advocates such as Robert Smith, who at the time was a Republican senator for New Hampshire, had increased the pressure from Congress for the Air Force to pursue weaponization aggressively. The core of the Air Force leadership, however, would not be stampeded into pursuing weaponization. In the words of one interviewee,

> If space makes sense because it is cheap or it is the only way we can do it, . . . then spend the money. But to merely build Luke Skywalker's fancy space plane because we can . . . doesn't make a lot of sense. . . . We've looked at . . . an application through space like the ICBM. . . . It could bomb a tank one half a world away if we wanted it to. [But] why would we want to do that?

In addition to concerns about the future of space distracting attention from the 1996 vision, the endless pressure on the Air Force to respond to multiple crises around the world was wearing out personnel and equipment. Morale problems associated with long-term separation of personnel from their families were presenting especially serious challenges. In response, General Ryan became a champion of the Expeditionary Aerospace Force (EAF), whereby combat units would take missions on rotation and for relatively short intervals. He made a huge investment in accelerating the implementation of the approach, which required a thorough review by the Corona council. In fall 1998, respondents strongly drove home to us the extent to which the development and implementation of the Expeditionary Aerospace Force was devouring much of the Air Force leadership's intellectual energy. The program was responding to a crisis in the operation of the Air Force, but it also called for a reconfiguration of the way in which the service conducted its business. As one respondent remarked, "I don't think EAF is designed to be an evolutionary change. I think EAF is designed to turn the Air Force upside down, shaking it a bit and putting it back together from scratch." This observation underscores the degree to which Ryan's more pragmatic approach to issues that the Air Force faced in no way spelled a vacation from wrenching institutional challenges.

The context for the Ryan visioning round partially suggested that a further investment in visioning and planning might face substantial resistance or even stiff opposition. Much of the luster had worn off the concept of space as a new frontier, and the operational side of the real-life Air Force found itself struggling just to keep up with the contingencies served up by post–cold war geopolitics. However, Ryan and many close to him became absorbed with the impending change of administration. They believed that regardless of which party won the White House, the advent of a new political team provided an opportunity for the Air Force to press its case for increased budget resources.

This mating game between a new administration and the Pentagon now formalizes itself in congressionally mandated Quadrennial Defense Reviews (QDRs) that must occur after each presidential election. It was felt that the previous visioning process had placed the Air Force in a good position for the 1997 QDR, even though the 1996 election had not resulted in a change of administration. Such positioning for opportunities, especially developing a reservoir of arguments for claims for additional resources, increasingly asserted itself as the core animator of the 1999 visioning process. An Air Force strategist described the gaming involved:

> [When] updating the vision, . . . [we] should identify programming issues likely to dominate the next QDR, . . . cut our deals with the Office of the Secretary of Defense, and then, when we hit the QDR

frenzy, we just hold our cards. For instance, the time to decide about the future of the Joint Strike Fighter (JSF) is not in the middle of the QDR; it's in advance of the QDR.

Two developments around this time gave new impetus to the need for a serious reassessment of the 1996 vision: the conflict in Kosovo and evidence from the Aerospace Future Capabilities War Games, or futures games, regarding the implications for U.S. national security if a hostile power could impose an exclusionary zone exceeding 500 miles within the next fifteen or twenty years. On one level, Kosovo seemed to validate the Air Force's capacity to halt aggression without waiting for the Army to marshal its divisions and engage. Many well-placed players, however, believed that Kosovo did not constitute a full test of Major General Link's view, as discussed in chapter 2, that the Air Force could check an enemy without the involvement of an overwhelming ground force. A colonel deeply acquainted with the logistical elements to sustaining the Kosovo intervention pointed up the strains that the episode produced from the standpoint of supply. He asserted that the conflict did not last long enough to tell the Air Force much about the benefits of new approaches such as real-time supply and prepositioning of equipment. More profoundly, this respondent also shared the view that the service's success in Kosovo seemed to have generated an unwarranted public optimism about what airpower could achieve almost single-handedly: "What discourages me about this is that there was all this discussion, 'Can airpower win this battle on its own?' Now people are saying, 'Yep, airpower did it. What a surprise; everybody said airpower couldn't.' Well, I don't think that's what I'd conclude from what I saw."

The problem goes beyond whether Major General Link's view was validated by the way Kosovo unfolded. The Powell doctrine of overwhelming force would certainly anticipate that, even if the Air Force could halt aggression before the Army engaged, the principle for determining the level of firepower to apply to the problem would remain the same—in the words of one respondent, "Figure out what you will need, and double it." NATO was strongly involved in determining the severity and the pace of attacks, including target selection aimed at eschewing situations in which civilians might be injured or attacks that might send the wrong message. This circumstance deviated seriously from the situation in Desert Storm, in which the United States took a clear lead in relation to alliance partners. However, the Kosovo model might prove at least as common as Desert Storm in determining Air Force engagement in the future. This means that concepts such as parallel warfare—whereby the Air Force modulates target selection so that attacks on command-and-control systems combine with those on directly hostile troops to optimally confound the enemy—prove increasingly difficult. The Kosovo experience, in fact, provoked a groundswell in the fall 1999 Corona meeting to reexamine the Air Force's concepts of operation in such contingencies.

The results of futures games provided the second stimulus for revisiting the 1996 vision. The 1999 game centered on the consequences should an aggressor establish a zone of more than 500 miles in which the basing and free movement of aircraft was proscribed. Such a perimeter would exceed the ranges of both the F-22 and the Joint Strike Fighter. It would also impinge on the feasibility of an Air Expeditionary Force by limiting the deployment and engagement of aircraft within a specific region. The games revealed huge differences in the time required to neutralize an exclusionary zone exceeding 500 miles, depending on the number of satellites available to provide surveillance. In 1999, the Air Force could call on fewer than ten surveillance satellites for monitoring enemy movement of missiles, which implied that neutralizing an exclusionary zone would be a matter of weeks rather than days. To fit within the latter parameter, the Air Force would require sixty-four surveillance satellites—giving it the capacity to monitor closely, for instance, all the efforts by the hypothetical aggressor to move missiles. The ability to prosecute standoff warfare of this nature, the 1999 game suggested, would require $5 billion additional resources to the Air Force's annual budget. Such price tags for satisfying future requirements began to shift the Air Force toward the belief that it should be more assertive in pressing for increased defense expenditure in the QDR.

The Ryan-Peters Visioning Process: General Ryan's Approach

General Ryan brought to his new position about as good an Air Force pedigree as a person could have: his father had served as chief. He emerged as the consensus choice of his four-star peers in deliberations over succession. Even General Fogleman preferred Ryan as his successor, recognizing that a different style of chief could move the implementation process forward steadily as the players recovered from overexertion in the first round. General Ryan made it clear from the outset that he viewed the 1996 vision and the 1997 plan as the Air Force's, and he corrected anyone who referred to them as Fogleman's.

Many participants in the 1999 visioning process noted that General Ryan's approach contrasted sharply with General Fogleman's. Ryan's absorptions tended to gravitate to practical issues more readily than to far-term visions. As a close observer with long experience in the Air Force noted, however, more immediate operational issues such as the Expeditionary Aerospace Force (EAF) rightly absorbed the new chief's attention, because the Air Force had to increase mobility if it were to fulfill its new role in national security. A political appointee echoed this assessment: "It's hard to find fault with Ryan's emphasis [on] EAF because the Air Force is going to fall apart if he doesn't find a different way to manage these crises that arrive on such short notice."

Perceived differences in Ryan's style engendered reflections about the degree to which he valued Fogleman's emphasis on deliberative bodies. Some noted that Fogleman's concept of buy-in created an overly formalistic approach to consultation. As one respondent stated, "The whole collegiality thing has run amuck. . . . The need for buy-in paralyzes people." Another critically placed respondent stressed that Ryan's preoccupations with the current pressures of war fighting contrasted with Fogleman's long-range concerns: "Ryan's game is preserving the institution of the Air Force . . . trying to keep pilots, keeping their families committed, maintaining capable units. He's trying to preserve the Air Force's core as a fighting instrument. . . . Ryan in that sense is a bit more of a war fighter."

Understanding of future challenges broadened and deepened within the Air Force leadership under Ryan. Kosovo was unfolding in the midst of the preparations for the fall 1999 Corona conference. The episode drove home the singularity of the Air Force's ability to halt aggression in a limited war with minimal danger to U.S. personnel. The latter standard, of course, operates as a crucial condition given public reaction to casualties. In addition, the development of future demand constructs, if not full-blown scenario building, and war gaming took huge strides in the period between the two visioning exercises. The investment in futures games was working effects beyond the Air Staff. The games gave key major command representatives direct exposure to likely exigencies far into the future. They also provided a wealth of information for briefing the board of directors and the Corona council on the types of challenges the Air Force would face in the future. Thus, while long-range visioning perhaps came less naturally to General Ryan than it had to General Fogleman, the sense of urgency surrounding the need to adjust programmatic commitments to future challenges had, if anything, intensified.

Ryan brought an element of pragmatism to both visioning and planning. Viewing much of what had been envisioned in the space domain as science fiction, he opted for more realistic parameters. These, he believed, would still fit within the confines of earth-orbiting vehicles and, therefore, the compass of aerospace. He believed that adaptations of programmatic commitments to future challenges would have to strike a balance between evolutionary and revolutionary approaches. As an example of the latter, he cited the decision under General McPeak to disestablish the Strategic Air Command—by merging bombers with fighters in the Air Combat Command—on the grounds that targets, not weapons, are strategic or tactical. He believed that maintaining capabilities imposed the greatest constraints on such dramatic adjustments: "We need a slower, more iterative type of strategic planning. . . . We can't afford to get rid of all the old and downsize, dissolve, and take profits from that dissolution, and hope it works. . . . We have to bound our jumps and leaps by sustaining capability. . . . We need to balance the revolutionary and the evolutionary."

A Greater Involvement of the Political Executive

As noted above, a degree of ambiguity entered into General Ryan's leadership role through the greater involvement of the secretary of the Air Force than had pertained under Fogleman. The secretary during the Fogleman round, Sheila Widnall, kept her distance from the process until issues surrounding the possibility of weapons in space emerged in the fall 1996 Corona conference. Some observers attributed Widnall's comparative detachment to the overpowering nature of Fogleman's personality, although participants highlight Fogleman's deference to Widnall when she did weigh in.

Widnall's successor, F. Whitten Peters, served for a lengthy period in an acting capacity owing to an eventually abortive process in which a nominee for secretary failed to obtain congressional confirmation. The uncertainty did not deter Peters from asserting himself while the Air Force struggled with the disjunction between planning and programming. His preoccupations contrasted with those of General Ryan. Ryan tended to view planning through the lens of specific projects with long-term implications, such as setting up the Expeditionary Aerospace Force, staking out a legitimate claim to space through the concept of Aerospace, and preparing for the next Quadrennial Defense Review. Peters sought from planning more immediate and specific guidance for budgeting and acquisitions battles that he had to fight on a day-to-day basis. A three-star general captured for us the secretary's viewpoint:

> The secretary wanted some strategic basis for making resource decisions. Right now he has a twelve-hour turnaround on major decisions,

and does it for expediency and with no strategic foundation. . . . [That was the case] with taking the C-141s [a transport aircraft] out of the fleet, which leaves us with a huge deficit in air capacity.

While a supporter of a greater role for space, Peters stressed realism, seeking "a long-range plan that isn't the long-range plan of the Space Command, which would have us fighting Martians in twenty years." He was concerned about preparing for the next QDR. Above all, however, he sought a budget for 2002 that would not only work off a vision for the Air Force, but also win the day with key players in the next administration and Congress. He believed that the 1996 vision was not translating into feasible budget decisions: "The programming and planning process takes spending out fifteen to twenty years, when we cannot at this point meet the requirements for the next five years. . . . We need an iteration of the plan that covers the gamut of core competencies that General Fogleman proposed in a realistic way for the next five or six years."

The contrast between what the Air Force was serving up by way of strategic guidance and what the secretary required raised the issue of whether to go forward with a board of directors meeting in the fall of 1998. Issues arose after this event, but less poignantly. For instance, after the Fall 1999 Corona conference, the secretary sought to enshrine as many details as he could, using the annual Air Force posture statement to Congress as a vehicle. General Ryan, meanwhile, wanted to emphasize brevity as he took the lead in developing the revised vision statement. Remarkably, the resulting dialectical process kept within constructive limits. As one close participant noted, "They are not working well together, but that's not bad." In other words, despite their contrasting views and approaches, the secretary and the chief worked closely with one another. They developed a degree of synergy around two shared values: a passionate concern that visioning be realistic and the need to strike a functional mix between dramatic and incremental adjustment.

Problems with the Board of Directors

When Peters and Ryan agreed to a major effort to recraft the vision in the fall 1999 Corona conference, the board of directors regularized its meeting schedule and assumed responsibility for preparing issues for discussion by the four-star generals. It failed to operate effectively, however, throughout most of the preparatory period. Even under Fogleman, concerns had arisen among political appointees and the Air Staff that the board of directors should include assistant-secretary-level officials and three-star generals in the Pentagon, and not simply vice commanders of the major commands. Staff three-star generals gained entry during the Fogleman round, whereas political appointees did not begin attending regularly until Secretary Sheila Widnall developed concerns about weapons in space during the 1996 Corona meeting.

The eventual inclusion of a wider circle of participants had two effects. The group dynamics of the board of directors changed as a result of its size, as participants became cautious of airing their views in such a diverse assembly.

The situation became awkward when F. Whitten Peters, while acting secretary, continued to participate on the board of directors through the auspices of his position as undersecretary. This dual role spawned some tension between Peters and General Ralph E. Eberhart, who had succeeded General Moorman as vice chief of staff and chairman of the board. This peaked in fall 1998 in discussions over the agenda for a November 4 meeting of the board of directors, which General Ryan ultimately cancelled. A frequent observer at the board provided a glimpse of the difficulty:

> It was a classic Air Staff versus secretariat problem. Eberhart eventually said that he wasn't going to deal with Peters any more at this level. Ryan said, "OK, we're going to pull everybody together and decide where to go from here." A core meeting took place [meaning the three-star generals in the Air Staff with Eberhart] on November 4 instead of the board of directors.

Even without Peters in attendance, the political appointees on the board frequently based their interventions on how they thought the secretary might react, which tended to dampen the discussion of sensitive issues. As one three-star general argued,

> Expanding the board of directors to include the secretariat has to have a chilling effect of, "You cannot decide that; that's for the secretary to decide." If we do not want to get the secretary in too early [on an issue], then we do not want to expose his men to the fact that we are even thinking about it, so we don't even put it on the agenda. This kind of dumbs down the agenda—we are afraid to show our hand prematurely, and it probably will not be a candid discussion.

Adding to the awkwardness, a cultural gap frequently made itself felt, centering on issues like space weaponization, terminology such as war fighting, and the perception among appointees that bluesuiters act is if they know their business best. The combined effects of appointees trying to anticipate the secretary's reactions and the cultural divide between them and the three-star generals made it all the more difficult for the board of directors to function as a bridge between the Air Staff and the major commands. The commanders thus took less interest in its proceedings, which compromised the capacity of vice commanders to communicate views each way between the major commands and the board. As one regular observer noted, "Three-stars are doing most of the discussion, and sometimes they are talking to their four-stars and some times they are not."

It seems natural that the decision in November 1998 to revisit the vision in an October 1999 Corona meeting would have provoked an effort to recapture the pivotal role of the board of directors. The Fogleman-created committee had left many participants and observers with a favorable impression following the first round. Such an expectation might prove unrealistic, however, given the disparate impressions among committee members of the board's previous role and effectiveness, the degree to which it would complement the leadership styles of the new chief and the new secretary, and the goodness of fit between a mechanism such as the board of directors and the exigencies of the moment.

First, the expectations of participants on the board of directors were truly disparate. Not only had the group been expanded to include Staff-based three-star generals and their political-appointee equivalents, but it also brought together a few three-star generals with direct experience of the board under Fogleman, who had become devotees of its potential role; three-star generals with little previous exposure, who held agnostic views of the board's potential and who were thus less willing to commit very substantial amounts of time without seeing tangible progress toward issue resolution; and political appointees coming to grips with the folkways of their uniformed opposite numbers.

Second, the different leadership styles of General Ryan and Secretary Peters translated into different parameters for the operation of the board of directors. General Ryan, although more pragmatic than General Fogleman, shared with his four-star colleagues a strong sense of his predecessor's immensely constructive role in defining and addressing crucial issues to be faced not just by the Air Force, but by the entire Pentagon. One current four-star general pressed this point strongly with us: "[General Fogleman] was one of the most remarkable chiefs in the Defense Department. As chief [he] started a process and a sequence of events that each subsequent chief, Ryan and Jumper, continued to build upon, . . . [namely,] posturing the Air Force to . . . be very agile, very flexible."

Whether because of this shared mentoring or his approach to leadership or both, General Ryan resorted to a relatively fluid consultative process that involved a great deal of direct, often one-on-one contact with fellow four-star generals in addition to the formal Corona processes. This intensity of engagement tended to make formalized interaction at the level of the board of directors somewhat redundant, in that the relatively fluid communication between likeminded four-star generals trumped that taking place between their deputies. Furthermore, General Ryan and Secretary Peters maintained a robust direct interaction, collaborating closely despite their different perspectives. While this was a strong plus from the standpoint of the Department of the Air Force, it clearly impinged on the latitude for mutual issue definition and option identification between bluesuiters and appointees in the expanded board of directors.

Third, the exigencies challenging the Air Force during the Ryan-Peters period differed from those confronting the service during Fogleman's term. Fogleman had to convince his colleagues that way beyond the horizon lurked peril for the service's viability. Ryan, on the other, had simply to remind the choir of a shared vision of the future and point up its implications in a timely fashion. The four-star respondent quoted above clearly differentiated between Fogleman's and Ryan's circumstances:

> Ron Fogleman saw . . . a monumental task, and he saw the board of directors as a way to pull all this together, to really get the four-stars prepared. The three-star generals did an awful lot, the lion's share of the work. . . . With regard to Ryan, it was a very subtle change to revisit the vision . . . and he had some of his own ideas pretty crystallized, so he came in quite prepared to make a much smoother process and didn't need this major muscle movement that Fogleman needed.

As noted above, General Ryan himself told us that the actual implementation of a vision would likely involve "iterative" rather than "revolutionary" steps. He posited a four-year vision-implementation cycle in which the board of directors would play an increasing role as the Air Force prepared for a Quadrennial Defense Review (QDR), while the Corona council would become the chief's principal sounding board during implementation.

Despite such convincing rationales, considerable frustration emerged surrounding the actual operation of the board of directors in the preparation for the October 1999 Corona meeting. This was most evident among those

who developed a high regard for the roles of the board under General Fogleman and those in major commands who were annoyed that issues they
considered critical did not seem to attract serious, concerted attention from
the board. The critiques centered largely on personalities, in particular on
the vice chief during the most crucial phase in the build-up for the October
1999 Corona conference, General Eberhart. The dissatisfaction may have
stemmed from the chief's view that issue preparation would require less
assistance from deputies in his round of visioning than pertained under
Fogleman. Some of the disenchanted respondents even seemed to touch
upon this possibility. As one keen observer put it, "I think [Eberhart] just
didn't think what we did would make much of a difference, so why invest
the energy?"

In any case, the negative views of the board's role under Ryan and Peters
might spill over into future visioning exercises for two reasons. First, the
next members of a visioning board of directors will be at least two genera-
tions removed from the Fogleman board. Nobody will bring to the exercise
direct experience with a highly successful board, and most will have
acquired reservations about the utility of the mechanism from their second-
hand knowledge of how the committee operated during the Ryan-Peters
round. Second, the Air Force Staff, especially XPX (which shoulders responsibility for strategic planning), filled much of the breach during the run-up
to the October 1999 Corona conference. However, we find in its success the
seed for the possible misfires in future rounds. Future visioning exercises—
which, according to General Ryan's scenario, would take place before
QDRs—will involve four-star generals who have not been clearly affected
by the strong consensus that emerged during the Fogleman years. Insofar as
this becomes the case, a new premium will emerge on issue preparation. If
the board's weakened legacy makes it unappealing as a venue for such activity, the work would concentrate on XP and perhaps set it up for serious
overload.[7]

One three-star general's criticisms of the board of directors during the
Ryan-Peters round alerts us to the danger that staff cannot compensate for
a lack of guidance from deputies working on behalf of their principals
through a group like the board of directors. He asserted that during the
preparations for the October 1999 Corona meeting, the board had become
a "façade for Staff actions" pressed by XPX. The view from this member's
major command perhaps reflects what he would have said in an unguarded
moment. In the words of a colonel working under the three-star general in
question,

[The board of directors is] a waste of high-paid, high-powered, intellectual talent the way it's currently structured. . . . It's used by the Air Staff XPX folks for a grab bag of topics. Here we have a bunch of three-star generals—some of the sharpest minds we've got in this country—sitting around this table dealing with minutiae, garbage, a potpourri of topics, and that is mind-boggling.

General Lester L. Lyles succeeded General Eberhart as vice chief and chairman of the board of directors in June 1999, with less than six months left before the October Corona conference. The board's lack of progress toward distilling issues for the conference had engendered soul searching among its members. Concerned about the difficulties, Lyles ultimately canvassed board members for their views about what could be done to make it more effective. From what we gleaned from our respondents, the answers raised issues connected with perceived problems with the Air Force's approach to corporate decisionmaking—a topic we probe at length in chapter 6. By the time Lyles arrived, it was probably too late to recapture the effectiveness that the board had achieved in preparing issues for the fall 1996 Corona meeting. Even so, the experience seemed to drive home two important issues for participants. First, the Air Force had to do a better job of narrowing the issues surrounding the linkage between planning and programming to those that required immediate attention, lest agents of change miss their window of opportunity. Second, the leadership required mechanisms for linking the secretary, the chief, the Air Staff, and the major commands so that planning and the effects of this on programs and budgets would become less ad hoc.

The Fall 1999 Corona Conference

The Air Force proceeded cautiously, much more so than in the previous round, in producing outputs from the fall 1999 Corona meeting. The development of its Posture Statement for 2000—the rationale it provides in congressional testimony for its annual budget requests—delayed the generation of a vision document until June 2000. The Corona council did arrive at a new strategy concerning the types of resource enhancements that would enable the service to pursue its vision of an integrated aerospace force. This development owed both to the dynamic that emerged in the meeting and the urgency conveyed by the briefing on strategic issues. It amounted to the Air Force taking a direct tack in communicating to Congress the implications of competing force-structure commitments in terms of meeting envisioned future demands. The vision would drive the identification of issues, but the Air Force would try to center discussion within a tighter and, presumably, more comprehensible time frame—focusing twenty years into the future.

We had an opportunity to discuss the performance at the fall 1999 Corona conference with several members and participants. Their observations ranged from enthusiastic to skeptical. One participant in the former camp asserted soon after the meeting that "this Corona [conference] was the most historic in three years in terms of the kinds of topics discussed and their far-term consequences and the passion that they generated." No other respondent stepped up to this glowing characterization. A key major command commander stated, "The historic nature should be based on results, not the process." Perhaps the most assiduous contributor to the board's preparations for the Corona conference described the fall 1999 meeting as a "reaffirmation and some adjustment of the previous vision." He asserted that "no decisions were made."

The mixed signals perhaps derive from different interpretations of the same data. The Corona meeting did not focus entirely on the issue of updating the vision, in that the chief also brought to the table Air Force identity matters associated with its efforts to improve recruiting. The ensuing deliberations even involved lengthy discussions in response to concepts presented by advertising executives. One observer suggested that precious Corona time was consumed by a matter that probably should not have been brought to a visioning conference, even if four-star generals wanted to review available options:

> They had been looking at some new designs for the Air Force symbol.
> . . . There were some good ideas from the marketing firms on better
> slogans . . . [and] it created a tremendous amount of controversy. . . .
> Some of the ideas were pretty silly. . . . Ultimately, it's the chief and the
> secretary who decide, and they'll do that in concert with the four-
> stars.

By all accounts, the segments of the Corona meeting dedicated to revisiting the 1996 vision did effectively concentrate on dilemmas faced by the Air Force in positioning itself for the long-range future. Maj. (now Lt.) Gen. Norton Schwartz, who at the time was the director of strategic planning, carried most of the weight for briefing the options for the Air Force vision. The presentation asked what thematic direction the vision should take with regard to "what is achievable with improved capabilities through modernization." It developed options along two intersecting axes: an emphasis on theater-specific capabilities versus global reach; and a balance between investments in shooting platforms and enabling systems versus a stress on shooting platforms.

The brief concluded that the current resource baseline projected out to 2020 would not be able to achieve a balance between investments in shooting platforms (for instance, fighters) and enabling systems (for instance, air transport). This would result in sacrifices in sufficient munitions, air transport, battle management, and intelligence, surveillance, and reconnaissance to effectively support the fighting force. In addition, the baseline would remain theater-focused, whereas the likelihood of potential aggressors being able by 2020 to establish exclusionary zones beyond 500 miles would necessitate longer-range, global-power capabilities. The Corona council galvanized around so-called option 4b, which entailed a commitment by the Air Force leaders to press for an increase in the service's total budget resources in order to achieve a balanced, globally capable force by 2020. Fulfilling this objective would require annual increases in the Air Force budget on the order of $15 billion—a total of $150 billion over ten years. The Gore presidential campaign called for $100 billion additional funds for the entire Pentagon over ten years, while the Bush campaign confined itself to a $45 billion pledge over the same period. In the event, the Bush administration actually chose to make no additional resource commitments for defense over the Clinton administration's budget proposal for fiscal year 2002. The Joint Chiefs of Staff, on the other hand, had argued, just with respect to procurement, that the services collectively required $90 billion per year rather than the $53 billion on offer if they were to meet future challenges.

Just as had occurred in the aftermath of the 1996 visioning Corona conference, the Air Force leadership had failed to face up to divestiture as a means of achieving its objectives within the framework of a constrained budget. For instance, it was not willing to sacrifice fighters for bombers or vice versa. Neither would it soon trade existing force structure for new acquisitions. That is, it would be parsimonious in redistributing budget resources so that modernization could occur more quickly. As one well-connected informant noted, the Corona participants appeared to have eschewed tough trade-offs and opted for a pipe dream:

> [There was] a really stunning presentation on what some of the trajectory choices look like. . . . Some of the options called for divestiture . . . [but] because the Air Force would not face up to those, they went to 4b, a pipe-dream strategy in my view. . . . It required no pain. They could all agree that was what they wanted.

History must serve as the final arbiter of whether the Air Force, through the 1999 visioning process, chose correctly in deciding to vie for a Cadillac force when the political leaderships of both parties seemed to think that a Chevy would do just fine. No rational observer would entirely dismiss the four-star generals' assessments of what the Air Force will require in the future to meet present and future demands and the inherent limits to trade-offs between programs in terms of real-time preparedness.

In this regard, the 1999 Corona meeting enshrined a new approach in the Air Force for presenting its positions in the policy arena. The vision statement issued in June 2000, in turn, identifies critical capabilities that the Air Force believes it must service by the year 2020. Earlier in this chapter, we discussed how the Air Force was adopting a more pragmatic approach to the task of linking plans and programs than prevailed in the aftermath of the 1996 exercise. This approach seems to have crystallized into what we term guided incrementalism—that is, one that falls well short of a one-to-one fit between long-range plans and budgetary resource commitments, but that nonetheless advances strategic choices selectively when opportunities to do so present themselves.

The Air Force has plotted a broad outline of where it would like to be in twenty years. Many believe that the Air Force will not even come close to connecting the dots in this vision unless it comes clean with the nation about where it must head and how much it will cost. The conservative factions do not want to compromise national security for what might prove to be speculative ventures, and they do not want to press for preferential treatment relative to other services for fear of worsening interservice conflicts. Guided incrementalism requires a doggedness more likely practiced by a Navy commander than an Air Force pilot. If successful, it will look more like a maneuver executed by an aircraft carrier than a fighter jet. As one crucial player in the process following the 1999 Corona conference put it, "We can change one degree per year every year over twenty years, and we eventually make a major course correction."

Conclusions

The Ryan-Peters round served as a significant test of the degree to which General Fogleman's approach to visioning and planning had begun to take root institutionally in the Air Force. The emergence of a number of new issues or difficulties in addressing matters identified in the 1996 Corona conference, rather than provoking an abandonment of the 1996 vision, fostered a commitment to reengaging the Fogleman process. Significantly, participants believed that the 1996 process helped the Air Force in the 1997 QDR. This served as an additional motive for pursuing another round as the 2001 QDR cycle loomed on the horizon by the end of 1998. The Air Force's investment in developing envisioned demand constructs and war gaming far into the future had paid off. It had given participants a shared sense of urgency over the need for the Air Force to align itself programmatically with future challenges. The engagement of Secretary Peters from the outset made direction of the process more complex than under General Fogleman. However, Secretary Peters and General Ryan did develop a positive working relationship in guiding the process. The board of directors did not work well in preparing issues for the Corona conference; this constitutes a significant failure for which the Staff partially compensated. Had Fogleman not made the investments in the strategic planning unit of XP and Ryan not maintained it, one certainly would have anticipated a less auspicious outcome than actually occurred. The brigading of planning and programming staffs under XP thus constituted the Air Force's institutional investment toward greater integration between the two disciplines.

CHAPTER 5

Understanding Strategic Visioning as a Practice

Having described the Fogleman and Ryan-Peters rounds of strategic visioning, we now turn to an analysis aimed at drawing lessons about the process of preparing for the future. Such lessons are best drawn from an empirically grounded understanding of practices that effectively perform the function of strategic visioning. Otherwise, efforts to prepare for the future would be based on little more than good intentions.

Some readers may wonder whether the key empirical insight to be drawn from the Air Force experience is that effective strategic visioning requires that the organization's top executive indulge a passionate interest in long-range planning. We cannot wholly discount this inference, since Ronald Fogleman surely displayed such an interest. The supposition appears less convincing, however, when the Ryan-Peters round is taken into account. General Ryan, while a military planner, radiated intensity about military readiness and focused his attention on stopping the loss of aviators and other personnel to civilian life. Despite these differences at the top, efforts to improve the Air Force's strategic vision were broadly effective in the Ryan-Peters round, just as they were in the Fogleman round. This analysis suggests that a passion for long-range planning is not an essential ingredient of effective strategic visioning after an organization has begun to institutionalize a serious practice. Such passion may be essential, however, in efforts to achieve a dramatic increase in an organization's strategic visioning capacities over a short period, as occurred during the Fogleman round.

The interpretation of the Air Force experience presented in this chapter starts from the assumption that practitioner readers have come to accept the principle that preparing for the future is an important responsibility in government, one that falls heavily on the shoulders of executives leading departments and agencies. Effectively discharging this broad responsibility requires an understanding of how an organization can develop a mature practice of strategic visioning. Like the Air Force in 1994, most governmental organizations face the task of developing their strategic visioning practices from a modest base, rather than introducing variation in their mature practices. Since a practice develops from local experience, it is important to discuss how an organization can approach the design of strategic visioning processes in particular settings.

Such doctrinal issues lie in the background of our analysis of strategic visioning in the U.S. Air Force. To shed light on these issues, we examine two empirical questions. First, how did the Air Force's practice of strategic visioning become mature? Second, why did the process of strategic visioning operate effectively in both the Fogleman and Ryan-Peters rounds? The first question highlights the dynamics of administrative innovation within a time frame of more than five years; the second highlights the dynamics of collective decisionmaking within a time frame of six to eighteen months. Both analytical focuses and time frames are relevant to the battery of doctrinal questions posed above.

Throughout this chapter, we are concerned with a single broad type of strategic visioning, defined by its intended proximate outcome. The proximate aim of any given round of strategic visioning is to improve the organization's strategic intent.[1] Strategic intent is a committed interpretation, shared by the organization's leaders, of how the organization's capabilities should evolve so as to remain effective in performing future tasks. Such organizational tasks will be shaped by imperfectly foreseeable changes in both policy objectives and the circumstances of implementation. As a committed interpretation, strategic intent is not a plan or even necessarily a set of authoritative, formal decisions. Rather, it represents a policy and institutional argument about how a particular organization seeks to create public value over the long run.[2] A round of strategic visioning is effective when the outcome is a plausible argument—well-rehearsed and internally endorsed—on how the organization's envisioned evolution will contribute to satisfactory government performance in the relatively distant future.[3]

The chapter begins by examining how the Air Force developed a serious practice of strategic visioning under General Fogleman and then matured this same type of practice in the Ryan-Peters period. The remainder of the chapter seeks to understand what makes for an effective round of strategic visioning. To derive the most insight from the case experience, this major research issue is pursued in three steps. First, we seek to account for the effectiveness of the Fogleman round using a version of smart practices analysis developed by Eugene Bardach.[4] Second, we conduct a similar analysis of the Ryan-Peters period's revisit of the strategic vision that had been established under Fogleman. Third, we compare the Fogleman and Ryan-Peters rounds. This third step provides insight into a number of process design issues, such as whether permanent planning staffs can substitute for shortcomings in working groups of senior leaders. All told, the chapter provides an analysis of strategic visioning as a practice for performing the organizational function of strategic planning and policy management.

Innovating the Strategic Visioning Practice

While Fogleman was the original source of what became the Air Force's distinctive strategic visioning practice, he did not design—let alone execute—the Corona issues process single-handedly. As seen in chapter 3, most of the procedures and content frameworks, such as the issue analysis process and the core competencies construct, respectively, were established in the midst of conducting the Corona issues process. The proximate sources of these improvised procedures and substantive frameworks were Fogleman's followers, rather than the leader himself. The Fogleman round must therefore be analyzed as an organizational-level innovation process, rather than as a heroic tale about a demonstrably talented and skilled leader.

A Leadership Intervention with Minimal Structure

Fogleman's role can be described as conducting an organizational intervention. This concept focuses attention on the dynamic interplay between the individual conducting the intervention and others in the situation. The case evidence suggests that Fogleman's intervention provided just enough structure to enable the followers to move forward collectively in a compatible direction. The essential, or minimal, structure that Fogleman provided through his organizational intervention can be analytically divided into three facets. The first facet was his conceptual approach to strategic visioning, as expressed in the core principles of collective buy-in and backcasting from the future. The principle of collective buy-in capped an argument that the impact of any strategic visioning effort depended on the level of understanding and commitment it produced, at least among the current senior leaders and the population of available successors. The idea of backcasting from the future encapsulated the argument that strategic visioning is meant to raise the likelihood that the Air Force's future tasks would be operationally feasible, because the institution would have effectively developed the necessary capabilities in the meantime. The backcasting principle helped participants recognize the value of the core competencies framework, which had been developed to evaluate divestment options. It also led to the definition of end states, an idea that grew out of the inductive method of first identifying and then selecting and analyzing long-range planning issues while applying the backcasting principle. End states were a key construct for establishing that the long-range plan would identify capabilities needed for the future, while leaving decisions about how to attain those capabilities to more appropriate venues.

The second facet of Fogleman's organizational intervention was to outline the strategic visioning process as a whole. Participants knew from the beginning that the effort would culminate in a dedicated Corona conference to be held more than a year later. Not all participants had intimate knowledge of Corona conferences, but they did know that every four-star general in the Air Force would be there. They also knew that the process included an extended period for study and analysis in the early phases. Thus, while much of the content and procedures was up for grabs, the overall shape and timing of the effort were clear from the start.

The third facet was to identify organizing devices for the effort. These devices included the Long-Range Planning Board of Directors and Special Assistant to the Chief for Long-Range Planning. The Corona forum was tapped as an organizing device for reaching conclusions about the strategic vision. Beyond this, the chief designated his four-star vice chief to serve as chair of the board of directors and allowed him to devote most of his time to the effort.

The overall effect of these facets of Fogleman's organizational intervention—consisting of a conceptual approach, an outline of the phased development of the overall effort, and organizing devices—was to give direction to his followers, who proceeded to improvise the Corona issues process. The interaction between the purposive creativity of Fogleman's followers and the threefold structure enabled the leader and followers to collectively improvise analytic constructs and working methods. The serious practice of strategic visioning thus originated in an organizational intervention that provided sufficient structure to allow followers to improvise the specific means to produce a strategic vision consistent with the distinctive approach marked by the buy-in and backcasting principles. The subsequent interplay between leader and followers supported the improvisation of these means, in part because the leader consistently placed a high priority on formulating a collectively supported strategic vision over a period of more than two years.

Cumulating Experience after the Leadership Transition

The Air Force only developed a mature practice of strategic visioning because the organization continued to pursue the same approach after Fogleman's retirement in 1997. A simple explanation of why the organization did so is that his successor as chief, Michael Ryan, found the approach to his liking. However, such an explanation is much too simple. It does not take into account organizational commitment dynamics, the effects of structural changes within the institution, and the incentives generated by competition among the services for budgetary resources as played out in the policymaking process. We investigate these influences here.

Air Force leaders became committed to the activities and ideas associated with strategic visioning as a result of participating in the Fogleman period's Corona issues process. This effort, symbolized by the fall 1996 Corona conference and the publication of the *Global Engagement* strategic vision, won accolades from its participants, especially for the collective planning process. Their positive attitude toward the process of strategic visioning contributed to further efforts to improve the practice. In the theoretical terms of Karl Weick, the Corona issues process thus functioned as a small win.[5] A small win is constituted by a highly favorable interpretation of a given effort, and its effect is to motivate participants to invest their time and energy in future efforts of the same type. The concept is apt despite the huge scale of effort involved and the intensely positive feeling for the experience.

The small-win effect was enhanced by the public character of the effort.[6] The Air Force went to some lengths to publicize its strategic vision throughout the defense policy subsystem and beyond. The vision also became well known within the Air Force, not least because Ronald Fogleman personally briefed all domestically based general officers in a session that lasted several hours. At the same time, the fact that the senior leadership as a whole contributed to formulating the strategic vision was routinely stressed.

Another key factor was Fogleman's effort to hardwire the long-range planning function into the Air Force's informal constitution and its formal structure at the headquarters level. Successive leaders in the Strategic Planning Directorate believed their duty was to assist the senior leadership in improving the content of the Air Force's strategic vision. Successes led to efforts to refine the process and constructs, whereas disappointments, such as the terminated effort to develop Thrust Area Transformation Plans, led to a renewed search for workable practices for strategic visioning. Accommodating the different styles of General Ryan and Secretary Peters produced changes in the directorate's routines. The interplay of organizational identity and situation produced a steady stream of adjustments in analytic constructs and procedures that, as a whole, constituted a long-lived managerial innovation process. This analysis suggests that Ronald Fogleman was wise to seek to institutionalize strategic planning by incorporating a well-placed strategic planning unit into the organization's technostructure after completing the Corona issues process.

Reinforcing the small-win and institutionalization effects was an incentive effect provided by the broad Defense Department policymaking process for organizing, training, and equipping the military services. Except for the total level of defense spending, authoritative decisions affecting the Air Force's programmatic direction and expenditures are largely made within the higher-level defense policy subsystem, specifically in such venues as the Joint Chiefs of Staff, the Office of the Secretary of Defense, the Congressional Armed Services Committees, and the Congressional Appropriations Committees. The Air Force's dependence on these externally provided resources produces an incentive effect, because the organization can be seen as possessing preferences for larger budgets.

The Air Force competes with the other services for a limited pool of funds. One key mode of competition is to present convincing policy arguments whenever the opportunity arises. The Air Force, accordingly, faces an incentive to use its routine access to decisional venues in the defense policy subsystem to proffer credible arguments in favor of policy decisions that coincide with its policy preferences. This incentive has fostered a positive attitude, at least among top officials, toward going public with well-conceived and widely endorsed strategic visions. This positive attitude has translated into a series of specific periodic efforts to formulate a strategic vision, in no small part because of the predictable opportunities (and threats) presented by the legislatively mandated Quadrennial Defense Reviews (QDRs). A by-product of each of these successive efforts has been a wave of innovation in strategic visioning practice.

All three elements, in sum, shed light on why the Air Force stayed with the task of enhancing its strategic visioning capacity long enough to develop its distinctive approach into a mature practice. The fact that the Corona issues process functioned as a small win meant that a large number of highly placed individuals with a positive attitude toward strategic visioning, including Michael Ryan, populated the senior leadership after Fogleman retired. The attempt to institutionalize Air Force long-range planning by establishing a permanent directorate formalized and validated the staff's role of providing the best possible assistance to the senior leadership as they discharged their responsibility to prepare for the future. The competitive defense policy subsystem provided strong incentives to put forward compelling arguments about the Air Force's future contribution to achieving national security objectives in such events as the Quadrennial Defense Review. All three factors—commitment dynamics, structurally derived organizational identities, and external incentives—contributed to the extended managerial innovation process evident in the Air Force's experience with strategic visioning. Together they contributed to the development of the Air Force's serious practice of strategic visioning into a mature practice.

Analyzing Process Designs for Effective Strategic Visioning: The Fogleman Round

We now set aside the dynamics of administrative innovation over the course of several years and focus our attention on the dynamics of collective decisionmaking within a time frame of six to eighteen months. The specific question, initially, is why the efforts undertaken in the Fogleman round led to an improvement in Air Force strategic intent. We address this empirical question with an eye to suggesting an intellectual procedure for designing a strategic visioning process in other contexts.

We begin by introducing a framework for explaining outcomes of strategic planning efforts. This framework is processual, in that the outcome is attributed to how a process unfolds over time. A process is influenced by causal factors, which are seen to interact with one another in time. We identify three groups of causal factors on the basis of theory. The first is process design features, that is, an interlocking array of design elements that are crafted by the organization to make the strategic planning process workable. An example of a process design feature is the year-long duration of the Corona issues process. The second group encompasses process context factors. These factors can broadly be considered as givens in the situation, at least for purposes of designing a single round of strategic visioning. Such givens include the organization's constitution and its policymaking environment. An example of a process context factor is the structuring of inter-service policy and budgetary competition through the Quadrennial Defense Review. The third type of factor is the quality of participation in the strategic visioning process. Participation quality is a product of the process design, to an important degree. For instance, the efforts of the board of directors were enhanced by the extended socialization period at the outset of the Corona issues process and by the pressure of having to present at the fall 1996 Corona conference, but neither process design nor process context provides an entirely satisfactory explanation of how individuals respond to opportunities for participation. Overall, we do not identify the separate effects of these different types of causal factors, since we favor a processual (or narrative) explanation for purposes of understanding outcomes of strategic visioning efforts.

This section proceeds by identifying the key process design features and process context factors in the Fogleman round. The quality of participation, while not addressed further here, should be kept in mind as an additional factor determining the effectiveness of the process. We then break the process of strategic visioning into its component functions and finally use these functions as the basis for analyzing performance in the Fogleman round.

Process Design Features in the Fogleman Round

The first process design feature we discuss is the five-day Corona conference held in fall 1996. This conference of the Air Force four-star generals and the highest-ranking appointed officials served as the culminating event of the entire strategic visioning process. Fogleman's decision to bring strategic visioning to a climax at the fall 1996 conference helped to organize the senior leadership's participation in the process. In addition, the prospect of presenting to the Corona conference helped to secure the full participation of many of the three-star generals who worked on the board of directors. The decision to dedicate five days to discussing the subject further contributed to achieving consensus about strategic intent. This process feature—a culminating event—thus contributed in several ways to the outcome of the strategic visioning exercise, especially the marshalling of collective support.

A second process design feature encompasses the explicit conceptual approach to strategic visioning. The principles of collective buy-in and back-casting from the future governed the process. The perceived need for collective buy-in provided a substantive rationale for dedicating well over a year of high-level effort to the process. The backcasting principle structured and simplified the intellectual task of conceptualizing strategic intent. For instance, it meant that participants did not have to become experts in the Air Force's planning processes that putatively forecasted from the present, including the mission area modernization plans and the Air Force programming projection, but rather could focus on deciding strategic intent in light of future policy objectives and the circumstances of implementation. As no one was an expert in this subject, it made no sense for senior leaders to delegate responsibility for strategic visioning to functional specialists or the long-range planning staff. The explicit conceptual approach thus created an ethos that greatly shaped the strategic visioning process.

A third process design feature is the Long-Range Planning Board of Directors. This design feature included a phased development of the group. Vice Chief Tom Moorman referred to the first phase as socialization. In this phase, the group began to see itself as responsible for preparing the Air Force's collective future, as opposed to just representing the usual organizational, functional, or career field perspectives. In a subsequent phase, the group bounded the task of strategic visioning by developing a shared representation of long-range planning issues. A further phase involved dividing up the work of preparing Corona issues papers. In a final phase, the group readied itself collectively to present options on the issues at the Corona conference. The phased development of the group contributed to members' sense that they were performing an extremely demanding intellectual task in a satisfactory manner. Such confidence provided a psychological footing for members' participation at the Corona conference, where they briefed the long-range planning issues and laid out options for their corresponding end states.

A fourth process design feature involves project research and analysis. The strategic visioning effort certainly did not lack studies and analytical inputs. Contributing organizations included the RAND Corporation's Project Air Force, Air University, the Air Force Studies and Analysis Agency, and defense contractors. These projects were important for collecting and making sense of information about the future policy environment, as well as conceptualizing strategic intent.

A fifth process design feature is Fogleman's reading and study. As noted in chapter 3, the chief became very knowledgeable about such defense policy issues as the revolution in military affairs. He was known as a voracious reader on this and related subjects, and he stayed close to the flow of research and analysis provided to participants in the strategic visioning process. Fogleman's substantive command of the issues played a key role in achieving consensus on—and declaring—the Air Force strategic intent.

A sixth process design feature involves disseminating the strategic vision. In the Fogleman round, the chief briefed general officers assembled in Omaha for three and a half hours. In addition, the strategic vision was published and distributed externally, while the long-range plan circulated widely within the Air Force.

In sum, the main process features include a culminating event, an explicit conceptual approach to strategic visioning, the phased development of the board of directors, numerous studies and project analyses, Fogleman's reading and study, and dissemination methods. These factors complemented one another. For instance, the culminating event was more successful in achieving consensus because Fogleman himself was extremely knowledgeable about the issues under discussion. He was in a position to lead his fellow four-star generals toward conclusions that they might have resisted if he had not been so well informed and articulate on the substantive issues. Such complementary relationships among process features are common among high-performing designs in organizational, as well as technical, systems.

Process Context Factors

This section describes the process context factors that we consider important for explaining the successful outcome of the Fogleman round. The choice of factors is informed by theory, to facilitate a comparison of the Air Force situation with that of other governmental organizations. The categories are the organizational constitution, the organizational cultural bias, the installed base of strategic thinking, and the policy subsystem.[7] We begin with a brief summary of each category and follow with a more detailed description.

—Organizational constitution. The central characteristics of the organizational constitution are that the Air Force displays a unitary organizational form; the Air Force has two chief executives, namely, the chief of staff and the secretary; the statutory role of the Air Force chief of staff is to advise the president and Congress on organizing, training, and equipping the Air Force; and within senior (military) leadership, the chief is first among equals.

—Organizational cultural bias. As a military organization, the Air Force is relatively high on the "groupness" dimension of cultural bias; as a bureaucratic organization, it is relatively high on the "gridness" dimension of cultural bias. High groupness plus high gridness add up to a hierarchist cultural bias.[8]

—Installed base of strategic thinking. Key elements include the air campaign doctrine of force employment and the *Global Reach—Global Power* vision.

—Policy subsystem. Military services compete for mission responsibilities (and funds); strategic policy reviews, such as QDR, occur regularly; national security apparatus produces authoritative outlooks on the future policy environment; and the Joint Chiefs of Staff consolidate service views.

ORGANIZATIONAL CONSTITUTION. The Air Force's organizational constitution prescribes a key role for its chief of staff. The chief is nominated by the president and confirmed by the Senate; the normal term of office is four years. Conventionally, the candidate pool for chief of staff is limited to general officers serving in other four-star posts. The secretary of the Air Force, a presidential appointee, oversees the chief and is directly responsible for numerous functions assigned to the secretariat, including acquisition and budgeting. In the Air Force's lexicon, the chief and the secretary are referred to as the department's chief executives. As a matter of practice, the two coordinate authorities—a presidential appointee and a career official—jointly occupy the Air Force's strategic apex.[9] This arrangement is common within the Department of Defense but rare in the U.S. federal government.

The chief's responsibilities are defined in the same statute that establishes the Air Force, known as Title X of the U.S. Code. These responsibilities include advising the president and Congress on matters pertaining to the Air Force. The main matters include organizing, training, and equipping the service, as the unified commands are responsible for employing forces in theater operations. (For instance, U.S. Central Command was responsible for military operations in Afghanistan and Iraq.) The chief of staff does not need to clear his statements with administration officials and is thus statutorily recognized as a source of professional military advice on Air Force matters.

Within the Air Force, the chief is typically described as first among equals. The reference is to his relation with other four-star generals, the majority of whom head the major commands: Air Combat Command (ACC), Air Education and Training Command (AETC), Air Mobility Command (AMC), Air Force Materiel Command (AFMC), Space Command (SPACECOM), U.S. Air Forces Europe (USAFE), and U.S. Pacific Air Forces (PACAF). Consistent with his first-among-equals status, the chief enjoys extensive prerogatives in such matters as general officer assignments, organizational structure of Air Force headquarters, expenditure planning, and doctrine. The chief sets the agenda for the Corona conferences, which convene three times a year. He also chairs those meetings.

The Air Force's constitution gives it more of a unitary form of organization than a multidivisional or holding company form.[10] Senior-level personnel tend to move among major commands. While the Air Force personnel system recognizes career fields, the service is not itself composed of separate corps, unlike the Army and Navy (for example, the Naval Supply Corps). The Air Force's organizational form has not always been unitary, however. During the cold war, the Air Force's organizational form was better described as multidivisional, with the major units being the Strategic Air Command (SAC) and the Tactical Air Command (TAC).

ORGANIZATIONAL CULTURAL BIAS. The Air Force's cultural bias is more hierarchist than it is the other polar types in cultural theory: individualist, egalitarian, and fatalist. Hierarchism involves strong identification with the institution to which members belong. This so-called groupness dimension of cultural bias is reflected in the official values of the Air Force, which include putting service before self. The Air Force displays some egalitarian characteristics, which insiders attribute to the fact that officers are directly engaged in combat more often than enlisted men and women, but it is essentially a bureaucracy in which appropriate behavior is prescribed in detail. In cultural theory terms, the Air Force is high in gridness. As such, extensive rules attach to roles.[11] These rules relate to expectations of collegiality among officers of the same rank as well as among individuals of different ranks within the same work unit. Expectations of deference to expertise and hierarchical superiors are also part of the rule set.

INSTALLED BASE OF STRATEGIC THINKING. This process context factor takes into account the learning path of organizations.[12] The installed base of strategic thinking serves as a platform for addressing how to match future capabilities with future tasks. If an organization has already developed a strategic vision, then attention can focus on remedying its perceived limitations. These two hypotheses suggest the possible importance of the prior development of strategic thinking in the Air Force, as codified in the air campaign doctrine and in the *Global Reach—Global Power* vision issued by Secretary Rice and General McPeak.

POLICY SUBSYSTEM. Every organization participates in at least one policy subsystem and its corresponding policy domain. The policy subsystem relevant to Air Force strategic visioning relates to the domain of organizing, training, and equipping the military services. The participants in the policy subsystem include the Congressional Armed Services Committees, the Office of the Secretary of Defense, the National Security Council, the Chairman of the Joint Chiefs of Staff, unified command commanders in chief, and top officials of the military departments. Some institutional properties of this subsystem are not common to all policy subsystems. For instance, the military services energetically compete with one another for mission responsibilities. While bureaucratic competition in government is pervasive, it appears unusually intense in this policy domain.[13] Another property is the institutionalized process of strategic policy reviews. While all policy subsystems involve annual budgeting exercises, few involve strategic reviews timed to track the presidential election cycle.

Introducing Component Functions of Strategic Visioning

The strategic visioning function can usefully be divided into a number of component functions, such as those depicted in figure 5-1. The function of organizing participation is performed effectively when senior leaders and experts are mobilized to make significant contributions to the strategic visioning effort. The function of making sense of the future is performed effectively when participants formulate an explicit, plausible interpretation of the organization's future policy objectives and the circumstances of implementation. This outcome could be described as a shared viewpoint on the implications of trends and discontinuities in such areas as technology, geopolitics, demographics, partisan politics, life-styles, and environmental stresses.[14] Conceiving strategic intent—the third component function—is performed effectively when it provides an intellectual format and language for describing how the organization is meant to adapt, in an anticipatory manner, to its leaders' current interpretation of future policy objectives and circumstances of implementation. The fourth function of agreeing on strategic intent is performed effectively when the organization's current and prospective leaders have a sophisticated understanding of the central elements of the argument and are prepared to defend it to internal and external audiences alike. The fifth function, declaring strategic intent, is performed effectively when participants in the wider policy subsystem consider the plausibility of the policy and institutional arguments set forth in the strategic vision.

This detailed conceptualization of the strategic visioning function is useful for reasoning carefully about process design issues. For instance, managers could ask how a given process design feature would contribute to the effective performance of any of the five component functions of strategic visioning. Managers might also ask themselves whether the process design features currently in the running are sufficient to perform the overall strategic visioning function to a high standard.

Figure 5-1. *Functional Hierarchy Representation*

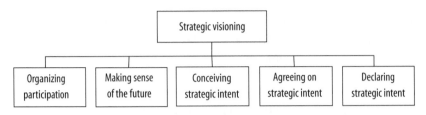

There is no reason to assume a simple, one-to-one relation between process design features and the five identified component functions of strategic visioning. The Air Force case, in fact, points to a more complex relation. The fall 1996 Corona conference, for instance, was undoubtedly crucial in performing the function of agreeing on strategic intent, but it also helped to mobilize participation in the Corona issues process, thereby contributing to organizing participation. Anticipation of the Corona conference further contributed to making sense of the future and conceiving strategic intent by piquing the interest and motivation of participants in the preparatory process.

Putting It All Together: Explaining Performance in the Fogleman Round

Our explanatory argument's basic structure is that the outcome of a strategic visioning exercise stems from the interplay of process design features and process context factors, considered as classes of influences.[15] A useful format in which to present analysis of why the Fogleman round was conducted effectively is to discuss each of the component functions of strategic visioning in turn. This format for organizing knowledge about strategic visioning not only simplifies exposition, but also helps to provide insight into how the functional requirements of strategic visioning can be satisfied by a combination of process design features and process context factors. Each row of table 5-1 represents a distinct component function of strategic visioning, with a list of the process design features and process context factors that contributed to the effective performance of the row's specific function.

ORGANIZING PARTICIPATION. The importance of organizing participation is self-evident, since attaining collective buy-in is impossible if an organization's elites do not participate in the strategic visioning process. In the Fogleman round, this functional requirement was largely satisfied by such devices as the Corona conference and the Corona issues process centered in the board of directors. The effect of such devices on participation was enhanced by the Air Force constitution. For instance, Fogleman enjoyed

Table 5-1. *Explaining the Performance of the Fogleman Round*

Component function of strategic visioning	Key process design features	Key process context factors
Organizing participation in the strategic visioning process	Anticipated culminating event Collective buy-in principle Long-Range Planning Board of Directors process Research and analysis project assignments	Air Force constitution Air Force cultural bias
Making sense of information about future policy objectives and circumstances of implementation	Long-Range Planning Board of Directors process during socialization phase Research and analysis projects Fogleman's reading and study	Defense policy subsystem
Conceiving strategic intent	Backcasting principle	Installed base of strategic thinking Air Force constitution Defense policy subsystem
Achieving organizational consensus about strategic intent	Culminating event Fogleman's reading and study Collective buy-in principle	Air Force constitution Air Force cultural bias Defense policy subsystem Hierarchist cultural bias
Declaring strategic intent	Briefing to general officers Publication of strategic vision Written long-range plan Participation in QDR	Air Force constitution Defense policy subsystem

the institutional resources to mobilize not only high-level officers and officials serving in Staff positions under him in Washington, but also his four-star colleagues heading major commands headquartered in Colorado, Hawaii, Illinois, Ohio, Texas, Virginia, and Germany.

MAKING SENSE OF THE FUTURE. Making sense of the future is obviously central to attaining foresight about policy objectives and circumstances of implementation. In this instance, performance was highly sensitive to process design features, such as issuing specific requests for studies and analysis to Air Force components, the RAND Corporation, and contractors. In terms of synthesizing the results of such work, a crucial process design feature was the Long-Range Planning Board of Directors, which was heavily supported by a small Staff unit called the Special Assistant to the Chief for Long-Range Planning (AF/LR). Fogleman's own reading and study was part of the mix of process design features, as well. The defense policy subsystem—a process context factor—contributed to this function by allowing for Air Force studies and analysis to concentrate on trends other than geopolitical ones. The board of directors regarded some aspects of the future policy environment as a settled matter for purposes of their discussions, since they had the option—and even the incentive—to defer to the authoritative outlooks contained in the National Security Strategy (a report published by the National Security Council) and the National Military Strategy (published by the Office of the Secretary of Defense).[16]

CONCEIVING STRATEGIC INTENT. Although the intellectual work carried out during the strategic visioning process was impressive, participants were not handed a clean slate. Indeed, members of the board of directors, as well as Fogleman himself, were presented with systematized ideas that seemed to have proved their worth just a few years before. As discussed earlier, considerable strategic thinking was embodied in the theory of the air campaign, which became official Air Force doctrine in the wake of the Gulf War. To some extent, conceptualizing strategic intent involved reformulating existing beliefs, rather than developing a completely new body of thinking. As an indication, some of the core competencies—especially, air superiority, precision engagement, and global strike—had been part of the Air Force's mind-set for decades.[17] The process context factor we call the installed base of strategic thinking thus contributed to the function of conceptualizing strategic intent.

AGREEING ON STRATEGIC INTENT. One of the keys to achieving consensus was the immense preparation for the culminating event. The three-star members of the board of directors, who opened discussions at the fall 1996 Corona conference by presenting the issues and laying out options, had begun their work over a year and a half earlier. The very concepts of a strategic vision and long-range plan, as elaborated during the Corona issues process, were another important design feature. Deciding on core competencies and distant end states did not require agreement on a concrete plan of action. The abstract character of strategic intent, which owed much to the backcasting principle, meant that the discussion skirted conflict-prone issues of how to pay for the actions required to move from the present to the future. This process design feature minimized conflict over many of the strategic issues discussed. While the abstract character of strategic intent might be viewed as a serious limitation of the Fogleman round, it did facilitate reaching a consensus.

All four of the process context factors contributed to achieving consensus over strategic intent. First, the installed base of strategic thinking, with which senior generals were at least familiar, meant that the area of agreement was already fairly wide before the event. Second, the defense policy subsystem provided an organizational incentive for senior leaders to agree on a common position. Since the community of interests between the Air Force and Army appeared to have dissipated during the Rice-McPeak period and since the nuclear mission had plummeted in importance to national security, the incentive to present a united front in the QDR and other policy events was strong by historical standards. Third, the Air Force constitution allowed the chief to chair the Corona conference in an active manner, as befitting his status as first among equals. When Fogleman sought to express the group consensus, his words carried substantial weight. In this fashion, the constitutional position of the chief of staff facilitated consensus about Air Force strategic intent.

The Air Force's hierarchist cultural bias—the fourth context factor considered here—had a similar effect. A simple interpretation is that the Air Force's high degree of groupness dovetailed with the organizational incentive to maintain a united front in the defense policy subsystem, while its similarly high level of gridness prescribed deference to the chief. What cultural bias helps one to appreciate is the effect of Fogleman's own reading and study. This process feature made the chief not only an organizational authority, but also an expert or intellectual authority. The Air Force is an institution that takes expertise extremely seriously; in many respects, the culture exudes the ethos of Frederick Taylor's philosophy of scientific management, in which the leaders who occupy the strategic apex of an organization should defer, on many matters, to experts, such as those who staff units in the organization's technostructure.[18] The Air Force might thus be considered a variant of hierarchism.[19] In this instance, deference was owed Fogleman for two distinct reasons: his expertise on subjects, like the revolution in military affairs, and his position as chief.

This analysis can be more fully appreciated if one reflects on the psychology, as contrasted with the internal politics, of strategic visioning. This process involves grappling with extremely complex and speculative questions. In Karl Weick's terms, the information considered in such a process is inescapably equivocal. Reducing equivocality is part of the psychology of achieving consensus on both the future policy environment and strategic intent. The interviews we conducted revealed that the board of directors struggled until some of its members sought to reduce equivocality, in effect, through informal communication with Fogleman (see chapter 3). We speculate that Fogleman's ability to reduce equivocality was substantially aided by the culture of deferring to expertise, a mechanism activated by his own reading and study of the issues. This same mechanism may have also been at work during the culminating event, when Fogleman did not simply play the role of moderator, but also weighed in with his own thoughts on the subjects at hand.

DECLARING STRATEGIC INTENT. The importance of declaring strategic intent lies in its potential to link the outcome of strategic visioning with medium-term expenditure planning, strategic human resource and organizational planning, and, ultimately, strategy implementation. The communication process was enhanced by the fact that the Air Force had something to say. Two process context factors also mattered. First, the Air Force constitution empowered the chief, together with the secretary, to speak out on behalf of the service and department on the subjects addressed in the strategic vision and the long-range plan. Second, the defense policy subsystem made the strategic vision somewhat notable, since it foreshadowed the arguments that the Air Force would soon set forth in the formal proceedings of the Quadrennial Defense Review. Aspects of process context thus enabled the leaders occupying the strategic apex to speak out, while aspects of the policy subsystem ensured that at least some would be listening.

SUMMARY AND IMPLICATIONS. The success of the Fogleman round can partly be explained in terms of the process features, which together formed a coherent design. This design, as a whole, could well represent a smart practice for improving strategic intent and for performing the higher-level function of strategic planning and policy management. This conclusion is a major hypothesis stemming from this detailed case study. Still, the success of the Fogleman round is not explained by its process design alone. Its outcome was helped by the process context factors outlined earlier in this section. For this reason, the process design may not operate as effectively in other settings, even if fully transferred.

Process context factors appear to vary significantly across the U.S. federal government. Many policy subsystems are less competitive than the one dealing with organizing, training, and equipping the military services. Many organizations are more closely characterized by the multidivisional organizational form than the unitary one, while career officials are only sometimes placed within the strategic apex. While a hierarchist cultural bias may be typical, many organizations are not as high in groupness as a military service. Finally, the installed base of strategic thinking may not be quite as rich in organizations with leaner technostructures and fewer opportunities for mid-career executive development than are found in the Air Force and the broader Department of Defense. However, a process design patterned on the one analyzed here may still lead to satisfactory outcomes of strategic visioning even in process contexts vastly different from the Air Force.

Explaining Performance in the Ryan-Peters Round

We turn now to analyzing the Ryan-Peters round, which revisited the Air Force's strategic vision. This process was conducted mainly during 1999, with the Corona conference in the fall of that year taking place just beyond the halfway point in Michael Ryan's term as chief. We use an identical explanatory framework to explore the similarities and differences between the Fogleman and Ryan-Peters rounds, so as to gain further insight into the process of strategic visioning.

The Ryan-Peters round improved Air Force strategic intent over the baseline represented by the Fogleman era's *Global Engagement* vision and long-range plan. The clearest evidence that this cycle improved the Air Force's strategic thinking lies in the development of critical future capabilities. As table 5-2 shows, these identified capabilities added a level of detail to the core competencies construct, although they remained abstract in the sense that they contain no specific references to equipment or even to whether the assets providing the capability would operate from space or the atmosphere. At the same time, critical future capabilities expressed a more refined understanding of the desired performance attributes of the systems that the Air Force would increasingly operate as it evolved during the coming decades. In addition, the outcomes of numerous specialized debates that had been conducted in the intervening years were selectively funneled into the organization's strategic vision. Insofar as the views emanating from these debates constituted improvements in strategic thinking (which we take at face value), then it is fair to conclude that the Ryan-Peters round performed well in this respect.

To say that the Ryan-Peters round was satisfactory is not to say that it was perfect. Indeed, the Long-Range Planning Board of Directors functioned poorly during this round, as discussed in chapter 4. The strong disappointment expressed by three-star major command vice commanders serving on the board stemmed largely from the relative absence of genuine dialogue at its meetings. The fact that the board of directors process was unsatisfactory, however, does not automatically translate into a similar eval-

Table 5-2. *Core Competencies and Critical Future Capabilities*

Core competencies	Critical future capability
Aerospace superiority	Rapidly dominate (within days) adversary air forces and air defenses to allow joint and coalition forces freedom from attack, freedom to maneuver, and freedom to attack.
	Consistent with international agreements, render an adversary's cruise, land attack cruise, and ballistic missile assets ineffective before launch or soon after through timely and effective interaction with national and theater missile defense assets.
	Protect our space assets and deny, when directed, an adversary's ability to exploit space.
Information superiority	Provide continuous, tailored information within minutes of tasking with sufficient accuracy to engage any target in any battlespace worldwide.
	In conjunction with joint and national capabilities, ensure our use of the information domain unhindered by all attempts to deny, disrupt, destroy, or corrupt it; and also ensure our ability to attack and affect an adversary's information and information systems in pursuit of military objectives.
Global attack	Create desired effects within hours of tasking, anywhere on the globe, including locations deep within an adversary's territory.
	Provide deterrence against weapons of mass destruction attack and coercion by maintaining a credible, land-based nuclear and flexible conventional strike force.
Precision engagement	Create precise effects rapidly, with the ability to retarget quickly, against large target sets anywhere, anytime, for as long as required.
Rapid global mobility	Provide the airlift, aerial refueling, and en route infrastructure capability to respond within hours of tasking to support peacetime operations or a crisis (up to a Major Theater War) while maintaining the capability to rapidly swing priority forces to another Major Theater War.
Agile combat support	Build an aerospace force that enables robust, distributed military operations with time-definite sustainment.

uation for the strategic visioning exercise as a whole, unless one makes dialogue among senior officials like the vice commanders an independent, rule-like success criterion. Our theoretical model of preparing for the future identifies dialogue among the next generation of leaders as a likely contributor to consensus, not as a necessary condition of effectiveness. In the case of the Ryan-Peters round, the strategic visioning process was robust to the failure of one of its components; we return to this issue below.

Finally, a brief description of the process design provides a factual basis for explaining why the Ryan-Peters round performed satisfactorily. In many important respects, the process design was similar to the Fogleman round. For instance, the two rounds shared three specific features: an explicit conceptual approach to strategic visioning, a formal board of directors process, and a culminating event at the Corona conference. The process design was not, however, identical to the Fogleman round. First, the board of directors operated differently: the Fogleman round's socialization phase was not replicated, officials serving the secretary participated more actively, and the chair's meeting leadership style was less encouraging of extended dialogue on open-ended, strategic issues. Second, the duration of the process was about six months, whereas Fogleman's Corona issues process lasted more than a year.[20] Third, Ryan's engagement with the issues seems to have been more typical of chiefs, with a substantial reliance on staff briefings. Fogleman, by contrast, pursued a program of extensive reading. Fourth, the culminating event was different in notable respects. The four-day conference agenda included subjects unrelated to strategic visioning; the time devoted to discussing strategic issues was therefore approximately two days, compared with five days during the fall 1996 Corona meeting. Also unlike the fall 1996 conference, none of the principal presentations on strategic visioning issues were delivered by major command vice commanders. The conference therefore reflected a conventional division of labor between staff units at Air Force Headquarters and the major commands. All told, the process was geared more to improving the substantive content of Air Force strategic intent than to educating future Air Force leaders about long-term issues.

Case Comparison: Toward Generalization about Strategic Visioning Practice

After comparing the two satisfactory rounds, it is reasonable to entertain the thought that their common design features are essential characteristics of a strategic visioning process. More precisely, successful strategic visioning may require adherence to the principles of collective buy-in and backcasting, a knowledgeable chief executive, and a culminating event. The case comparison also suggests that those process design features of the Fogleman round that were not replicated in the successful Ryan-Peters round may be inessential for a satisfactory strategic visioning exercise. These features included an effort lasting more than one year, intense personal study of policy issues by the chief executive, and a high-performing group like the board of directors. The theoretical arguments developed above further suggest that process context factors are important. These factors include the surrounding policy subsystem, the organization's constitution, the organization's cultural bias, and the installed base of strategic thinking. In sum, we may have discovered smart practices for strategic visioning—namely, the three process design features common to the two successful rounds. We further hypothesize that certain institutional factors are strongly conducive to a satisfactory outcome.

From a smart practices perspective, however, these propositions are not completely satisfying. For instance, the board of directors process was an important process feature in the Fogleman round, yet the outcome of the Ryan-Peters round, which we defined as an improvement in the Air Force's strategic intent, was relatively insensitive to the virtual collapse of the Long-Range Planning Board of Directors. We must reconcile the single-case and comparative analyses if we are to fully understand strategic visioning as a process.

A plausible explanation for why the Ryan-Peters round proved successful despite the failure of the board of directors is that a substitute was found. When the board of directors lost momentum, the role of the Strategic Planning Directorate (AF/XPX) changed from supporting this collective process to taking responsibility for preparing the Corona conference. This permanent staff unit within Air Force headquarters, together with the three-star deputy chief of staff for plans and programs who oversaw it, had the capacity to provide input to the decision conference. This substitute was not available during the Fogleman round, since this structure had yet to be established. The Fogleman round was thus more dependent on the board of directors process than was the Ryan-Peters round. If the board of directors had lost momentum in the Fogleman round, the burden of preparing the Corona conference would have fallen to Fogleman and the small, temporary unit called the Special Assistant to the Chief for Long-Range Planning. The inputs to the fall 1996 Corona conference would then have been perceived as the chief's own views rather than as a collective product, and collective buy-in might not have been achieved. In sum, the Fogleman round probably would not have succeeded if the board of directors process had failed, and in this sense it was a critical process feature. On the other hand, the Ryan-Peters round was successful despite the board's ineffectiveness because a functional substitute was available.

This brief discussion goes some distance toward harmonizing the single-case and comparative analyses, but it leaves open the question of why AF/XPX proved a fairly close substitute for the board of directors. The answer lies with the Air Force constitution, a process context factor. Simply put, the Air Force constitution construes the senior leadership as comprising the four-star generals and the secretary. The three-star board members are not part of this echelon, so collective buy-in was not especially sensitive to opportunities for three-star participation. Now the question remains as to why the four-star generals were willing to give much credence to the inputs provided by a headquarters staff unit. One explanation is that strategic planning had become institutionalized as an Air Force function. This change in the Air Force constitution was one of Fogleman's main objectives as chief, and his intentions were realized during the early Ryan period. AF/XPX also came to be accepted as the organizational unit bearing principal Staff responsibility for performing the strategic planning function. This modest change in the Air Force constitution, in conjunction with the service's hierarchist cultural bias, licensed reliance on AF/XPX organization as a source of advice on strategic intent.[21]

The upshot of this analysis is that a strategic visioning process may be enhanced if a strategic planning unit is built into the permanent organizational structure. A liaison device like the board of directors faces inherent difficulties, especially when it is composed of individuals with different loyalties (for example, some to the career service and others to political appointees), as suggested by the case analysis presented in chapter 4. Still, there is no guarantee that a strategic planning unit will make a strategic visioning process effective, most notably with regard to achieving consensus. Much depends on whether the process design includes the smart practices identified earlier and whether the process context factors are conducive to the exercise.

From the standpoint of smart practices, the Ryan-Peters round offers a further opportunity to understand strategic visioning as a process. The round was not just satisfactory; it was highly successful in terms of improving the strategic vision's content and direct relevance to defense policy debates. The explanation for this success lies in large part with the organizational incentives provided by the defense policy subsystem, as well as with changes in the installed base of strategic thinking. First, the Air Force anticipated another Quadrennial Defense Review soon after the 2000 elections. If anything, the organizational incentives to agree on desired force structure, as well as more abstract and conceptual dimensions of strategic intent, were even stronger than in 1997, due to the prospect that a defense-minded Republican Administration would come into office in January 2001.[22] Thus, the anticipated opening of a policy window provided a stimulus to make the strategic vision sufficiently concrete so as to be highly germane to policy discussions at the outset of a new administration.

Second, the installed base of strategic thinking grew considerably during the 1998–99 period, just prior to the process of revisiting the vision. The explanation for this increase is manifold. One influence was Michael Ryan's desire to remedy what he believed was a problem with *Global Engagement*, namely, the idea that the Air Force was evolving into a space and air force. As discussed in the previous chapter, he believed that the concept of an aerospace force was better, for substantive military and institutional reasons. This view was the impetus for the work of the Aerospace Integration Task Force, which we examine in chapter 8. Although this effort was not entirely successful, its emphasis on military effects (such as disabling a target) over media (such as space or the atmosphere) reinforced functional thinking as a key intellectual discipline in strategic planning. A second influence was the desire, especially on the part of the AF/XPX organization, to improve how strategic intent was conceptualized. Participants were dissatisfied with the conceptual disjointedness of the three components of *Global Engagement*, namely, Air Force core competencies, long-range plan end states, and the anticipated evolution toward a space force. Such dissatisfaction partly explains the effort to define Thrust Area Transformation Plans. While this effort eventually collapsed, the lessons AF/XPX learned from it led to the development of the more streamlined construct of critical future capabilities, which elaborated on the core competencies. A third influence was the Aerospace Future Capabilities War Games (see chapter 8). This series of war games was designed to identify strategic issues that had not been recognized when *Global Engagement* was debated and crafted. The futures games put the issue of so-called asymmetric, anti-access strategies pursued by potential military opponents, which had been moving up the defense policy agenda for some time, squarely within the mainstream of the Air Force strategic planning agenda. This issue's importance came to be reflected in the *Global Vigilance, Reach, and Power* vision, and it then grew in importance during the Rumsfeld policy reviews in 2001.

The threads woven through this story relate to organizational learning. The process of strengthening the installed base of strategic thinking was mainly one of remedying the organization's declared strategic intent. Dissatisfaction with the status quo came from diverse sources, including the chief and the staff bureaucracy responsible for strategic planning. Not all attempts to improve on the earlier product were successful. Even so, commitment to performing the function of strategic planning and policy management remained firm, owing to such factors as the Air Force constitution (for example, the chief's role and the institutionalized strategic planning function) and the defense policy subsystem. These factors underwrote the developmental dynamics that allowed the revision of the Air Force strategic vision to produce a substantially improved conception of strategic intent.

In sum, smart practices analysis takes account of process context factors—specifically, the policy subsystem, the organization's constitution, the organizational cultural bias, and the installed base of strategic thinking. These factors seem likely to influence the effectiveness of any strategic visioning process in government.[23] The inquiry also sensitizes public managers to the importance of process design features, including the candidate smart practices identified above: the doctrinal principles of policy management, backcasting from the future, and collective buy-in; substantive knowledge on the part of the chief executive; and a culminating event. In addition, the inquiry finds that liaison processes (like the board of directors) and bureaucratic processes may be substitutes for preparing a culminating event, albeit imperfect ones. Finally, the installed base of strategic thinking needs to be continually cultivated, and doing so may require the sort of determination that comes from specific organizational responsibility (like that of a strategic planning directorate) and a career chief executive with specific responsibility to advise the administration and Congress on substantive and institutional matters.

The Air Force Experience in Broader Focus

The Air Force experience is a source of case evidence not only about the strategic visioning process, but also about the broader function of strategic planning and policy management. The innovation process has advanced sufficiently in the past decade for the Air Force experience to serve as a concrete example of the approach to public management that we call preparing for the future. The remainder of this book examines aspects of preparing for the future other than strategic visioning and analyzes the processes through which the Air Force has criticized its own established vision.

CHAPTER 6

Continuing Institutional Issues: Planning, Resourcing, and Governance

In a seven-year span, the Air Force went through two relatively far-reaching efforts to discern and implement a new corporate direction. Like any such organization that has worked so intensively to position itself for the future, the Air Force has only just begun to process the consequences of its tremendous efforts. Many participants and observers will conclude that it has been spinning its wheels without producing tangible results. Others will argue that it has been positioning itself for those rare occasions when the alignment of political forces invites advocacy of dramatic changes in the Air Force's aggregate resources and their allocation among programs. Still others will point to identifiable changes in resource commitments as evidence that we can already see consequences of the Fogleman and Ryan-Peters rounds of corporate strategic planning. At the same time, however, the process of realization that has unfolded since 1994 has driven the Air Force to a clearer view of the challenges it will face in the future and has provided key players with a better grasp of how they might alter their core competencies. Perhaps more critically, it has pushed the leadership toward making a significantly more robust effort to define and resource requisite capabilities in a timely fashion.

This chapter and chapters 7 and 8 together provide a detailed assessment of how well the Air Force has done in processing the outputs from the two rounds of corporate strategic planning. This chapter focuses on the degree of institutional learning that occurred as a result of the seven-year effort to enhance the role of planning in the Air Force's decisional processes. It first examines whether planning enjoys a higher standing in the service now than it did in 1994 and, if so, whether it has gained sufficient recognition to sustain its newfound profile. Second, we look at the connectivity of planning to program and resource commitments. Granting that planning has gained new status in the Air Force and occurs more authoritatively, we examine whether it actually makes a difference in developing and promoting claims for aggregate resources and committing those claims programmatically throughout the Air Force. If not, what remains to be done to achieve greater real-world relevance for planning? Third, the chapter measures the extent to which the Air Force governance structures and cultures have contributed their share toward improving corporate coherence, focusing on how internal decisionmaking within the Staff, relations between the Staff and the major commands, and practices within the major command community have evolved so that the service may better rise to the challenges and opportunities underscored in the past seven years.

Planning and Shifts in Fiscal Circumstances

Planning receives regular incantation in the Pentagon because it is one of the elements in the Planning, Programming, and Budgeting System (PPBS). Robert McNamara presided over the development of PPBS while defense secretary during the Kennedy and Johnson administrations.[1] Charles J. Hitch, McNamara's comptroller, actually masterminded the approach. PPBS sought to place services' specific programmatic commitments within the broader context of the entire defense effort within a given capability. McNamara argued, for instance, that funding of the Polaris—a nuclear submarine that composed the Navy's main contribution to deterrence during the 1960s and 1970s—ultimately should depend on how the program stands up in comparison with other strategic retaliatory forces, not just those in the Navy's arsenal. Within this framework, Hitch believed that the Joint Chiefs of Staff and planners in military departments would review big-picture projections annually so that these would guide resourcing decisions.[2]

Aaron Wildavsky directed an incisive critique at PPBS soon after President Johnson embraced the approach as applicable to all departments in the United States government.[3] To Wildavsky, PPBS's promoters had failed to see that most domestic agencies lacked the capacity for strategic planning displayed by the Department of Defense in the 1960s. In implementing PPBS in the Pentagon, McNamara could tap a strong analytic legacy that dated back to the important role played by the RAND Corporation in generating analysis of defense policies after World War II.

Wildavsky believed that planning and analysis go hand-in-hand. Rigorous policy analysis provides the capacity to transcend "the fire-house environment of day-to-day administration" and trace out "the consequences of innovative ideas" rather than "projecting the status quo" into the future.[4] He noted that the originators of PPBS in the Pentagon wanted to close the gap between planning and budgeting: "They wanted to stop blue-sky planning and integrate planning and budgeting."

Importantly, Wildavsky noted that, at least until the Vietnam war began to drain U.S. resources, McNamara's efforts to prioritize through PPBS did not meet stiff external resistance because defense budgets remained flush and contractors routinely amassed sizable backlogs. In other words, neither pressures from fiscal constraint nor especially intense concept-to-program entrepreneurship placed a premium on the continual prioritization anticipated by Hitch. In the Pentagon, PPBS stressed programmatic sorting of claims much more than strategic planning.[5]

The assertion that planning is the silent P in PPBS has become an old saw among budgeting aficionados. Wildavsky's observations reflect the degree to which this was the case by the mid-1970s. This reality corresponded with thinking about budgeting systems emerging from public choice economists. Public choice advanced the position that analytic approaches involving planning and programming simply leave the door open for bureaucrats to pursue their favorite pastime, namely, dreaming up ways to maximize their budgets. William Niskanen, a former Department of Defense analyst, produced in 1973 a public choice agenda for altering the budgeting process so as to constrict budget maximizing. The program sought to institute automatization as a means to keep budgets within tight aggregate fiscal frameworks and to constrain severely programmatic entrepreneurship on the part of both political appointees and career officials.[6]

Planning and programming received a further blow in the form of stagflation in the 1970s, which seemed to add urgency to the public choice prescription. The United States, along with several other advanced economies, found itself short on revenues and overextended in entitlement programs. The resulting fiscal pressures triggered a spiral effect, whereby mounting deficits undermined economic performance. In response, the public became highly receptive to arguments for downsizing the government.[7] Within this context, Niskanen-style automatization became the plat du jour even for scholars like Wildavsky, who had previously viewed

budget as inherently incremental: "To the extent that governments are serious about limiting spending, . . . they will become concerned about overall
spending limits. . . . [C]ountries that desire to keep spending from growing
to a greater proportion of national product than it already is will move
toward some mechanism for imposing limits."[8] Wildavsky goes on to
describe the dire consequences of the emergent regime for budget review
based on analysis:

> Where the budgetary reforms to which we are accustomed are con-
> cerned with the quality of spending, the new wave will emphasize the
> quantity. . . . Where [reforms are] . . . avowedly apolitical, drawing on
> economic or management science for legitimacy, spending limits will
> be openly political, resting on explicit choices about total spending and
> its major subdivisions.

In the United States, the Reagan administration sought to impose such a
regime of fiscal restraint, especially over discretionary domestic spending.
The reality, of course, fell short of this level of discipline. Even to key players in the administration, it became obvious within the first term that
reductions in spending on domestic programs had failed to cover the losses
of revenue from Reagan's dramatic tax cuts.[9] The administration's indul-
gence of defense expenditure exasperated the fiscal strain, causing
monumentally high deficits that provided a huge drag on both the economy
and domestic programs well into the 1990s. An Office of Management and
Budget official conveyed in a 1983 interview the degree to which the Reagan administration had turned Wildavsky on his head by eschewing analysis
but at the same time encouraging Pentagon profligacy:

> There was no big assessment of defense. It was like they just didn't
> want to do it. They just wanted to add dollars. . . . Our advice . . . was
> . . . [to] add a few billion [dollars]—from five to ten, depending on
> how far they wanted to go—then do a big study and decide how to
> allocate. . . . But they didn't follow that advice. They just added
> twenty-six or so billion. This was beyond our wildest imagination. It
> probably was even beyond the wildest expectations of the defense
> establishment . . . There was no substantial new initiative [to exam-
> ine how best to use the new funds]. It was just a lot more of the
> same.[10]

A great deal has occurred since these bleak days for planning and programming. The collapse of the Soviet Union and the end of the cold war

completely dispelled the view that the United States was engaged in a mortal struggle with a Communist evil empire. This change in global politics, combined with fears over the mushrooming deficit, ushered in a period of austerity for the Pentagon in the early 1990s. General Fogleman's predecessor, Gen. Merrill A. "Tony" McPeak, responded to the dramatic shift in opinion with huge cuts in Air Force personnel and an extensive reconfiguration of force structure. McPeak pressed these responses in an effort to preserve some funds for investment in future programs.

Generals Fogleman and Ryan both faced two problems not perceived during the McPeak years. First, the United State's role as the sole global superpower had subjected the Air Force to an operations tempo that frequently stretched beyond its funded capacities. Second, the Air Force had recognized two threats that had not been anticipated immediately after the collapse of the Soviet Union. First, one or more peer competitor nations could emerge within twenty years so as to reproduce cold-war-like conditions. Second, rogue nations could play havoc on world security. Either of these two conditions could pose an especially grave danger if the Air Force failed to make the sacrifices in current programs to invest sufficiently in programs designed to address likely future threats.

Fogleman's and Ryan's commitments to corporate strategic planning attempted to dislodge the Air Force from the horns of this dilemma. In addition, more auspicious circumstances for defense expenditure seemed imminent around the time in which the Ryan round culminated in the fall 1999 Corona conference. Unparalleled economic prosperity and the emergence of surpluses in the late 1990s introduced what now appears as a brief episode—namely, a politics of choice characterized by intense struggles between claims for increased domestic and defense expenditures and tax cuts. Participants believed that with the emergence of a Republican president, the Air Force could capitalize on its investment planning and make aggressive claims not just for additional aggregate funds for the Pentagon, but for a significantly enhanced share of new resources in relation to the other services.

In the wake of the terrorist attacks on September 11, 2001, the Bush administration shifted dramatically from somewhat anemic plans to enhance defense expenditures to increases that now rival the Reagan build-up.[11] In addition, its budget proposal for fiscal year 2003 favored the Air Force over the other services. Bush thus outlined a spending trajectory that would take the aggregate defense budget far beyond the $45 billion increase over ten years to which he committed during the 2000 presidential campaign. The fiscal year 2003 proposal envisioned an addition of $120 billion by fiscal year 2007, taking the total defense budget, in real terms, almost to the level attained under Reagan. The Air Force garnered not only the largest share of the proposed expenditure among the services, with a total of $107 billion out of $379 billion in fiscal year 2003, but also the most procurement dollars.

As discussed in chapter 4, the fall 1999 Corona conference led to the selection of so-called option 4b, which entailed pushing for increases in the service's total budget resources on the order of about $15 billion annually. The plan considered no appreciable sacrifices of two Air Force objectives— namely, global reach as opposed to theater-specific capabilities and a force structure that balances shooting platforms and enabling systems rather than favoring the former at the expense of the latter. The Air Force found some support in diagnoses elsewhere in the policy arena about future funding requirements. In the summer of 2000, the Joint Chiefs of Staff tallied their aggregate needs for additional funds at $30 billion each year.[12]

At the time, this seemed to reflect irrational exuberance on the part of the Joint Chiefs, premised on the expectation that a Bush administration would prove more willing to fund the Pentagon than would a Gore administration. The Congressional Budget Office chimed in by September 2000 with a recommendation for an additional $50 billion.[13] The bulk of this sum would go toward closing the $37 billion gap between the $53 billion procurement budget and projected requirements.

Fiscal reality did not appear conducive to executing option 4b, however, over and above the political vulnerability of specific items on the Air Force's programmatic wish list.[14] Around the time of the fall 1999 Corona conference, Michael O'Hanlon, the highly regarded Brookings Institution defense analyst, observed that Bush's vision for the military would cost $25 billion each year.[15] This stood at odds with the central plank in Bush's platform— a tax cut within a fiscal framework that would prove affordable only with substantial containment of expenditures. During the nomination and election campaigns, the future administration made several efforts to articulate how it would reconcile new claims for funding the military with general fiscal strictures. In a September 1999 speech at the Citadel in South Carolina, candidate Bush asserted that his administration would "skip a generation" of acquisitions, thereby saving money by investing more strategically. However, palpable strains on the military associated with servicing the United States' global commitments seemed to cry out for an immediate infusion if the administration were to live up to its campaign promises.

Notwithstanding his campaign rhetoric, President Bush proposed no new funds for the Pentagon for fiscal year 2002 beyond those outlined by President Clinton in his final budget submission. Donald H. Rumsfeld—the defense secretary, who before Bush's decision had been overseeing the preparation of supplemental appropriations for fiscal year 2001—found himself explaining to the top brass that the administration wanted a full strategic review before pressing for new funding. Rumsfeld assigned the job of ringmastering this task to Andrew W. Marshall. At the time seventy-nine years old, Marshall had a long career as a Pentagon planner and a reputation for not hesitating to air his reservations about such programmatic icons as the F-22, heavy tanks, and aircraft carriers in twenty-first century warfare.[16]

Marshall had distinguished himself as an advocate of the view that the United States has emphasized preparation for a possible conflict in Europe at the expense of developing capabilities to respond decisively in Asia. Marshall's role in the strategic review thus bore good and bad tidings for the Air Force. On the negative side of the ledger, an emphasis on Asia meant that lessons from the Kosovo conflict might not trump the other services quite so readily as thought in 1999. The Air Force believed that its success against Serbia demonstrated the need for stealth in its platforms, which stood as evidence favoring the F-22 against the Joint Strike Fighter, and precision in its enabling systems, which supported greater investments in unmanned aerial vehicles and satellites.[17] "Measured war" became a key consideration operating behind these conclusions: Kosovo represented future engagements that did not stem from an immediate threat to the security of the United Sates and that were set within the framework of consensual responses implemented collegially with allies. The attacks on New York and Washington on September 11, 2001, of course, could not have contrasted more sharply with such circumstances.

The emphasis on the emergence of a so-called peer competitor in Asia (a euphemism for China) suggested before September 11 that the Air Force would have to dramatically trim its wish list and focus on a narrower array of prospective capabilities. Option 4b likely would not have survived this winnowing process. On the positive side, however, an emphasis on Asia still put the Air Force in a strong competitive position relative to the other services. One found, among the menu of possibilities, evidence that the Fogleman and Ryan investment in planning had channeled thinking to long-range programmatic commitments that would enhance the Air Force's stature among the services.

Even before the arrival of the new administration, Asia-focused visioning had underscored the tyranny of distance associated with the emergence of a peer competitor across the Pacific. This had led to discussion of a reprioritization of programmatic needs so that lift (that is, air transports) and long-range bombers would receive new emphasis.[18] By fall 2000, key players in the Bush campaign were advancing precisely this view.[19] Subsequently, the weaponization of space and the development of information warfare capabilities entered the discourse, on the grounds that the United States would want to protect its own satellite and cybernetic systems from possible attack and conduct aggression against hostile parties' assets.[20] This concern was evaluated in a congressionally mandated commission chaired by Rumsfeld before he became defense secretary. It echoed language assumed by the Air Force leadership over the past few years when discussing future challenges.[21]

The Air Force's emphasis on planning gave it acumen in canvassing the issues associated with the potential rise of China as a peer challenger, including the consequences should China or any other Asian power obtain the ability to enforce an exclusionary zone that would impose clear limits on theater-based, heavy, or readily detectable assets. In focusing much of its visioning of the future on such an eventuality, the Air Force had accumulated a diverse menu of prospective systems that would help neutralize such a threat. It thus began to appear that many programmatic roads led to the Air Force. The degree to which the Air Force had invested in intense corporate strategic planning meant that it could take advantage of these new mission opportunities.

In the aftermath of the September 11 attacks, the Bush administration proffered budget figures that brought new life to option 4b. The Air Force found itself under less pressure to sacrifice theater-specific capabilities for global reach, development of enabling systems for acquisition of shooting platforms, and short- for long-range combat aircraft. The Air Force had so positioned itself that, given an upsurge in demand, it could present a number of programmatic options with seemingly unquestionable appeal. It did not hurt that the Air Force had turned its contribution to the campaign in Afghanistan into a demonstration project for the utility of unmanned aerial vehicles, spaced-based sensors, and conventional ordnance (1,000 pound bombs) with high IQs (precision guidance systems). The Air Force's investment strategy had given it just the tools it needed to parade its potential contributions to future conflicts associated with the efforts to combat terrorism.

Career Establishments and the Politics of Strategic Visioning

We do not find uniform approbation of the concept of a career establishment engaging in such anticipatory positioning. It is thus important to briefly examine the legitimacy of an organization dominated by career officials—in this case, the leaders of an armed service—using planning to position itself advantageously in anticipation of changes in the preferences of its political masters and Congress. Such a practice would likely strike abhorrence in any devotee of the public choice view of the relationship between bureaucrats and politicians. Public choice holds a strict dichotomy between the role of the politician, which is to define policies, and that of the bureaucrat, which is to implement them. Such a sharp distinction between the two cadres and their functional domains often proves untenable in practice, however, although conditions within a given political epoch might constrict the policy roles of officials whereas other circumstances might facilitate them.[22]

New Zealand underwent the most thorough effort to impose the policy-administration dichotomy. Ten years after the imposition of the reforms, a renowned American authority on budgeting systems, Allen Schick, was retained to analyze the failure of the approach. The New Zealand attempt at dichotomization, which derived directly from American public choice economics, sought to constrict relations between political executives and officials into contractually formalized purchaser-provider arrangements, in which the former would establish the outcomes they sought and the latter would simply provide the requisite outputs.[23] By the mid-1990s, the New Zealand political leadership concluded that the purchaser-provider format had obscured long-term strategic goals and the integration of these with on-going policy decisions, especially those concerning the budget.[24] The government eventually embraced the view that senior officials' contracts should allow for collaboration in ownership between political executives and senior bureaucrats, which would lead to better alignment of outputs with desired outcomes.[25]

Schick seized on this realization to promote the benefits of more strategic approaches to budgeting as part of greater mutuality between the obligations of political masters and their senior officials. While praising the revolutionary zeal of the New Zealand reformers, Schick highlighted a number of weaknesses in the evolving system. The bill of particulars could easily read across to the current condition of many U.S. government agencies, including the Air Force: considerable unevenness in departments' sense of mission and performance; the straightjacket effect of the sinking lid on operating budgets; the failure to incorporate cost and performance data in budget decisionmaking; and, generally, the tendency for narrow concerns to crowd out collective ones and for the short-term to obscure the long-term.[26] Schick employs words that would sound like music to the ears of senior career officials concerned about the long-range mission of their agency. He issues a strong admonition to political executives about the importance of taking on board matters associated with their organizations' long-term viability: "Ministers must also be mindful of the organizational strength of their departments; they should be institution builders, and they should forbear from demanding so much by way of outputs and from pushing the purchase price down so far as to jeopardize the department's long-term capacity to perform."[27]

In another work, one of us notes that different standards and perspectives can affect budget systems by either furthering balance or introducing distortions.[28] For instance, a politics of constraint took hold in the 1980s and early 1990s in response, first, to economic stress and, ultimately, to mounting deficits. Fiscal competence became the order of the day. Specifically, individuals within the political executive responsible for setting fiscal targets enjoyed ascendancy in devising the contours of budgets. As Wildavsky correctly anticipated, this emphasis tended to rely on automatization of the budgeting process and to skew discourse toward matters concerning inputs and relatively short-term objectives.

Under normal circumstances, incrementalism prevails in budget politics. Wildavsky cited this reality in his critiques of efforts to achieve greater programmatic rationality through devices like PPBS.[29] Incrementalism thrives when politicians can indulge their efforts to maintain political support. Elected politicians who succeed at this function and the political executives who advise them on policies that will sustain support have become adept at what is called responsive competence. Outputs count most in this sector of the budgeting system equation. Responsive competence takes a longer-term perspective than does fiscal competence because it focuses on programs rather than inputs. However, the prominence of the approach rests on the frequency with which, for example, the district or state in which a fighter jet will be produced trumps other considerations in garnering congressional support for increases in defense spending. We find this despite the fact that focusing on such output vectors almost invariably harms the development of the capabilities required for the country's future national security position. Even presidents benefit when programs cherished by voters in a state they need for reelection survive cutting rounds.

Strategic competence finds a more natural home among the career establishment of an agency than among those trying to hold the line in the fiscal framework or those seeking to obtain and maintain political support. This does not imply that neither of these groups is capable of strategic competence. It simply recognizes that permanent officials tend to take a longer view of their organization's requirements. U.S. government departments in which career officials do not work closely with political executives normally display little or no pressure from within their own cadre to integrate strategic perspectives across units responsible for different programs. A different dynamic might emerge in apex agencies, however. The Air Force presents as an apex agency because one official, the chief of staff, assumes formal responsibility for the interface between the political executive and the career establishment, in this case the uniformed leaders of the Air Force.

From what we know about General McPeak, the imperatives of the drawdown of resources associated with the end of the cold war probably meant that he had little option but to pursue aggressive spending cuts. Fogleman and Ryan, however, found themselves in a position from which they could give considerably greater attention to the long-range future consequences of resource decisions, although their approaches contrasted in several regards. To be sure, they operated under overarching circumstances that normally invite gaming for greater resources, namely, the emergent politics of choice associated first with a shrinking deficit and later with an expanding governmentwide surplus. However, they were also motivated by the extent to which the post–cold war drawdown had put the Air Force under immense strains and impeded its ability to adapt programmatically to future threats and challenges.

The conditions faced by Fogleman and Ryan thus seemed to favor a stronger role for strategic competence. The resurgent investment in planning responded to these conditions. Questions remain about the extent to which it worked lasting institutional effects, but it is significant that the Air Force leadership articulated the problematic in terms strikingly close to our own. A May 2000 Staff document on the resource allocation process acknowledged that the Air Force successfully engaged in strategic planning to identify options.[30] However, the document maintained that subjective judgments about the fiscal reality and political impacts continued to hold excessive sway in the process whereby the Air Force evaluates options and allocates resources.

Persistent Disjunctions between Planning and Programming

The lessons from the disjunction between the Air Force's immense investment in planning since 1994 and the relatively tenuous effects on resource allocation have not fallen on deaf ears in the service's leadership. Assessments of the difficulties point to weaknesses in the programming process and in the corporate connectivity between programming and other elements of resource allocation as crucial drags on performance. In spring 1999, Secretary Peters and General Ryan commissioned the Air Force headquarters 2002 initiative to address the issues emerging from the shortfalls of the corporate structure adopted in 1995 in achieving integration of planning, programming, requirements, and acquisitions.

The Air Force leadership determines the service's corporate structure, to the extent that there are no externally imposed mandates guiding how the Air Force makes internal decisions regarding its prerogatives. However, while the Air Force Staff takes the lead in both planning and programming, the acquisitions and requirements processes operate somewhat independently from Staff oversight. In fact, the acquisitions process is controlled by civilians in the Office of the Secretary of Defense, and the requirements process largely revolves around advocacy for equipment associated with major commands' jockeying for operational relevance. The Air Force headquarters 2002 Air Force Corporate Structure report advocates bringing requirements and acquisitions more clearly under the ambit of the Air Force corporate structure.[31] This objective might prove elusive because of the institutional barriers to such a reform, but the Air Force might yield a high return from a more robust and rigorous connection between planning and programming, on the one hand, and between requirements and acquisitions, on the other.

General McPeak—General Fogleman's predecessor—streamlined the programming process when he assumed office in 1990. The acute budgetary challenges that arose with the end of the cold war prompted McPeak to establish a process centered on the chief and relying heavily on his decisiveness. Previously, programming had operated through four filters: fifteen specialized panels fed into four committees, which then fed into the Air Force Board (consisting of Pentagon-based two-star generals) and, finally, the Air Force Council, made up of the Staff three-star generals and chaired by the vice chief. McPeak eliminated both the Air Force Board and the four committees and replaced the fifteen panels with five resource allocation teams. The old structure allowed a great deal more participation from major commands, including direct participation on the part of four-star generals in discussions of Program Objective Memorandums (POM) with the chief. A current four-star general with a long background in programming captured the dynamics of such involvement:

One aspect of the process was the complete involvement of the Air Force four-stars in the programming process. They came into the building for POM briefs and often had spirited debates on the programs and vision! McPeak chose to remove much of that process in order to facilitate his decisions, which might have faced problems in a collaborative environment.

As cumbersome as the old structure might have appeared, it allowed the chief essentially to delegate the thorough preparation of issues on his behalf, while he addressed the specific issues that only he could resolve. One close observer noted that General Fogleman inherited a process that, though streamlined, perhaps overloaded the chief with matters that might have been reconciled earlier in the POM process but were not.

> I was in the chief's office when . . . [he received] the 1996 POM. [It was quite] thick, with a thousand stickies in it. Each of them was broken glass—meaning the council had decided not to fund something that would seriously affect a program and undercut something important to the Air Force. . . . Fogleman went through every one of them and said, "Fund this; don't fund that," and reordered the POM.[32]

General Fogleman reinstated the Air Force Board and panels. He added a colonels committee—the Air Force Group—that reviewed the recommendations of the panels and the seventy-two corporate integrated process teams that prepared issues for the panels. The overarching expectations of the new corporate structure, as identified in the 2002 Air Force Corporate Structure report, resonated with Fogleman's preference of collegial decisionmaking in the Air Force: (1) bolster the quality of information and options for senior leadership decisionmaking; (2) provide institutional support for key decisions; (3) serve the development of future leaders; (4) enhance cross-functional decisionmaking; (5) facilitate major command involvement in the corporate process; (6) address a wide range of issues for senior leadership; and (7) improve staff communication and integration.

As we have already noted, Fogleman later modified this Staff-centered corporate structure to include a separate planning unit. Through the inclusion of all Air Force four-star generals in the Corona meeting and the incorporation of major command vice commanders on the board of directors, the new planning structure reflected a relatively encompassing view of the Air Force corporate process. Programming was another matter, however.

Not only our respondents, but also the Staff members interviewed by the team preparing the 2002 Air Force Corporate Structure report indicated that the machinery in place for programming frequently fails to advance support for key decisions, improve cross-functional decisionmaking, and facilitate major command involvement in the corporate process. Among the issues that emerged from our interviews, the so-called bow-wave factor seemed to provoke the greatest concern. This problem derived from the tendency of programmers to embrace and promote overly optimistic projections of the costs of developing and maintaining programs. Anxious to win or continue administration and congressional support for programs, programmers would advance projections that ultimately proved unrealistic because they did not include inevitable development or operational costs. A three-star general aptly characterized the difficulty as management by wishful thinking—a common feature of processes through which officials press their cases for programmatic resources.

Several respondents registered concerns that the cumulative impact of unrealistic programming that focused on gaming the administration and Congress proscribed reinvestment toward the Air Force's future. One key Air Force Staff civilian highlighted the consequences of the 2000 POM submitted in 1998, which was more than $3 billion over the target established by the Office of the Secretary of Defense (OSD). He stressed that this gap necessitated abandoning commitments made in response to the 1996 vision, which would have greatly enhanced investments toward the development of space-based programs. Specifically, the programmers decided to cut $218 million from the science and technology program as proof of their willingness to meet OSD half way, and the Staff at headquarters "never got an opportunity to make its case about the consequences."

Secretary Peters shared with us his concern that defective programming was having serious effects even in more prosaic areas than space, such as the transport required to fulfill the 1996 Vision. In one interview, he noted that "really hard choices about progammatics were being made in a very compressed period at budget's end." He later warned of a loss of capabilities: "If we keep going with budgets like today's, we will fall off a cliff. . . . Stuff like tankers will be irreplaceable at today's budget level, and if we can't replace them we won't have the global reach we have now."

Such criticisms did not necessarily chasten those who served as programmers. Programming calls for a higher tolerance of ambiguity than does planning, and it requires an ability to make judgment calls. One three-star general long associated with the craft defended it vigorously: "The joke among programmers is that the planners can go away and plan all they want, but the reality is that the programmers own the money and they will put it where they think it ought to go. They decide the future of the Air Force." However, the deft gaming of the administration and Congress to develop and maintain support for the areas of expenditure deemed most desirable and politically achievable might bear an unreality of its own. Incremental adroitness might well leave the Air Force too clever by half in terms of its preparation for future opportunities and challenges.

Notwithstanding the realpolitik that dominates the programming world, support is increasing for the view that the lack of corporate connectivity in programming has undermined the legitimacy of the resource allocation process in the Air Force. Concerns center on the concept prevalent among the Staff that it represents the Air Force's corporate interests because, by their nature, major commands are too biased to take the wider view. One key Pentagon player articulated the Staff view starkly in describing how the council was truly corporate while the board of directors was not:

> The council is corporate because we leave our baggage at the door. We come in and put on our corporate hat. . . . Fogleman said that major command vice commanders should belong to the board of directors to get buy-in. That means that the board comes with baggage. . . . [Its] advice and buy-in are only required at critical times. At other times it isn't needed because there are corporate issues to be handled.

This perspective flies in the face of the immense devolution of planning and programming operations to major commands that occurred under General McPeak. Indeed, it implicitly discounts evidence that for the resource allocation regime to be effective, the Staff must go beyond garnering support for its vision of the future and achieve a better connectivity with major commands over programming.

The mounting brief against the Staff-centric view of Air Force programming emanates from three concerns. First, several respondents indicated that bridging dynamics between the Staff and the major commands should operate continuously rather than sporadically. A highly experienced consultant stressed that this argument takes root in the de facto decentralization of the Air Force corporate structure: "Once they decentralize programming and budgeting, they have to come up with a new mechanism. . . . The council . . . is an utterly irrational mechanism because it's a headquarters planning operation [managing] a decentralized planning process." A major command three-star general elaborated on the connection between sporadic deliberations about corporate strategy and the continued drift of programming:

> The idea that [we] can do strategic planning in one meeting of the principals like we tried this past fall [at the 1999 Corona conference] and get buy-in is fallacious. . . . The decisionmakers of the organization need to spend time personally and get engaged in the issues. . . . Either the four-stars must work consistently and continuously with one another, or they must invest that authority in the three-stars and the board of directors. . . . The Staff can't decide the strategic direction of the organization. . . . [These are] tough choices that can't be based on analysis; they can only be based on what the leadership collectively believes is going to happen.

Second, some respondents, including a critically placed four-star general, noted that the Staff had not even internalized the investment in strategic planning sufficiently to redefine programs and panels according to the core competencies identified through the visioning processes. A former colonel (now a consultant) noted that this was in line with the Air Force's tolerance of doctrinal ambivalence—in contrast with the Army, which, he surmised, would conclude, "These are our core competencies. It will be taken as doctrine and hut-two-three."

Third, respondents in both the Staff and major commands noted that the major commands are open to receiving clearer guidance, but they doubt whether the Staff has the capacity to provide it cogently. A relatively newly minted major at the major command level put his finger on the problem:

> Every year we go through a POM process and we put together a plan. . . . It goes to the Air Staff, and immediately it gets criticized as a house of cards. There is no integration of plans. At the Air Staff level it is personally and politically driven as to which of the plans and their appropriate programs get center stage.

Fixing the Corporate Structure

On a fairly regular basis, we read newspaper articles that make us wonder whether the huge investment in strategic planning that General Fogleman instigated led to any improvements in the way the Air Force balances planning and programming. One such item appeared in the *Washington Post* in August 2001.[33] It probably made Fogleman wince. The piece maintains that the Air Force dug itself into a hole by deriving too much of its contribution to the peace dividend from cuts in funding for procurement and maintenance. The article conjures a dire image by noting that even the prestigious First Fighter Wing kept two F-15s hangared at Langley Air Force Base to face ignoble decommissioning as so-called can birds, or a source for spare parts.

The *Post* article also demonstrates that keen observers of the Air Force continue to condemn its judgment in pressing forward with plans for the next generation of fighter—the F-22 and the Joint Strike Fighter. It cites Brookings defense analyst Michael E. O'Hanlon as asserting that the F-22 would prove so expensive to develop and fly that it would hurt the United States in future warfare by draining money for spare parts and precision munitions.[34] It quotes Steven M. Kosiak, a defense analyst with the Center for Strategic and Budgetary Assessment, as arguing that the funds sought for the Joint Strike Fighter would provide greater bang for the buck if the Air Force simply bought more updated versions of the F-16. This move, Kosiak claims, would accelerate the modernization of the tanker fleet while leaving funds for other priority items.

Significantly, the *Post* article only skirts the question of whether the Air Force can pursue its expansion into space and respond to the tyranny of distance associated with potential threats in the Pacific while at the same time aspiring to both the F-22 and Joint Strike Fighter (JSF) programs. Before the terrorist attacks on September 11, it appeared that George W. Bush's ascendance to the White House implied that the Air Force, along with the other services, would have to tighten its belt in relation to another dividend. This is the surplus dividend, which the Bush campaign rhetoric had cordoned off as the taxpayers' money and not Washington's. The surplus was rapidly eliminated, both because of Bush's success in gaining congressional approval of his $1.35 trillion tax cut and as a result of the economic downturn beginning early in 2001. The likelihood that the Air Force would realize any significant augmentation of resources had thus declined dramatically by summer 2001. This meant that the administration's plan to "leap ahead" to the new frontiers of defense technology would require much greater sacrifices in force structure—the people, organizations, and programs through which the Air Force produces its capabilities—than anticipated even in the gloomiest scenarios reviewed by the Corona council when it devised the 2000 vision. Indeed, the Pentagon's civilian program analysts recommended a 10 percent cut in force structure, including significant cuts in Air Force squadrons.[35]

The Joint Chiefs of Staff dug in their heels during the summer of 2001. One Defense Department official described the service chiefs' reservations about the thinking of the people advising Donald H. Rumsfeld: "[The civilians] are saying, 'Take on a ton of risk so we can get where we want to be twenty years from now,' [but] everybody on the uniformed side is saying, 'No, you've got enough risk now.'"[36] If, however, new acquisitions money ever came on tap, whether derived from new funds or reallocated from cuts in force structure, the Air Force had many programs on the agenda that dovetailed with administration priorities. Examples include the missile national defense shield with spaced-based interceptors, the space-based infrared system, the space-based laser, and the Boeing-747-based airborne laser.[37] Yet the Air Force ran into a brick wall when it attempted even a relatively modest effort at reductions in force structure in summer 2001: a proposal to cut the oft-criticized B-1 fleet from 93 to 60 bombers seemed doomed when the congressional delegations of the states in which the aircraft were based launched a spirited rearguard action.[38] This event suggested extra- as well as intramural resistance to streamlining existing programs to accomodate budgetary limitations.

Rumsfeld submitted his Quadrennial Defense Review (QDR) on October 1, 2001. Following so closely the September 11 attacks, the document, not surprisingly, identified homeland defense as the Pentagon's top priority and advocated no cuts in force structure. The review strongly exhorted a shift to "transformational" technologies in information technology, intelligence, and space, but it did not indicate the levels at which it would fund these objectives and from where the money would come. The Air Force's success in the subsequent combat in Afghanistan further bolstered the QDR's preference for transformational technologies. More important, the Afghanistan experience gave wider currency than ever before to the case that the Air Force could fulfill major strategic objectives for the nation without the Army and Marines having to deploy substantial numbers of ground forces.[39]

The events surrounding September 11 nudged the Bush administration toward an expansive budget for the entire Pentagon.[40] The elimination of eighteen relatively small projects in the Army, the inclusion of fewer new vessels than expected for the Navy, and cancellation of the Navy's short-range antimissile system prompted some grumbling in those services. Meanwhile, Air Force players seemed anxious to muffle any glee over what the president submitted to Congress. Traditionalists in the service could point to the $1.3 billion of additional funds for the F-22, a program that had come under heavy fire from both Congress and civilian advisers close to Rumsfeld as a cold-war holdover. The transformationalists garnered a near doubling to $815 million of the resources for a surveillance satellite system that forms part of the projected missile defense shield, $1 billion to develop or speed up production of unmanned aerial vehicles, and $1.1 billion for expanded production of laser and satellite guided bombs.

Earlier in this chapter, we outlined the contrasting standards associated with fiscal, responsive, and strategic competencies, asserting that the balanced integration of these perspectives lends itself to policy competence. Policy competence emerges when political leaders and career executives do as much as possible to reconcile conflicts between fiscal exigencies, political pressures toward incrementalism, and investments required for an organization's ability to adapt to future opportunities and challenges. A skew toward one standard can, on the other hand, proscribe the possibility of policy competence in the long run.

This reality was evident even before summer 2001, when the Air Force seemed to be staring into tax-cut-induced fiscal austerity. It had become clear in the months that followed the fall 1999 Corona conference that the four-star generals had deceived themselves by opting for option 4b, even given the rosier view of the fiscal frameworks that would prevail under Bush versus Gore. They had elected to attempt to pursue a 2020 Air Force with minimal sacrifices of current capabilities. This betrayed a bias toward responsive competence, which reflected not only inertia in the Air Force itself, but also the expected resistance from Congress to each attempt to cut back existing programs. Beyond this less-than-optimal output from the Ryan-Peters strategic planning exercise, the Air Force leadership faced the imposition of an extremely stringent fiscal framework by summer 2001. This would make the attainment of policy competence exponentially more difficult. The Air Force would have to pay for its 2020 vision—which, incidentally, Bush implicitly trumpeted during the campaign when he said his Pentagon would "skip a generation of technology"—out of its own hide. The Air Force met stiff resistance from Congress, however, when it began moving toward such austerity, as seen in the case of B-1 force reductions. The events surrounding September 11 intervened not only to buy time for the Air Force, but also to drive home the highly relevant nature of many of its new programmatic initiatives to modern warfare.

Faced with such radical changes in circumstances, many organizations might resign themselves to their lack of control over their destiny and succumb to pressures to suboptimalize policy competence. The Air Force, however, underwent a gradual process of realization, whereby the organization has deepened its recognition of internal institutional impediments to policy competence. Furthermore, efforts to strengthen the link between planning and programming reflect the degree to which learning has occurred over the period since General Fogleman first identified the enhancement of the Air Force's strategic competence as the key to sculpting its future.

Addressing Institutional Impediments

We noted above that the iterative network of bodies that review programs—that is, the integrated process teams, the panels, the Air Force Group, the board, and the council—lacks legitimacy from the perspective of the major commands. Key players in the Staff indicated that a Pentagon-driven process guarantees that the corporate interest will prevail in resource decisions. The major commands simply do not accept this rendering of the corporate process in the Air Force. They believe that the service has to find an approach to programming that regards the concerns of the major commands as legitimate inputs to the distillation of a corporate resource allocation.

A brigadier general who had never done a tour in the Pentagon but who headed up programming for a major command expressed dismay with what he witnessed when in late 1998 he attended a session of the Air Force Board, a committee composed of Staff two-star generals that reviews the POM before submission to the council. Our respondent had expected that the board's decisions would reflect a coherent effort at prioritization. Instead, he described a process in which the squeaky wheel got the grease:

> I was disappointed. . . . It [initially] appeared that we weren't going to spend our money haphazardly because a lot of people had done a lot of coordination to attempt to define what the plan was for modernization. . . . My sense was that it was not sufficiently grounded, and that the items that were debated had not been prioritized. It seemed like he who spoke the loudest and the most eloquently won the day.

However, the general did not come away from the experience with a clear idea of how the process might be changed: "My head started to hurt when I tried to figure out how they could do that prioritization better."

Around this same time, key players began trying to formulate structural arrangements that might better connect the Staff and the major commands in the programming process. Indeed, Secretary Peters became well acquainted with the problem and its structural origins. First, major command commanders did not have access to the council when it deliberated over their programs. Second, the board of directors did not advance connectivity, although it consisted of three-star generals from both the Staff and the major commands. As often as not, commanders and vice commanders did not communicate sufficiently well on issues on the board's agenda. Peters took a small step toward providing a forum for interaction between the Staff and the major command commanders by including the latter in his quarterly acquisitions reviews with the chief:

> The major command commander, who, I think, is the key in the way the Air Force runs, does not personally appear in the corporate process of planning and the early stages of budgeting . . . It's often obvious [at the Corona conference] that the vices haven't been in communication with their commanders. . . . The major commands aren't given clear direction, so all this structure can do is propagate the past.

Some of our respondents believed the board of directors should take on the dual role of preparing planning issues for the Corona meeting and identifying priorities for the POM. This idea emerged in the face of some of the difficulties encountered by the board of directors in the build-up to the fall 1999 Corona meeting. Such an arrangement, many believed, would create a forum for a more robust nexus between the Staff and major commands in the resource allocation process. It would provide a more organic link between the vice chief's two roles as chairman of the board of directors and of the Air Force Council.

One especially incisive major command colonel believed the failure to develop a more robust connection took root in the policy directive that mandated the board of directors to support the Corona conference in strategic planning but did not provide it authority to devise guidance for programmers. By the same token, the colonel noted, XPX—the Staff unit that supported the board of directors—lacked an authoritative connection to the council. This meant that the deputy chief of staff for plans and programming (XP) was responsible for both planning and programming, but bereft of sufficiently clear authority to advance integration of the two realms. The colonel pointed up these flaws in institutional arrangements cogently, especially in highlighting the degree to which ambiguity in authority hobbled the board of directors:

> I've been there for briefs and debriefs over the past two years, and unfortunately [the XP staff] have wasted a lot of senior executives'

time. . . . [Mostly they have] been informational briefings, with the Air Staff in transmission mode and the vice commanders in receive mode. . . . If there are one or two decisional briefings in there, that is a miracle! . . . There is a distinction between having a mandate and having authority. . . . The corporate decisionmaking process in the Air Force is the council. XPX does not have a link there. . . . For the Air Force Staff to have authority to do the integration, . . . it would have to come from the secretary, not from the chief, because one half of the council is made up of the secretariat [civilians].

Disillusionment, even disaffection, about the board of directors peaked in summer 1999. Frustrations came to a head over the way in which the board's efforts to prepare for the fall 1999 Corona meeting had been much more limited than in Fogleman's visioning round. Many felt this prevented the board of directors from contributing as effectively to the preparation of issues for the 1999 conference as it had in 1996. General Lester Lyles, who became vice chief and chairman of the board of directors in summer 1999, tried to heighten the committee's relevance. His efforts included canvassing board members for ideas about how to improve deliberations. Several of those we polled conveyed that their advice was to place the board of directors more directly in the nexus between planning and programming. Soon after the 1999 Corona conference, General Lyles moved on to become commander of the Air Force Materiel Command, and General John W. Handy became vice chief. Handy brought with him a deep understanding of programming acquired through a succession of Pentagon tours. He initially wanted the board of directors to meet less frequently, preferably only with the major command vice commanders in attendance. He scrapped this idea, however, and the board of directors fell into disuse.

Ultimately, the Air Force pursued a piece of advice originally tendered to Lyles by Lt. Gen. David McIlvoy, then vice commander of the Air Force Education and Training Command. McIlvoy, a seasoned student of Staff–major command relations, suggested that major command commanders brief their Program Objective Memorandums (POMs) directly to the Air Force Council. In the February 2001, major command commanders assembled for two days to jointly brief the secretary and the chief, together with the other four-star generals, on their submissions for the 2003 APOM (the adjustment to the POM, carried out in odd-numbered years). The briefings constituted a highly significant departure from the view that the Air Force Council stood as the pinnacle of the corporate process because it was a Staff-only body. The gradual process of realization appeared to have produced substantial fruit. The preparation of the 2004 POM in 2002 followed this approach, as well.

The innovation formally emerged from an initiative called the Air Force Resource Allocation Process, or AFRAP, which was designed to improve the budgeting process. Maj. Gen. Daniel Hogan, who headed up AFRAP, took his team out to several private sector companies to benchmark best practices in corporate resource allocation processes. In direct contradiction to the prevailing Staff view of the requisite Air Force corporate mechanisms and processes, the team found that when private sector concerns make highly significant resource decisions, they involve both the headquarters and division leadership. Such meetings, the study asserted, serve as the equivalent of the Staff and major command four-star generals all meeting together:

> [What is] so starkly different from the Air Force is that in Caterpillar or Pfizer [visits were also made to Boeing, Chevron, Ford, Lilly, United, and UPS], when big decisions are made, there's a powwow and it's the big guys. . . . In the Air Force it's remarkable how little participation the major command commanders have had in the planning, programming, and budgeting process. . . .

Accounts of the major command commanders briefing their 2003 APOMs in 2001 to the secretary and the chief suggest that it occasioned their taking a keener direct interest in programming and budgeting. A Staff two-star general received a resounding endorsement from the major command briefing teams:

> Each major command had its own entourage of action officers . . . who had come in to support the briefings. . . . I would talk to them during the breaks. . . . They unanimously said, "This is terrific. Our commander has never had this kind of interest in and understanding of our budget and our programs."

Even more convincing confirmation of early success came from a four-star general who was nudged from deeply skeptical to cautiously impressed by the experience: "They all got up to brief their POM. The fact that it was theirs put a whole different onus on the debate. Before, . . . they'd be throwing rocks at one person [the vice chief], . . . so the entire dynamic of the decisionmaking process has changed dramatically." Our respondent noted that the transformation carried over to greater accord once the Staff distilled the major command submissions into an integrated Air Force POM, thereby reducing the grumbling and special pleading that surrounding the unveiling of the final resource commitments:

> Now the planners and programmers brief the integrated POM, and all those decisions are in there. [The major command commanders] know what they asked for; they know what they didn't get. . . . At that final briefing, the buy-in from the four-stars locks them in. In times past, after the POM was done, the chief, secretary, undersecretary, and vice chief would constantly get phone calls from people saying, "Why did you do this? Why did you leave this out? Why did you modify that?"

The Emergence of Guided Incrementalism

We noted in chapter 4 that a penchant for mixed scanning differentiated the corporate strategic planning that occurred under the leadership of Secretary Peters and General Ryan from that which took place under General Fogleman. Amitai Etzioni coined this term in the 1960s to capture a midpoint between those who seek comprehensive rationality in policy decisions and those who maintain that the American system vests beneficiaries of the status quo with such leverage that change occurs only incrementally and disjointedly. Etzioni argues that change agents who position themselves in his middle ground can devise an overarching strategy for achieving evolutionary success and then focus their energies on the most pertinent issues for fulfilling this objective.

Mixed scanning was certainly a factor in the 1999 Corona conference, but we hesitate to employ the term here for two reasons. First, the 2000 vision that issued from the 1999 Corona meeting, which focused on the attainment of option 4b, adopted an overly optimistic view of the Air Force's future resources. This rested on the expectation that a new administration would greatly enhance Air Force Total Obligation Authority (TOA)—some thought to the tune of $15 billion a year. It would do so by both providing more cash to the Pentagon and acknowledging Air Force claims for a larger share of the defense budget. Second, congressional intractability preordains a bias toward an incremental approach, as evidenced in the resistance to even modest attempts at divestiture such as the effort to cut the B-1 fleet by one-third. We find this despite the Bush administration's rhetoric strongly promoting a futuristic view of defense technology.

Even if the Air Force secured internal assent to a coherent view of its future, it would not be able to adapt its programmatic commitments with the agility of a F-15 pilot. At best it can hope for guided incrementalism

Figure 6-1. *The Air Force Migration to Guided Incrementalism*

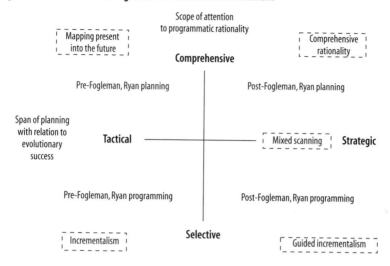

whereby, through calculated positioning, it can bring about iterative changes of course that in the long-run amount to its becoming a very different organization from what it is today.

We count this as a significant achievement. Figure 6-1 spatially represents the migration that the Air Force has executed. The vertical axis portrays the scope of attention to programmatic rationality in an organization—selective at one extreme and comprehensive at the other. The horizontal axis depicts the span of planning in relation to long-term evolution success, from tactical approaches to strategic ones.

The Air Force's tremendous investment in strategic planning and its attempts to institutionalize processes designed to tighten the relationship between planning and programming have accomplished two things. First, much of the play seems to be moving out of the left hemisphere of the figure, where major commands lamely project the status quo into the future and Staff programmers have to broker budget deals in the eleventh hour in the face of fiscal constraints and ad hoc political pressures. What has emerged in the Air Force over the past few years is an ability to gain consensus about a few investments that must move forward as essential steps toward evolutionary success and a greater degree of agreement on divesting some programs so others might develop in a timely way. Second, this migration to the area we label guided incrementalism has occurred at a time when the gap between the perceived vocations of planners and programmers has narrowed. Most important, planners have realized that comprehensive rationality is unattainable and that they need to focus on the issues where timely decisions can make a substantial difference. In other words, they began to embrace mixed scanning. Programmers, on the other hand, began to consider the adaptations necessary for the Air Force to survive and thrive in the future.

Two innovations in the budgeting system stand to advance guided incrementalism and perhaps leave the door open to the attainment of mixed scanning as the system matures. First, planning and programming are now focused on what is required to advance critical capabilities and identify decision points at which the Air Force must reallocate resources to future programs or miss the opportunity to adapt in a timely fashion. Second, the Staff has devolved much of the responsibility for fiscally constrained programming to the major commands. This should allow the Staff to concentrate its energies on providing support for the secretary and chief in the resolution of fork-in-the-road decisions involving critical trade-offs between future capabilities and current requirements.

CRITICAL CAPABILITIES AND FORK-IN-THE-ROAD DECISIONMAKING. The shift in focus from core competencies to critical capabilities and associated decision points first emerged during the 1999 Corona conference. It evolved significantly in the period between the seminal Corona meeting and the formal publication of the revised vision document over six months later. The delays in publication owed in part to differences in opinion between General Ryan and Secretary Peters about what shape the vision should ultimately take, with the former preferring a short document and the latter pressing for a detailed one.

The process surrounding the pair's preparation of the Air Force Posture Statement and associated testimony to Congress during much of this period reflected the conflict and also revealed deeper political calculations by both men. That is, the Air Force should not undermine congressional funding of current programs by revealing its aspirations for the future prematurely. In any case, many respondents found it difficult to distill what had transpired in the fall 1999 Corona meeting. A consensus had emerged that the vision should elevate vigilance to parity with the Air Force's missions of achieving and maintaining global reach and power. However, the unrealistically ambitious nature of option 4b suggested that the leaders still had little stomach for tough choices. As a major command three-star general noted, the four-star generals seemed more to be positioning for the 2001 Quadrennial Defense Review:

No connection to programming and budgeting will come out of this. We are very clearly optimistic because of increases in the budget that the administration gave us. We think we will solve the budgeting disconnect with an infusion of money after the 2000 election. . . . What came out of the process was very specific: how do we posture ourselves for the QDR? Everybody was happy to work on that question.

Notwithstanding the delays and ambiguity, a seed planted at the Corona conference germinated and began to take root. Gregory "Speedy" Martin, who at the time was a lieutenant general and principal deputy to the assistant secretary for acquisitions, outlined in exceedingly cogent terms the need for the Air Force to establish clearer objectives and strategies for achieving these. This sparked a realization on the part of the four-star generals that they had to give much greater attention to assessing the interconnectedness of programs and systems from the standpoint of the capabilities that they sought to maintain or obtain within a specified period of time. Martin argued that critical capabilities transcend core competencies in that they focus on the desired effects that the Air Force hopes to achieve through its investment in people, training, tactics, and hardware. For instance, he argued that two core competencies discussed in the 1996 vision document—namely, precision engagement and global attack—align functionally to provide the capability to successfully engage targets around the world. Subsequently, the Air Force *Strategic Plan* conveyed the dynamic and integrative nature of the capabilities. It characterized them as combining "organized and trained people, force structure and/or equipment, [and] robust command and control, with CONOPS [concept of operations] and infrastructure for performing a particular function or set of tasks."[41]

The inclusion of concepts of operations marked an effort to flesh out the idea of planning based on core competencies. Gen. John P. Jumper—who succeeded General Ryan as chief in summer 2001—stressed their importance in the fall 1999 Corona meeting while commander of U.S. Air Forces in Europe. He followed through when he took over the Air Combat Command early in 2000. As chief, he has pressed for a systematic integration of critical capabilities with six concepts of operations.

One four-star general explained to us in great detail why concepts of operations had to play a key role in the planning and programming process. He argued that the Air Force has tended over the years to plan for what it will buy rather than determining how it is likely to fight in the future:

We have always planned for what the Air Force will buy, which sets up a concept without a construct. . . . If we look at what we're doing, it lacks a description of how it will fit together and fight. This is linking long-range plans to programs without an operational filter. The program elements in today's Air Force are the same as in 1978, even though what we do and how we fight and how we integrate are profoundly different.

The respondent then widened the claim with an example of how the Air Force had not even learned how to adapt programs to real-world experience:

We haven't even learned to incorporate lessons from Desert Storm, Bosnia, and Kosovo. . . . In Kosovo, we put a laser on the Predator [the unmanned aerial vehicle designed for reconnaissance, surveillance, and target acquisition]. . . . The [fighter pilot] wouldn't be able to locate the tank that the [ground controller] was pointing out. We put a laser on the Predator so that . . . [the ground controller] could pinpoint the target for the [fighter pilot]. The minute the war was over, they took the laser off the Predator because that's what the program called for.

The Air Force's effort to focus on critical capabilities and link these to concepts of operations poses a similar problematic to that recounted in the above passage. It constitutes a comprehensive and strategic effort to overcome blinkered programming. The Air Force Resource Allocation Process (AFRAP) reengineering team—initially under Gen. John W. Handy while he was vice chief of staff—spearheaded efforts to devise a corporate capabilities investment strategy. By the 2004 POM, which occurred in 2002, a revamped process was supposed to focus on determining capability objectives, developing capability options based on these, allocating resources according to agreed priorities, and assessing major command performance in the fulfillment of objectives. The different products emanating from the various elements of the process would be coordinated through review by both the secretary and the chief, in tandem with the four-star generals. Major commands would gain access to the crafting of the strategic plan, the capabilities investment strategy, the POM and budget, and performance plans through Corona conferences and joint meetings with the secretary and the chief. We found that the capabilities investment strategy approach, while still alive, did not play as robustly in the development of the 2004 POM as hoped.

Fork-in-the-road issues, or decision points, have become the focus of the new approaches to integrating planning, programming, and budgeting. Even before the AFRAP recommendations came fully to light, the congressional appropriations process during summer and fall 2000 saw a considerable effort to keep score on how the commitments made for fiscal year 2001 tracked decision points for fourteen critical capabilities. The latter derived from the fall 1999 Corona meeting and input from the major commands. As discussed below, the major commands did not see the fourteen critical capabilities as perfect images of their programmatic aspirations. Nonetheless, the Strategy and Policy Division (XPX) of the Staff devised a methodology for flagging windows of opportunity in funding that, if missed, would seriously impair timely attainment of key capabilities. One deft participant described the interventions as follows:

> [In the case of] the science and technology investment stream, Congress might say, "We're not particularly interested in space radar; I think we will cut that." Now we can say, "OK, fine, but when you cut space-based radar from our budget, here is the impact on military capability over the next twenty years." We can build a compelling argument that that is a bad cut.

The respondent further pointed out that such tracking often led to the secretary of defense getting involved in a timely fashion. The critical capabilities framework also buttressed claims for urgency by providing "a framework to enter the debate with a firm operational rationale hooked to the vision."

To be sure, such tracking constitutes guided incrementalism more than full-fledged mixed scanning. That is, it reacts to specific assaults on bids for resources as much as it reveals positioning for opportunities. Attainment of the latter, however, served as the core objective of the AFRAP initiative. We have already noted that the fall 1999 Corona conference allowed the fiscal expectations of option 4b to become enshrined and, therefore, deferred discussion of hard choices still further. Before the tragic events of September 11, 2001, the harsher-than-expected fiscal realities of the Bush administration had begun to drive home the unattainability of option 4b.

The Quadrennial Defense Review submitted by Secretary Rumsfeld in October 2001 appeared to preordain that fork-in-the-road issues would increasingly become the order of the day for matching plans and programs.[42] The New Testament image of how difficult it is to get a camel through the eye of a needle might become more apt. The document went to Congress on the tail of a defense authorization bill for fiscal year 2002 giving the greatest increase to the Pentagon since the mid-1980s. Despite this windfall, however, the outgoing chairman of the Joint Chiefs of Staff, Army General Henry H. "Hugh" Shelton, asserted in an afterword to the QDR that the services might require an additional $40 billion to $50 billion for procurement.

Contrary to Rumsfeld's overtures toward reordering force structure early in the administration, the QDR assumed the status quo in aggregate— namely, ten Army divisions, twelve Navy aircraft carriers, fifty-five attack submarines, forty-six Air Force fighter squadrons, and 112 bombers. Innovation would thus occur through new operational concepts, advanced technological capabilities, and stronger coordination among the services. All of these efforts require reinvestment, however, and the document provided little guidance about how that would be financed. When we combine the failure to alter the core elements of force structure with the elevation of homeland defense as the Pentagon's top priority, we can excuse the Air Force leadership for feeling like a highly leveraged investor living in mortal dread of a margin call. The circumstances would not seem to favor mixed scanning even though the Air Force tried to follow the rubrics for this as it worked up to the preparation of the 2004 POM, which projects out to 2009.

In February 2001, the Corona council reviewed issues associated with the timing of investments for all critical capabilities. Based on this review, it identified four fork-in-the-road issues that called for urgent attention. If these capabilities did not receive substantial new investment in the 2004 POM, they might become seriously compromised. The identified issues included (1) wide-body transport, specifically whether to update the C-5 (first introduced in 1969) or build more C-17s (introduced in 1993); (2) the so-called fighter bathtub, or how to manage the preparedness gap caused by lags in the rate at which the next generation of fighters replaces the current one; (3) intelligence, surveillance, and reconnaissance, which had to be expanded to reflect the 2000 vision document's upgrading of the global vigilance mission; and (4) tankers, involving the need to replace the KC-135 refueling aircraft, whose average age exceeded forty years. The October 2001 Corona conference would then make decisions based on capability options developed by the Air Staff in dialogue with the major commands.

A two-star general working in the Staff put great stock in the advantages of involving the four-star generals early in fork-in-the-road issues that inevitably would emerge in 2002 as the Air Force developed the 2004 POM: "The fork-in-the-road [approach] was not new, but it was new to present these to the four-stars so early. . . . [By the fall Corona meeting] all of the four-stars sitting out there will know what we're doing with C-5s and C-17s." The 2004 POM reflected significant efforts to address each of the four fork-in-the-road issues.

DEVOLVING FISCALLY CONSTRAINED PROGRAMMING TO MAJOR COMMANDS. As mentioned earlier, reforms introduced by General Fogleman's predecessor, General McPeak, delegated to the major commands much of the analytic work associated with planning and programming. Owing to the lack of corporate connectivity between the Staff and the major commands, this format greatly exacerbated the tendency for planning and programming to function with little reference to fiscally constrained parameters. The Staff would thus have to forcibly integrate POMs, thereby leaving a great deal of unfulfilled expectations. The major commands would come away from a POM cycle convinced that the Staff had run roughshod over their plans and programs; the Staff would complain that major commands had completely lost sight of fiscal constraints and had behaved as if the sums involved were theirs to bid for regardless of the corporate interests of the Air Force.

This vicious circle seemed poised to perpetuate itself even after the fall 1999 Corona meeting. In the first attempt to devise critical capabilities, major commands believed that the Staff had ignored their inputs by hammering together a list that, they believed, scarcely accommodated their priorities. A major command colonel intimately involved in the process conveyed considerable dismay and frustration:

> They talk about encapsulating the corporate decisions and identifying priorities. We expect to see that, but we also need to understand how the Air Staff is going to do. . . . Around December or January . . . they went back to identifying their critical capabilities. It was based on what analysis? Basically on a bunch of guys saying, "Yes, those are the right things."

A similarly placed colonel concurred:

> They went about it the wrong way. They listened to us for two days, and in the last hour and half hours they said, "OK, guys, let us show you the answer." They brought the set solution with them. We looked at each other and said, "If they were going to do that, why didn't they do it yesterday morning at 9 o'clock?"

One key Staff player dismissed these objections in two separate interviews. He pointedly argued that the critical capabilities will not serve as venues for the major commands to project the status quo into the future:

> They tried to bring in a critical capability for each of their programs but we said no, we've tried this already and it doesn't work. . . . If the major commands are unhappy, it's because they misunderstood what we wanted, that is, not hooks for all their current programs. We want those things that are going to have to be done in the future that we cannot do today, like space control.

In an effort to resolve these continued tensions, the Staff introduced an innovation in the 2003 APOM (the off-year adjustment of the 2002 POM) that ultimately could revolutionize programming. It essentially devolved to the major commands decisions about changes in investments to cover requirements. One of us has previously encountered such devolution in the United Kingdom and Australia with regard to running costs—expenditures for personnel and administration that typically amount to less than ten percent of agencies' budgets.[43] However, funding for requirements serves as the lifeblood of programs and thus comprises an area of expenditure that central coordinators usually hold tightly to themselves. The Staff move was exceptionally bold. It was aimed at breaking the vicious circle whereby the major commands routinely sloughed hard choices between programmatic investments off to the Pentagon. One Staff respondent clearly expressed the Pentagon view of major command POM submissions:

> They always turn their hands up and say, "We gave [the POM] to you and you destroyed it." The answer is, "What you gave us was inexcusable, guys. We do not have extra money up here. You sent in a bill for $9 billion over what you could reasonably expect to get. Where do you think the $9 billion was coming from?"

The new approach establishes a cash limit within which the major commands must cover basic requirements as agreed in dialogue with the Staff: "We essentially give them a figure and ask them to structure that pot within their headquarters to cover all their requirements. In the past, we have asked them to come in with their requirements and then we've slammed them together up here." It is too early to ascertain how successful this approach will be in making programming at the major command level more fiscally constrained. The Air Force has only employed the approach through one APOM and one POM. However, one well-placed Staff informant asserted that the 2003 APOM submissions exceeded the cash available to the Air Force for programs by only $3 billion, whereas the figure was $14 billion in the 2002 POM cycle.

The Staff anticipates that the new approach, combined with increased participation on the part of major command commanders in deliberations on critical capabilities and fork-in-the-road issues, will produce several potential benefits that should help the players remain engaged. These include improving the connection between major command POM submissions and the process whereby resources are actually allocated; tightening the focus on effects-based critical capabilities, as opposed to program advocacy; involving the major commands in the effort to achieve fiscal discipline and accountability; making resource allocation decisions more visible and analytically based; and reducing superfluous work by both the major commands and the Staff. Unfortunately, the 2004 POM process, which produced a still tighter fit between major command bids and available resources, crashed into a $2.4 billion shortfall in funds available for the Air Force portion of Defense health. This prompted a last-minute search for savings, the urgency of which meant that the Staff had to make a number of tough decisions with little consultation of major commands.

Conclusion

This chapter has charted the odyssey of the Air Force, beginning in 1994, toward more robust planning and greater attention to future opportunities and challenges in the commitment of resources to programs. When General Fogleman initiated the process with which the Air Force still struggles, planning was extremely ineffective and disconnected from programming. Fogleman's efforts, combined with signs that the Air Force had to change its ways, generated a substantial willingness to invest immense time and effort in corporate strategic planning. In the early phases, however, disillusionment set in as programming both at the major command and Staff levels continued to operate as if planning still did not count. During the second iteration of a major planning thrust under General Ryan, attention increasingly focused on issues associated with confusion over corporate responsibility for programming. The leadership gradually realized that the often conflictive, self-absorbed perspectives of the Staff and major commands proscribed the emergence of coherence between plans and programs.

Since 1999, this process of realization has led to several innovations designed to focus discussion on critical capabilities and fork-in-the-road issues surrounding their attainability. One of the innovations was to expand the senior deliberations over the Air Force's programmatic commitments to include major command commanders and to largely devolve fiscally constrained programming to major commands. These innovations have already achieved a substantial degree of guided incrementalism, although to date they have fallen short of mixed scanning. The next chapter probes in much greater detail a prominent programmatic manifestation of this shift.

CHAPTER 7

The Process of Implementing Strategic Intent

The preparing-for-the-future approach is not exclusively concerned with formulating strategic intent and providing an administrative linkage between planning and resource allocation. Ultimately, it is concerned with matching bureau capabilities with the future policy environment. For this reason, a study of recent Air Force experience needs to examine how the service's technological capabilities actually evolved in relation to its strategic intent.

This chapter explores this issue by tracing the career of the Predator medium-altitude unmanned aerial vehicle. In its principal current uses, Predator provides commanders in theaters of military operations with real-time video images of situations on the ground. The richness and timeliness of such tactical intelligence is extremely valuable, especially for monitoring peace agreements and identifying mobile targets in combat missions. From an Air Force perspective, Predator contributes significantly to its desired capability of finding, fixing, tracking, targeting, and engaging any target of military significance. By compensating for limitations faced by satellite systems and the infamous U-2 jet, Predator has played a notable role in translating the Air Force core competencies of information superiority and precision engagement into actual force structure.

Predator became a household name during the war in Afghanistan. Reports about its combat employment were regular features in major U.S. and overseas newspapers throughout the intense air campaign. A main

155

source of journalistic interest in Predator was its relative novelty as a form of aviation technology: a medium-altitude, propeller-driven craft flown from a ground station rather than a cockpit. As an aircraft controlled from the ground, Predator represented the broader category of unmanned aerial vehicles (UAVs).[1] Predator made good copy because of its contrast with traditional manned aircraft, but it also symbolized the expanding military use of sensors and communication technologies to reduce risks of U.S. combat casualties and to give commanders unprecedented levels of information about the situation on the battlefield. Newspapers also indicated that Predator presaged a time when unmanned combat aerial vehicles (UCAVs), which are capable of firing weapons, would play a significant role in the nation's arsenal.

We focus on Predator for several reasons. First, tracing the career of this now familiar component of military force structure will be meaningful to readers who are not specialists in defense matters.[2] Such might not be the case if we were to focus on, say, directed energy or space-based radar systems. Second, scholars interested in military organizations and technology have written about the history of UAV programs. Our explanation can thus rely on expert work on this topic. Finally, Predator presents as a clear implementation success. The *Global Engagement* vision called for cultivating the core competencies of precision engagement and information superiority, and the long-range plan included a directive statement in favor of fully developing and fielding UAVs. In the words of a former deputy chief of staff for plans and programs whom we interviewed in mid-2001, "UAVs are the little-noticed stars of the last three or four years of Air Force planning."

The evolution of the Predator program unarguably brought organizational capabilities into closer alignment with strategic intent. In the context of a military service, the concept of capabilities translates, in part, into force structure. To understand how the strategy implementation process operates in this context, it is useful to examine how innovation in force structure actually occurs. Developing bureau capabilities involves technological (and organizational) innovation.[3] The central issue in this chapter is therefore how Predator became a growing, innovative component of U.S. Air Force force structure.

Origins of the U.S. Air Force Predator Program

Predator's story begins with early preparations for the U.S. and North Atlantic Treaty Organization (NATO) peacekeeping mission in the former

Yugoslavia, specifically Bosnia.[4] In planning this mission-other-than-war, the Department of Defense's Unified Command for Europe informed the Pentagon of a military requirement for what they called loitering surveillance. The European command desired the capability to obtain intelligence about specific areas of interest on a continuous basis. Existing systems were said to provide only episodic surveillance. A satellite, for instance, picks up information about a specific locale only when it passes overhead during an orbit. The U-2 jet aircraft did not meet the requirement either, because it moves too fast over too much ground to offer continuous surveillance over a specific area of interest. The European command concluded that some other kind of system was required to provide adequate loitering surveillance over Bosnia.

Soon after the Clinton administration took office in 1993, its high-level defense officials ran a major study on tactical airborne reconnaissance. This study led to powerful administration backing for the development of UAVs. A specific outcome was the decision to satisfy the loitering surveillance requirement by speeding up development of what administration officials called a tactical endurance UAV. The decision reflected two major considerations. First, domestic political support for engagement in Bosnia was assumed to depend on the near absence of losses in military personnel. As an unmanned system, the tactical endurance UAV promised to eliminate such risks, while fulfilling the need for loitering surveillance. Second, decisionmakers believed that the development of a high endurance UAV—one that could perform a mission of a day or longer before having to return to base for refueling and maintenance—was technically feasible in the near-term. The principal technological challenge appeared to lie in aspects of the system other than the platform, including communication links between the UAV and its ground station.

The decision to meet the U.S. European Command's requirement by developing a high-endurance, medium-altitude UAV quickly prompted efforts by defense contractors to develop a working system, which was eventually dubbed Predator. The new system's first test flight in July 1994 was a success, and the experimental Predator was put into operation by the U.S. European Command in mid-1995 as part of its peacekeeping mission in Bosnia, operated by the U.S. Army's military intelligence battalion.

Meanwhile, Ronald Fogleman was settling into the role of Air Force chief of staff. Early in his tenure, Fogleman was briefed on modernization plans that the major commands began writing under his predecessor, General McPeak. The Air Combat Command's briefing on the intelligence, surveillance, and reconnaissance mission area, more than any other single event, sparked the Chief's concern that Air Force planning had become excessively incrementalist in outlook. During the legendary session, Fogleman was told that the eventual replacement for the Airborne Warning and Control System (AWACS) would presumably be a later model Boeing with a dome mounted on top. At about the same time, the Chief also became aware that the Air Force was no longer actively engaged in UAV research and development. Fogleman concluded that the lack of UAV development was part of a growing pattern of technological incrementalism in the Air Force.

Historically, Air Force interest in UAVs had run strong. Drones were used extensively for reconnaissance purposes in the Vietnam War.[5] Although many operational UAV programs were terminated when the war ended, the Air Force spent hundreds of millions of dollars in the 1970s to develop UAVs for use in defending Western Europe against Warsaw Pact forces. These development programs were unsuccessful, however. Operators often did not know exactly where their airborne UAV was situated—a problem termed locational accuracy—with the result that NATO allies barred UAVs from their airspace. Their inability to provide satisfactory surveillance in bad weather, which is typical in the European theater, also undermined development programs. By 1979, all UAV programs had been cancelled. The Air Force later agreed to participate in two major UAV programs during the massive Reagan buildup. These troubled programs were cancelled by Air Force Chief of Staff Tony McPeak during the steep defense drawdown of the Bush years.[6]

The subject of UAVs came to occupy Fogleman's attention in 1995. Not only was he concerned about technological incrementalism within the Air Force, but he was also attentive to the wider defense policy subsystem, where the closely related issues of UAVs and tactical airborne reconnaissance were playing out.[7] These issues were highly important to Defense Secretary William Perry, Deputy Secretary John Deutsch, and Undersecretary for Acquisition and Technology Larry Lynn. The three looked on UAVs as a potential breakthrough in airpower that could permit the U.S. military to undertake dangerous missions without risking pilot casualties or capture.[8] By 1995, Fogleman came to share their conviction that UAV development should be energetically pursued, and he decided that the Air Force should become fully engaged with Predator, as well as the development of other UAVs.

An initial step was to establish a squadron within the Air Combat Command dedicated to operating Predators. The Eleventh Reconnaissance

Squadron was stood up in August 1995 at the command's Indian Springs Auxiliary Air Field near Nellis Air Force Base, Nevada. This organizational move was intended to signal that the Air Force was willing to take full responsibility for Predator's operational success.[9] Soon thereafter, the chief asked the Defense Department to designate the Air Force as its executive agent for managing the Predator program. At the time, the program was managed by the Defense Airborne Reconnaissance Office, a unit reporting to the Undersecretary of Defense for Acquisition and Technology. Following negotiations between the Air Force and the Army, the Joint Requirements Oversight Council (JROC), composed of service vice chiefs of staff, approved Fogleman's request in December 1995.[10] Secretary Perry ratified the decision a few months later, thereby initiating a significant deepening of the Air Force's involvement with UAVs.

Predator and Strategic Intent

Predator became an Air Force program some months before the Corona issues process hit its stride, as described in chapter 3. After completing its socialization phase, the Long-Range Planning Board of Directors inductively developed a list of issues that it believed the Air Force should resolve in formulating a strategic vision and long-range plan. The plentiful initial list was boiled down to thirty-two key issues, one of which was UAVs. Fogleman circled the issues he believed to be of greatest strategic significance. UAVs made the cut, and the subject was pursued in one of the Corona issues papers and discussed during the fall 1996 Corona conference. UAVs went on to feature in a directive statement and became an end state in the long-range plan.

The subject of UAVs was also closely tied to strategic thinking about Air Force core competencies, especially information superiority. This idea represented one of Fogleman's main contributions to Air Force strategic thinking while he served as chief. The wish to take full advantage of the technological revolution in microelectronics, with its powerful application to such broad fields as communications, was a key idea emerging from Fogleman's own study of strategic issues, and it became a significant current in the deliberations by the Long-Range Planning Board of Directors. The information superiority core competency, which touched on the long-established military functions of command and control as well as on intelligence, was expressed in a memorable phrase attributed to Fogleman: "We want to be able to find, fix, target, track, and engage, in near real time, anything of military significance." A two-star general who worked in the field of command, control, intelligence, surveillance, and reconnaissance during the Ryan period commented on Fogleman's affirmation:

> I think [that] was a real focusing statement by Fogleman. . . . We want to have global awareness, if you will. The Air Force Science Advisory Board had come out saying that it is technically feasible to be able to do that in the future. We own the high ground, since between us and the NRO [National Reconnaissance Office] we have a lot of the sensors. We probably have 80 to 90 percent of the data that comes from U.S. systems on what's really happening in the battle space. So we started to get a vision of where we wanted to go. After the visioning process, it was clearly a competency we wanted to have.[11]

The core competency of information superiority provided a rubric under which Predator's capabilities were strategically significant for the Air Force. The platform's loitering surveillance capability would potentially provide high-fidelity, continuous information about specific areas of interest. It was thus seen as fitting in with the information superiority core competency.

Concurrent Visioning and Implementation

The Air Force's deepening involvement with Predator thus took place concurrently with the formulation of Air Force strategic intent through the Corona issues process. This aspect of the Air Force experience underscores two characteristics of the Air Force approach to strategic planning. First, the purpose of strategic visioning and long-range planning, as indicated by the backcasting principle, is to align future capabilities with the future policy environment. In Fogleman's mind, this purpose was served by moving ahead with Predator. Second, the move to incorporate the Predator program into the Air Force reflected the rhythms and flows of the policy environment.[12] The bid for Predator was timed to ensure that the Air Force's request would receive strong support from the top executives in the Defense Department. The window of opportunity for taking UAV development away from central Department of Defense management could easily close once Perry, Deutsch, and Lynn moved on. Thus, the strategic planning and implementation processes were both grounded more in the rhythms and flows of the wider policymaking process than in classic models of the management process.

The Predator case nonetheless raises a question about the concurrent formulation and implementation of strategic intent. In his handling of this issue, Fogleman may have compromised the principle of collective buy-in.[13] After all, this decision was more like an executive action than the product of collective deliberation. What seems to have partially compensated for the adverse effect on collective buy-in was the eventual interpretation of UAVs as strongly related to the core competency of information superiority.

Implementation as Spiral Development

Earlier we discussed why the Clinton administration's defense officials decided to launch a program to develop a medium-altitude, high-endurance UAV. After doing so, they immediately turned to the Defense Advanced Research Projects Agency (DARPA) with a brief to rapidly pursue the development of UAVs. One of DARPA's mechanisms for acquisition and program management was an Advanced Concept Technology Demonstration (ACTD). The idea to use this mechanism to meet the unfulfilled requirement for loitering surveillance in Bosnia was formally approved in October 1993.

Within three months, DARPA awarded a prime contract to General Atomics Aeronautical Systems. Predator flew its first test flight just six months later, in July 1994. To speed the system development process, the prime contractor used off-the-shelf component technologies. Predator's airframe was designed along the lines of the earlier Gnat 750 UAV. The air vehicle was powered by an FAA-certified 80 horsepower piston engine, itself a modification of snowmobile engines. Predator's flight controls were also off-the-shelf items, including the autopilot that obtained its bearings from the global positioning system (GPS).[14] So, too, was the sensor payload, which included electro-optical imaging systems, essentially video cameras, as well as infrared imaging systems.

Predator came to the attention of the operational military when the services prepared for the annual air defense exercise, slated for April–May 1995. The exercise's planners decided to give Predator a mission, as a proof-of-concept demonstration. Participants in the Roving Sands exercise were impressed with how the prototype performed, and a decision was made soon thereafter to experiment with the Predator system in an actual theater of operations.[15]

By July 1995, a Predator system, including its ground control system and communication facilities, was in service at Gjader, Albania. Operated by the Army's military intelligence battalion, the system conducted reconnaissance and surveillance missions over Bosnia over the course of three months. A Predator was shot down during one mission while flying at 4,000 feet. It was operating at that level to stay below the clouds, which otherwise would have impeded the view of its video cameras.[16] Another Predator crashed a few days later, reportedly because of an engine failure. The system was removed from Gjader in November 1995.

Predator was back in the Balkan theater of operations by March 1996, deployed at a U.S.-operated facility in Taszar, Hungary. This time the air vehicle was equipped with synthetic aperture radar, a sensor technology that provided a series of still images rather than streams of video data and that could see through cloud cover. This modification to the sensor payload dealt with the problem of having to descend below clouds in order to obtain intelligence imagery. The new version performed better than the old.

During this second deployment, Predator flew sufficiently far from its operating base that direct communications between the ground station and the vehicle were no longer technically possible. Communications, including flight control messages and intelligence signals, were instead relayed by commercial satellites. The successful use of satellites to relay instructions and data was a technological breakthrough, enabling UAVs to move considerably beyond their previous limitation of maintaining direct (line-of-sight) communications between the air vehicle and the ground station.

The developmental process extended to using the video data that Predator provided. A decision was made to provide a direct video feed to command posts involved in the Bosnia operation. Implementing this decision required establishing a link between the satellite relay system and the military's worldwide intelligence communications system. The resulting availability of a Predator video feed in command posts did much to stimulate interest in the system.

At the same time, work was under way to incorporate Predator video streams into the larger system for processing intelligence signals and, ultimately, providing tactical intelligence products to operating commanders. This work was sponsored by the Combined Air Operations Center based in Vicenza, Italy. The initiative was taken by Col. Neal Robinson, who was leading the intelligence function within the center. Robinson saw the Balkans as an opportunity to exercise more capabilities and thereby improve the technology. He issued a request to include Predator imagery in a multi-source context, in which the other sources were still images. This request was directed to the Air Force's Electronic Systems Center (ESC), located at Hanscom Air Force Base near Boston, which was responsible for managing the development of numerous Air Force programs related to command and control and intelligence, surveillance, and reconnaissance.

The request did not come as a complete surprise: a few months before, ESC staff had been challenged to find a way to fuse Predator video data with other signals. One civilian participant, Steve Hansen, recalled:

> We were at Fort Franklin, doing our thing with intelligence-fusion systems, and someone walked up and handed us an ordinary VHS videotape that contained imagery from a Predator UAV. They said something like, "You guys claim your research program can represent virtually any kind of intelligence." We looked at that tape and told ourselves, "We're in big trouble now." We had never thought about things like moving pixels, and at that time, Predator was just an experiment flying around Nellis Air Force Base, Nevada. That night we were sitting in the Hanscom Officers Club, talking about what to do with that VHS tape. We first said, "We don't do this sort of thing," which then led to, "Well, video is nothing but still imagery presented at 30 frames per second, and we've been doing still imagery from aircraft and satellites." Over the next three days, we built a quick prototype around a video compression card.[17]

When ESC received the request to include Predator imagery in a multi-source context, it responded by sending its staff and the prototype to the users' locale, the Combined Air Operations Center in Vicenza. According to Hansen,

> We took our glorified hobby-shop project over to Italy, and they didn't care how rudimentary it was. That was purely a function of General Robinson, who was a colonel at the time. . . . We were in the [Combined Air Operations Center] for a month during the conflict, and we came out of it with an enormous amount of knowledge. We brought the lessons back and offered them to anyone who would listen— lessons including how fast the video card has to be.[18]

As this chronicle shows, the innovation process associated with Predator exemplified the principles of spiral development, including rapid prototyping and user involvement.[19] Rapid prototyping was most evident in the test flight that occurred within six months of the prime contract being awarded, in the upgrading of the sensor payload to include synthetic aperture radar during the winter of 1995–96, and in the development (within three days) of the software and hardware needed to harmonize video data with the more common still imagery. User involvement was most evident in the 1995 annual air defense exercise, in the Bosnia deployments, and in the movement of ESC staff to Vicenza to work with the Combined Air Operations Center's intelligence function in responding to the request for including Predator imagery in a multisource context. As a result of this spiral development process, the Predator system reached a substantial level of functionality within just three years of the decision to meet the requirement for loitering surveillance with a tactical endurance UAV.[20]

This situation established a foundation for the next stage in Predator's career, which included institutionalization and scaling up. The Air Force's involvement in Predator took hold during this stage. Predators officially entered the Air Force inventory in mid-1997, coinciding with the completion of DARPA's Advanced Concept Technology Demonstration project. At this time, the Air Force also established a second squadron dedicated to the operation and maintenance of Predators. In early 1998, the Air Force awarded a contract for production of an additional eighteen aircraft and their associated ground systems. Attention also turned to improving on what remained, in effect, a prototype air vehicle.

Predator's career really picked up momentum, however, during NATO's war against Serbia over Kosovo, which began in March 1999 and which involved Predator operationally in a combat mission, as distinct from a peacekeeping one. Commanders employed Predator to enhance the process of targeting fixed and mobile assets for attack by strike aircraft and to limit collateral damage, including civilian casualties.[21] Predator was also used to pinpoint mobile targets, such as camouflaged missile launchers. Operational commanders came up with the idea of using the platform to shine a laser beam onto an identified mobile target, improving the accuracy of munitions delivery by strike aircraft. Altogether, Predator flew more than fifty sorties in support of targeting operations.[22]

The effect of this episode in Predator's career, according to an Air Force strategic planner we interviewed, was "acceptance by a whole other class of leader—the most conservative: the war fighter group." As a result, the Air Force as an institution came to embrace Predator. In our respondent's words, "After Kosovo, we're in love with it." That sentiment was echoed by Gen. John Jumper, who served as commander of U.S. Air Forces in Europe (USAFE), during the conflict. Jumper, who is now chief of staff, told a gathering in Washington that "the UAV, especially the Predator, came into its own" in Kosovo.[23] The Air Force awarded a contract for the production of an additional seven air vehicles in July 1999. Predator was deployed in Afghanistan in October 2001, attracting the extensive publicity mentioned at the outset of this chapter.

Conclusion

Analyzing the career of the Predator program provides insight into how organizational capabilities evolve in line with strategic intent. This section moves beyond a narrative of Predator's career to develop an explanatory argument accounting for the system's development and impact on the service's force structure. The concluding part of the section then addresses wider issues surrounding the implementation of strategic intent.

Understanding Predator's career requires explanation of two key events: first, the Defense Department decision to initiate a fast-track program to develop what became Predator and, second, the expansion of the Predator program under the aegis of the Air Force. The first decision is analytically significant because it took place before Fogleman initiated the strategic visioning process. The Air Force was not then viewed by top defense officials or, evidently, by Congressional overseers, as willing and able to assume responsibility for filling identified gaps in the area of tactical airborne intelligence through the development of UAV technology. This perception contributed to the centralization of program direction and management at the Department of Defense, through such organizational instrumentalities as the Defense Airborne Reconnaissance Office (DARO) and the Defense Advanced Research Projects Agency (DARPA). Arguably, such perceptions have become more favorable in the years since 1993.

Once the decision to move in this direction was taken at the highest levels of the Defense Department, the career progression of the Predator medium-altitude, high-endurance unmanned aerial vehicle (UAV) appears to be due, in part, to the spiral development process through which the system's technical features evolved. This process included relying heavily on off-the-shelf components, including the airframe, engine, flight controls, sensors, and communications equipment. The use of off-the-shelf technologies helps to explain how a prototype took to the air in a test flight within a mere six months of a contract being awarded. Predator's career was marked by other instances of rapid prototyping and user involvement, such as Predator's inclusion in the 1995 annual air defense exercise—the first opportunity to try it out in an experimental environment controlled by the operational military. Another example of rapid prototyping and user involvement is the introduction of Predators just a few months later to perform missions in the former Yugoslavia. This move provided operational commanders with an opportunity to gain familiarity and experience with the system. It also triggered the developmental spiral that came to characterize Predator's career, including the addition of the capacity to see through cloud cover by incorporating synthetic aperture radar into the air vehicle's payload; efforts to use the system's capabilities through the broadcast of Predator video feeds to command centers around the world; and the systematic exploitation of "moving pixels" by intelligence specialists operating in a technical environment dominated by still imagery.

User involvement and rapid prototyping provided a foundation for the critical decision to advance Predator's career to the production phase. In this phase, Predator's career continued to reflect the practice of spiral development. During the hot war with Serbia, Predator's mission evolved from monitoring compliance with peacekeeping agreements to engaging in the planning, execution, and evaluation of lethal strikes. The technical part of this iteration included incorporating the capacity to project laser beams onto mobile targets, which then provided the tactical intelligence needed to make effective use of precision munitions delivered by strike aircraft. As far as theater commanders were concerned, the Predator came to play a variety of roles effectively. Because of theater commanders' institutional position in the Defense Department, this belief helped to trigger a decisionmaking process that provided resources to produce more Predators, as reflected in the series of contract awards that expanded the Air Force's inventory.

The spiral development approach worked effectively in this case in part because some of the players in Predator's career believed in it. In the early stages, these players included officials within DARPA and the company acting as prime contractor. This approach was gaining ground in the defense establishment in the same period in which Predator was developed. Not surprisingly, some of the strongest early adherents to this movement were responsible for programs meant to incorporate leading-edge information technologies into command, control, and intelligence systems. In that soft- and hardware-intensive arena, lengthy development cycles like those typical in the Defense Department virtually guaranteed that systems were already obsolete by the time they were fielded. The growing acceptance of spiral development as an approach to managing technological innovation is reflected in the Air Force's issuing an official instruction explaining and endorsing the idea in 1998.[24] This commitment to the principles of rapid prototyping and user involvement was arguably a crucial part of the technological innovation process, just like the belief in backcasting from the future, collective buy-in, and policy management was a crucial part of the strategic visioning process.

The effectiveness of the process design of spiral development was bolstered by process context, as defined in chapter 5. From the outset, that context included the belief that public acceptance of U.S. casualties was likely to be highly limited when military operations were not patently in support of vital national objectives, as would often be the case in the post-cold-war world. This strategic belief, propagated by Secretary Perry and others, helped to underwrite the view that developing UAV technology should be a high priority for the Defense Department. The process context for Predator's spiral development also included the belief that theater commanders needed more loitering surveillance capability, which spread through the relevant action channels via the established routines of the operational requirements process. These beliefs accentuated the positive reaction to each of a series of partial successes that Predator experienced as its career proceeded. These reactions, in turn, created opportunities for improving the system's technical design and for obtaining more practical experience with the system.

Technological maturity was another process context factor that contributed to the effectiveness of the spiral development process. Predator was able to draw on prior development of such technologies as satellite data links, GPS-based autopilot flight controls, synthetic aperture radar, and data fusion systems to rapidly exploit vast amounts of electronic intelligence. Some of these prior technological developments allowed Predator to overcome the severe operational problems, such as locational accuracy, that had doomed earlier UAVs. Others were crucial to whether the unmanned system would provide useful inputs to military operations.

A third important process context factor was Air Force strategic intent. Not long after the Air Force became executive agent for Predator, the Corona conference endorsed the core competency of information superiority and the directive statement in favor of UAVs. These features of strategic intent were relevant to Air Force decisionmaking concerning Predator. They contributed to commitment within the Air Combat Command to the operational success of the system, which required, among other factors, the assignment of experienced aviators to "pilot" the unmanned system. Although the UAV was a culturally disruptive technology, its backing by senior figures helped smooth the way for its integration into the Air Combat Command's organizational structure and the development of competencies to operate the system. In parallel, the intelligence, surveillance, and reconnaissance community set to work accommodating this disruptive technology for battlefield awareness. In this way, specialized functional communities within the Air Force cultivated the core competency of information superiority. Subsequently, the operational community in Kosovo experimented with using Predator in the target acquisition process, enabling more effective performance by strike aircraft. A specialized community thus set about cultivating the core competency of precision engagement.

The assessment that Predator's rapid evolution is attributable both to design features of a particular technological innovation process and to the process context of Air Force strategic intent provides some insight into the means for counteracting the powerful stabilizing force of technological incrementalism. A strategic vision provides a sense of urgency and focus for cultivating an abstractly defined set of organizational capabilities, such as information superiority and precision engagement. Strategic intent constructs a favorable context around the actors who are directly engaged in particular processes of technological innovation, such as developing Predator. The mechanisms that connect the process context of strategic intent to the inner core of the technological innovation process include the formation and dissemination of elite beliefs about what technological trajectories will close the gap between future capabilities and the future policy environment. These beliefs influence not only technology developers, but also users. For instance, the belief that UAV technology was such a trajectory appears to have shaped decisions within the Air Force intelligence, surveillance, and reconnaissance community to integrate video data into a system dominated by still imagery, and the same type of belief may have shaped the decisions of operators like Gen. John Jumper to develop tactics for employing Predator in combat missions. Indeed, strategic intent may provide an overlapping agenda between technology developers and users. If so, strategic visions lay a foundation for user involvement in the technological innovation process. User involvement, in turn, is a key enabler of spiral development.

User involvement is only one aspect of the spiral development method of technological innovation and thus the implementation of strategic intent. Another key aspect is rapid prototyping. This process design feature for fostering technological innovation and implementing strategic intent would seem essential for counteracting technological incrementalism. In sum, the effective implementation of strategic intent would seem to require a spiral development process and its component practices of user involvement and rapid prototyping. The Predator case suggests that spiral development is a smart practice for performing the implementation function, contributing to an organization's ability to counteract technological incrementalism in preparing for the future.[25]

CHAPTER 8

Processes for Corrective Visioning

This book has proceeded from analysis of strategic planning to implementation, implicitly following a model of a management cycle. To conclude with an analysis of strategy implementation would, however, leave the reader with distorted impressions of both the Air Force experience and the management approach we call preparing for the future. In practice, the functions of strategic planning and policy management, on the one hand, and strategy implementation, on the other, are not just sequentially interdependent. In the Air Force experience, these functions have been reciprocally interdependent, while the processes for performing them have run both serially and in parallel.

This realistic picture helps make sense of the fact that the Air Force undertook efforts to criticize its 1997 strategic vision, *Global Engagement,* starting just a year after the momentous fall 1996 Corona conference. An appropriate place to end the empirical analysis of this book is by examining closely the processes through which the Air Force's strategic vision was critiqued during the 1998–99 period. Our method is to analyze and compare three such processes, namely, the Aerospace Integration Task Force, the congressionally chartered space commission, and the Air Force Futures Games. These cases varied enormously in their design and effectiveness.

In honing in on this aspect of the Air Force experience, we seek to analyze a potential pitfall with the preparing-for-the-future approach. An organization runs the risk of making its strategic vision immune from internal criticism by investing it with the collective authority of its top leaders. What is a plausible argument concerning how an organization intends to contribute to creating public value in the future may become an article of faith. The possibility that a strategic vision would become immune from internal criticism may be especially high in public bureaucracies, where the organizational culture bias is typically hierarchist. This risk is serious, since a strategic vision could easily be ill conceived, and it presumably will become obsolete. Bearing this risk in mind, the Air Force's efforts to give impetus and structure to internal efforts to remedy perceived shortcomings of its own vision are analytically significant, as are efforts by Congress. An essential characteristic of the preparing-for-the-future approach is to operate effective processes for criticizing the incumbent vision. The three cases studied here provide an empirical basis for addressing the issue of how formal organizational processes work in compensating for the risks inherent in generating strong consensus on a particular view of strategic intent.

The Aerospace Integration Task Force Case

Six months after succeeding Ronald Fogleman as chief of staff, Gen. Michael Ryan signed a memo in April 1998 chartering the Aerospace Integration Task Force (AITF). The idea of air and space integration had been endorsed by the fall 1996 Corona conference, but the classified directive statements on this subject became overshadowed by the *Global Engagement* vision's public declaration that the Air Force was en route to becoming the nation's Space and Air Force. The "air to space" formulation had lost its luster, however, by the time the AITF was set up. The new chief thought that putting emphasis on the space versus air distinction was inherently divisive in a service where most airmen identified almost exclusively with the field of military aviation and others identified as strongly with military space. In the background was a full commitment to maintaining Congressional and administration support for funding the production of the F-22 and development of the Joint Strike Fighter. The concern was that opponents of these major programs might be strengthened if the service stood behind the idea that it was evolving away from the nation's Air Force. These concerns, among others, spawned a request by the Corona council in the fall of 1997 for Air Force headquarters to look deeper into the issue of air and space. This request eventually led to the avowed focus on aerospace integration and to AITF's establishment in April 1998.

Institutionally, the AITF was very different from the devices used during the Corona issues process, namely, the Long-Range Planning Board of Directors and the Corona council itself. The high-ranked participants in those venues were meant to offer the perspective of senior leaders, rather than to stake out positions reflecting their current assignments. By contrast, the AITF was composed of representatives of virtually all the Staff offices within Air Force headquarters. Pentagon action officers, who held the comparatively junior ranks of major or lieutenant colonel, were involved in the day-to-day work of the AITF. The job of action officers in this case, as in most others, was to coordinate tasks with their counterparts representing other organizational units, referring a given subject up the hierarchy only if consensus could not be achieved at their level. In this respect, the AITF was to operate just like many other cross-functional task forces within Air Force headquarters.

In pursuing the ascending agenda of aerospace integration, the AITF was charged with developing an aerospace integration concept, creating a plan, and formulating a communications plan. The primary task at the outset was to formulate the intellectual underpinnings of aerospace integration and to codify this conception in the form of a publishable document. The envisioned "white paper" was provisionally entitled *Beyond the Horizon*. The AITF was expected to complete this task in a matter of a few months and then move on to carry out the rest of its charter. Successive drafts of the document came under unrelenting criticism, however, and *Beyond the Horizon* never saw the light of day as a white paper. In this narrow sense, the effort was unsuccessful. More broadly, the AITF failed as an institutional mechanism for rethinking the Air Force's strategic vision, as evidenced by the fact that the chief and secretary in effect revoked the charter by working the issue themselves, with support from their direct subordinates, including the deputy chief of staff for plans and programs. This episode represents a cautionary tale about how to critique an incumbent vision and use formal organizational processes to undertake strategic thinking. The empirical aim of this case study is to understand why the AITF proved ineffective.

Origins of AITF

The concept of aerospace integration emerged as the antithesis of air-to-space migration. Space migration was the thrust of a planning effort performed by Air Force Space Command at the Corona council's request, starting in early 1997. In the words of one observer, Space Command went around to the other major commands saying, "We'll help you figure out how to migrate your capabilities into space."[1] The planning premise was that when systems operating in the atmosphere, like the Airborne Warning and Control System (AWACS), were retired, they would be replaced by systems operating from space. This space migration approach grew directly out of the *Global Engagement* vision, with its envisioned trajectory away from an air force toward a space force. According to the same observer, the planning issues included which platforms would migrate first and how to manage the transition so as not to lose current air capabilities.

This intense effort, centered at Space Command, gave rise to an elaborate plan covering a wide swath of Air Force mission areas. The resulting Air Force–wide plan, which was completed after Fogleman's early retirement in September 1997, even included an annex about moving military airlift capabilities into space. The space migration plan did not make it off the drawing board, however. According to those who followed the process, the space migration plan "died in coordination" at Air Force headquarters early in the Ryan period.

While the space migration plan was being written at Air Force Space Command, another strategic planning effort was underway at the headquarters: namely, thrust area transformation planning. This effort sought to build on parts of the *Global Engagement* vision other than the "air to space force" statement. The effort responded to a widely felt practical concern that the numerous end states in the long-range plan provided little guidance for determining what steps were urgently required in the short run. An additional impetus to undertake this effort came from the deputy chief of staff for operations (or XO), John Jumper. The XO wished to give more priority to strategic operational thinking than had characterized the Corona issues process. "I knew that the strategic plan could not work without a concept of operations that would guide it," he told us in a later interview.[2] Thrust area transformation planning was seized on as an opportunity to describe a concept of operations at a much more strategic level than was standard practice in the Air Force, where doctrine (outside the nuclear realm) has historically dealt with lower-level matters of tactics, techniques, and procedures.

Out of these concerns and aspirations came the thrust area known by its acronym of F2T2E, which stood for find, fix, track, target, and engage. These are the sequential stages in employing airpower against fixed or mobile targets in the atmosphere or on the ground. The idea of thrust area transformation planning included improving thinking about this fundamental operational process and forming a view about how to evolve the service's force structure accordingly. By and large, the exercise sought to refine thinking about the core competencies of air and space superiority, precision engagement, and information superiority—and to translate this thinking into terms that would more closely resemble an actionable plan than did either the *Global Engagement* vision or the long-range plan.

Thrust area transformation planning eventually ran into difficulties as a planning method, as discussed in earlier chapters. It nonetheless influenced how its participants thought about the issues addressed in *Global Engagement*. Analysis of the F2T2E process convinced them that the Air Force required a mix of space and air systems. This view collided head-on with the underlying idea of the space migration plan, a fact that helps account for why the latter eventually died in coordination. With the death of the space migration plan, the Air Force needed a different approach to the air and space issue. This sentiment was reflected in a Corona tasking handed to Air Force headquarters at its fall 1997 conference.

At its winter 1998 conference, the Corona council was briefed on this broad subject by the deputy chief of staff for plans and programs (or XP), Lawrence Farrell. Farrell's briefing marked the final demise of the space migration approach. The briefing put forward the assessment that airborne systems compensated for the limitations and vulnerabilities of space systems, and vice versa. Breaking with the idea of migrating systems to space, Farrell suggested that the sensible question to ask is how to integrate space capabilities with air capabilities to create the best mix. Beyond giving priority to integrating air and space, the XP's briefing underscored the semantic inconvenience of giving prominence to the air/space distinction. This distinction, as mentioned earlier, was considered divisive by the chief. In a chart entitled "Words Matter," Farrell retrieved the 1950s term *aerospace*. The concept of aerospace integration was thus inserted into Air Force strategic planning discussions at the highest level.

The approach reflected a meeting of the minds with Gen. Michael Ryan, who became chief of staff several months after Farrell settled into the new XP role. In our interview with Ryan in 1999, the chief stated the following:

> The division between Air and Space cannot be an artificial division. Things that we do in the atmosphere can't be separated from the things we do orbitally. . . . So splitting air and space right now doesn't make a lot of sense to me. . . . It's not space; it's not air. It's aerospace.

Farrell's Corona briefing proposed a list of subjects to be dealt with in pursuing aerospace integration. The first was called aerospace theory and doctrine. The briefing specifically called for developing the theoretical underpinning for employing aerospace power in the twenty-first century. The other subjects were described as an equipping strategy, a resourcing strategy, an education, training, and career management strategy, and an organizational strategy. To organize work on this full array of subjects, Farrell advocated chartering an integrated process team led by the Strategic Planning Directorate, with representation from all of the staff offices at Air Force headquarters as well as liaison officers from the field organizations. It was this proposal that became the Aerospace Integration Task Force, chartered by General Ryan a few months later.

Writing the White Paper

The group's initial task was to prepare *Beyond the Horizon.* This exercise corresponded to what Farrell described as developing aerospace theory and doctrine. "It was a very hard task," remarked one respondent who participated in the AITF. Participants who identified with the space community in the Air Force frequently locked horns with those who grew up in the larger aviation career fields. A lieutenant colonel identified with the space community explained the conflict in the following terms:

> The current war fighters—the pilots, the pointy-end-of-the-spear guys—see space as a mere force enhancement tool, . . . whereas the space guys see space as being an equal—and as having military effects just based on space. . . . The space guy, if he is really looking out twenty years, says, "We won't even have to put steel on targets. We'll just pick up the phone or send an e-mail to the guy, and say, 'We know what you're up to, and if you do it, then this is [what will] happen.'" We can affect his decision before he even acts, so why do we need to blow up the bridge? There was a big culture gap in how different people viewed space capabilities.

The perception of an intercommunity conflict was not limited to the space guys. A prominent aviation-oriented operator, who participated in the process from a senior position on the Air Staff, expressed his recollections in the following terms:

> We've gone through traumatic events like the first attempt at the air and space integration book. The book beat guys like me over the head

saying we didn't understand space, that space was a misunderstood orphan for years and years, and that guys like me have just got to change our minds. I wasn't going to buy into that.

One interpretation of the conflict is that the aviators sought to consolidate the still youthful doctrine that airpower, enhanced by command-and-control systems reliant on space-based assets, was not only essential but also potentially decisive in contemporary warfare. This military thinking had been viewed as radical before the Gulf War, as described in chapter 2. Meanwhile, some within the space community had been developing a different unofficial theory of future warfare that gave even more emphasis to the military use of intelligence; it relied on the prospective fielding of whole constellations of satellites with radar and communications payloads. Some had even concretized this theorizing in a catalogue of nonlethal means of military force. The space guys saw the AITF as an opportunity—the only one available at the time—for pressing their community's distinctive views about the theory and doctrine of force employment in the future. From their standpoint, the current operators were mired in a paradigm in which employing military force meant putting steel on targets. An observer from the space community described the situation as follows:

> There is a clear rift. One of the things we have a real problem with in the Air Force is how to conceptualize these nonkinetic capabilities— things that don't go boom or smash. . . . What it really boils down to is, what is the role of information in warfare? Is it indeed becoming a key center of gravity?

As originally conceived, *Beyond the Horizon* was meant to express consensus on a theory and doctrine of the aerospace force. The priority given to developing theory and doctrine reflected the subjects enumerated by Farrell in his important Corona briefing on air and space. Farrell's briefing, in turn, reflected two key influences. First, the Air Force had decided that it needed a strategic-level doctrine of conventional war; tactical-level doctrine no longer sufficed, as it had in the days of the air-land battle doctrine mentioned in chapter 2. The Air Force had already begun to set up a new Doctrine Center to write strategic-level doctrine. The new ideal was to analyze planning issues in light of official Air Force doctrine. The second key influence stemmed from thrust area transformation planning. The work done on the F2T2E thrust area amounted to a theory of airpower. It was this work that led to retrieval of air and space integration as a key issue. Against this background, skipping the step of formulating the intellectual under-pinnings of aerospace integration seemed retrograde.

A central objective of the consensus document was to get out the word that the Air Force was dropping the air-to-space formulation in favor of aerospace integration. The intended audience included both the Air Force as a whole and the outside world. The chief and secretary did not wish to delay broadcasting the new approach. At the same time, they were reluctant to go public with a statement that remained controversial within the Air Force, since discord was unlikely to remain within the service.

The challenge of writing a consensus document on the intellectual foundations of aerospace power was, however, vastly underestimated. In the words of one high-level observer,

> There was absolutely no consensus in the spring and summer of 1998 that the theoretical underpinnings of the draft version of *Beyond the Horizon* were correct. It was complicated by the fact that those who were trying to develop the attributes of space power were doing it as a derivative of the attributes of airpower—speed, range, and flexibility. The arguments for airpower in some measure extend pretty clearly into space—and in other places, they don't extend well at all. And there are subtleties that were causing endless arguments.

One controversial early idea was that air and space are one medium. This formulation reflected the chief's firm view, quoted above, that "it's not air; it's not space. It's aerospace." The idea that air and space are one medium was attacked for contradicting facts about the physical world. Critics pointed out that the physical principles that govern flight in the atmosphere (aerodynamics) are different from those that govern flight in space (astrodynamics). Consensus on this conceptual matter was reached by drawing a distinction between a medium and a domain. Aerospace came to be defined as an operational medium, whereas air and space were defined as distinct domains of flight.

The larger goal of setting out the theoretical underpinnings of aerospace integration still proved elusive. The installed base of strategic thinking in the space community was different from that in the aviation community. Whereas some hoped for an early consensus, others sought to make full use of this opportunity to give a wider berth to a space-centric perspective on information-intensive, potentially nonlethal warfare. The "endless arguments" outlived the first six months of the AITF's life cycle. By that time,

Lawrence Farrell had retired. Farrell's successor as deputy chief of staff for plans and programs, Lt. Gen. Roger De Kok, commented that "trying to do a comprehensive theory of aerospace power—and get any degree of consensus—by the fall of 1998 was probably a mission impossible."

From time to time, a draft version of the white paper was brought before the Long-Range Planning Board of Directors. As discussed in chapter 4, this body continued to meet, if irregularly, during the 1998–99 period. The compromises in language worked out by the AITF did not pass muster with the three-star group, chaired by the vice chief. According to De Kok, "*Beyond the Horizon* was reviewed several times by the board of directors. Frankly, there were wildly divergent critiques on the document." The ultimate effect was to abandon the effort to publish a white paper on the subject.

De Kok, who moved into the XP role after commanding the Air Force Space and Missile Systems Center, concluded that the debate "wasn't going to be resolved anytime soon." With his encouragement, the AITF's focus shifted away from a "theological debate about the attributes of space power and really started to concentrate on the effects that could be produced through air and space integration." Such effects were understood in operational terms, in the same spirit as the work on the F2T2E thrust area. According to De Kok, "Effects-based thinking had been coalescing elsewhere in the Air Force anyway. And it applied very well to this particular subject. The debate came to focus on how air and space can be complementary and on how space, in particular, can be supportive of air operations."

The focus of the staff work on aerospace integration shifted toward preparing a plan for internal discussion. At the same time, the institutional process for working the aerospace integration issue was modified. Developing a concept and plan for aerospace integration became an interest item for the chief and secretary, who, along with the vice chief, took charge of the review. They relied heavily on De Kok, who not only was deputy chief of staff for plans and programs, but who also was one of the two highest-ranking Air Force officers with extensive experience on space matters.

The XP staff office, which included the Strategic Planning Directorate, took matters into their own hands. As De Kok explained,

> The AITF produced a compendium of some fifty action items that they recommended. We cherry-picked the ones we thought were the most important and the ones we believed we could get some consensus on.

I briefed them at Corona and got some approval, and I ultimately used that to jump-start the process.

A major milestone in the process was the fall 1999 Corona conference that revised the Air Force strategic vision, which was later published under the title *Global Vigilance, Reach, and Power.* At that conference, De Kok briefed the highlights of the draft Aerospace Integration Plan, which "consisted of seven or eight clear statements of Air Force intent." These statements were approved at the Corona conference. They were later reflected in the strategic vision, as well as in Aerospace Integration Plan's first volume, which was approved by the chief early in 2000.

Analyzing the AITF Case

The Aerospace Integration Task Force is analytically interesting from two angles, as we suggested earlier in this chapter. First, the effort indicates that the Air Force engaged in seriously rethinking its strategic vision within about a year of its publication. The *Global Engagement* vision thus was not immune to internal criticism, despite the fact that it had been endorsed by the institution's senior leadership. Second, the effort was unsuccessful insofar as the AITF was unable to complete the task of writing the intellectual foundations of aerospace integration. To address these two issues, we analyze the AITF experience through the same lens as was used in chapter 5.

To begin, we can eliminate external factors as a spark for the rethinking effort. The administration had not changed as a result of the 1996 election, and the 2000 election was far off. While the U.S. military was engaged in numerous operations, none provided a focus for changing the climate of opinion about defense policy. Attention was increasingly focused on issues of readiness rather than on modernization, which, if anything, would have decreased interest in strategic visioning. The search for causal factors therefore belongs within the Air Force.

Executive turnover is undeniably part of the story. Ronald Fogleman unexpectedly opted for early retirement in August 1997, less than a year after the momentous Corona conference and not long after the Quadrennial Defense Review began to wind down. His successor, Michael Ryan, had been an active participant in the Corona issues process, as a four-star commander of U.S. Air Forces Europe (USAFE). On matters of process, Ryan was a strong supporter of this effort. He proved less enthusiastic, however, about some specific aspects of the substance published in *Global Engage-*

ment. In 1999, the chief expressed his difference of opinion to us in the following terms:

> In our past vision, we had air and space. I think it's a bad construct.
> . . . Space and air are places; they are not missions. . . . We had Air and
> Space Superiority, and I think it really is Aerospace Superiority, so
> that's one of our core competencies. Aerospace means that we want
> capabilities that are produced in aerospace, and we don't care where
> the vehicle is—on the ground, in the atmosphere, or orbital.

While turnover at the top definitely mattered, other internal factors were also clearly involved. One key factor was the continuing momentum of the long-range planning process. Such momentum was behind the efforts to write a space migration plan and to fashion the F2T2E (find, fix, track, target, and engage) thrust area. Why did the planning process exhibit momentum after the culminating event in 1997? Several interrelated factors played a role.

First, the strategic vision and long-range plan were not really plans at all, as was readily acknowledged. They were declarations of strategic intent. The Corona participants believed it would be useful to translate such intent into a proper plan. Their notion of what constituted a true long-range plan was clear: the obvious model was the major commands' modernization plans, which provided road maps for retiring equipment and replacing them with follow-on systems. Given this set of beliefs, the Corona council's call for a space migration plan is unsurprising, as is the fact that Space Command responded with a space migration road map along the lines of an equipment modernization plan.

Second, the deputy chief of staff for plans and programs (XP) and the Strategic Planning Directorate were committed to keeping the planning process in motion. Doing so was consistent with their mandate to institutionalize long-range planning. How to maintain momentum was a question without an easy answer, however, especially as Fogleman became distracted with the circumstances leading to his early retirement. Joining forces with the powerful deputy chief of staff for operations (XO), John Jumper, to sponsor work on the F2T2E thrust area was consistent with the XP's objective of keeping the long-range planning process in motion.

Third, competition for primacy over Air Force strategic thinking was part of General Jumper's motivation in collaborating with the XP. The thrust area effort provided a forum in which the operational community could try to gain acceptance for its distinctive intellectual approach, which centered on envisioning a production process for destroying a target. Such competition for intellectual primacy appears deeply embedded within the Air Force, for reasons that cannot adequately be explored here. Its effect was to draw energy into thrust area transformation planning and, thus, the long-range planning process.

These three factors encompass not only the initiative of particular individuals, but also the operation of two key social mechanisms. One powerful social mechanism was psychological buy-in. This mechanism was at work in prompting the Corona council to ask for a space migration plan; it was also at work in strengthening the first XP's resolve to institutionalize the long-range planning process. Another social mechanism was competition for intellectual primacy, which helped motivate the XO's collaboration in the thrust areas. The strength of this mechanism seems rooted in the particularities of military professionalism, the structure of careers in the Air Force's officer corps, and the department's formal organizational structure. That the social mechanisms of buy-in and intellectual competition gave rise to a structured process for criticizing the incumbent vision at such an early stage is partly attributable to a peculiar mix of situational factors: fresh memories of a positively regarded strategic visioning process, a weakly institutionalized function of long-range planning, and turnover at the top. In sum, two social mechanisms, a mix of situational factors related to strategic planning and executive leadership, and individual initiative all help explain why the *Global Engagement* vision was not immune to criticism in the U.S. Air Force.

We now turn to the question of why the AITF failed to deliver a consensus document on aerospace integration. As in chapter 5, we focus on the interplay between process design features and process context factors. The process design features in this case included the task of writing a white paper for public release and that of satisfying the perceived need to define the intellectual underpinnings of aerospace integration. These two purposes were conflicting. The prospect of publishing the document put a premium on omitting internally controversial statements, whereas a neutral document would provide an inadequate basis for resolving issues that would arise in writing an aerospace integration plan.

The institutional design of the AITF process did not compensate for the inherent weakness posed by these conflicting purposes. Various drafts were handed off to the Long-Range Planning Board of Directors, which, by this point, was more a collection of individuals than a team. The board of directors was no longer connected to a strategic visioning process in anticipation of another Quadrennial Defense Review. This forum therefore turned into a venue for expressing discordant views about whatever tentative consensus was served up by the AITF. Board members had no great incentive, or psychological motivation, to seek a meeting of the minds. This analysis suggests that the sort of process design factors highlighted in chapter 5 are truly significant for the effective achievement of institutional consensus on strategic thinking.

Process context factors exacerbated the difficulties faced by the Aerospace Integration Task Force. Consider the factor we call the installed base of strategic thinking. The Air Force harbored two distinct perspectives on aerospace power. One was built on the foundations of the air campaign theory and doctrine, which came to the fore in the Gulf War. This perspective was subsequently augmented by collective reflection on how the effectiveness of the Air Force's shooters could be enhanced by a rich flow of military intelligence collected from space and aviation platforms and processed by a sophisticated command-and-control system. The other perspective was essentially built on the foundations of a prospective universal space-based radar system and an innovative theory of conventional deterrence, in which information was considered the center of gravity.[3] These two perspectives were both elaborate and strongly held by their partisans.

Consider, too, the factor we call cultural bias. The type of hierarchist culture bias evident in the Air Force is one that makes it appropriate to defer to technical expertise. Arguments about technical matters cannot simply be ended by invoking organizational authority without going against the grain of the institution's culture. Technical expertise was undoubtedly relevant to the task of identifying the intellectual foundations of aerospace integration, as illustrated by the debate over whether air and space were the same medium. This aspect of Air Force culture, combined with the competing bases of strategic thinking, made it very difficult to achieve consensus on the intellectual foundations of aerospace integration within the time frame desired by the sponsors of the Aerospace Integration Task Force. To this analysis of process context factors can be added that of the defense policy subsystem. Attaining internal consensus on the theory and doctrine of aerospace power was not crucial to succeeding in any prospective policy event, such that strong incentives to resolve differences did not operate.

In sum, the AITF case shows that psychological buy-in to an institutionally sanctioned strategic vision does not have to mean that the organization's strategic intent is immune from criticism. Buy-in to the long-range planning process may generate momentum effects, leading to formalized efforts to think harder about issues that were supposedly resolved in the earlier strategic visioning process. These efforts may produce understandings that are at odds with the strategic vision itself, as occurred in this case. Such dissonance can give rise to efforts to formulate a more sensible and accepted body of strategic thinking. At the same time, the case suggests that the goal of achieving consensus on fundamental issues of theory and doctrine can be elusive, especially when internal intellectual competition is not checked by incentives rooted in the external policy subsystem.

The Space Commission: Corrective Visioning in the Defense Policy Subsystem

The central focus of this chapter, as we have seen, is to analyze processes through which an organization might subject its own strategic vision to criticism; this analytic focus led us to spotlight the Aerospace Integration Task Force. Before examining the Air Force Futures Games, we briefly consider a closely related analytical issue, namely, how overseers might influence an organization's strategic intent through formal processes. From a theoretical perspective, the issue merits attention because no governmental organization—not even the Air Force—is an island unto itself. Manifold avenues of influence over strategic intent are open to external power centers, including congressional ones. This facet of U.S. government is palpable in the Air Force's recent experience.

Aerospace versus Air and Space

While the Air Force was arguing internally over the intellectual foundations of aerospace integration, the advocacy coalition for a stronger emphasis on military space, situated in the broader defense policy subsystem, became increasingly uneasy with the service's emerging stance on the so-called air and space issue. A central figure in the space advocacy coalition was Senator Robert Smith, a New Hampshire Republican and member of the Senate Armed Services Committee. Smith gave voice to the view that the Air Force had yet to give space the importance it deserved. In pressing the issue, the senator won passage of an amendment to the Fiscal Year 2000 Defense Authorization Act calling for a thoroughgoing review of management and organization issues concerning uses of space for national security purposes. The six-month review was to be conducted by a blue-ribbon Commission to Assess United States National Security Space Management and Organization, commonly called the space commission. The questions for the commission to consider included whether the government should reorganize the military to establish a space force.

Leaders of the Senate and House Armed Services Committees selected a majority of the thirteen members. Donald Rumsfeld, then a private citizen, was chosen to chair the space commission. He had recently chaired the Ballistic Missile Defense Commission. Of the remaining twelve members, four were retired Air Force generals: Ronald Fogleman; Thomas Moorman, the Air Force space community's elder statesman, who as Fogleman's vice-chief had run the board of directors during the Corona issues process; Howell Estes, who in his former capacity as head of Air Force Space Command had overseen preparation of the space migration plan; and Charles Horner, who ran the air campaign in the Gulf War and later became head of Space Command. The commission thus included some highly credible people. In announcing the committee's membership on June 5, 2000, House Armed Services Committee Chairman Floyd Spence stated, "Space is becoming increasingly critical to the conduct of military operations. This commission will play an important role in ensuring that our forces are properly structured to gain maximum benefit from military and intelligence space operations."

The committee officially kicked off its six-month project on July 11, 2000. In that period, the panel met for more than thirty full days. In the words of one member, "It was a real working commission. Rumsfeld handed us writing assignments. We worked twelve hours a day. We didn't leave the room until we talked [an issue] through and came to something we could all agree with. It was a unanimous report."

The report was due for submission to the Armed Services Committees by January 10, 2001. Two weeks shy of the due date, President-elect George W. Bush announced that Rumsfeld would be his nominee for secretary of defense. Rumsfeld formally resigned his chairmanship of the space commission. He was destined to revisit the issues, however, since the authorization bill setting up the space commission required the secretary of defense to respond to the panel's recommendations within a matter of months. In the words of Roger De Kok, who was completing his tour as deputy chief of staff for plans and programs, the space commission's report suddenly became highly significant:

> The chairman became the secretary of defense. Once that occurred, the Air Force's interest in the space commission report escalated dramatically. The new secretary of defense had just spent the previous six

months getting an advanced degree in space culture and problems. He came to the position with some very definite ideas about what needed to be done, so frankly, whatever thoughts the Air Force might have had on this subject were overtaken by events.

The space commission's report led to structural changes in both the Air Force and the wider national security bureaucracy. The eventual outcome also included a change in rhetoric inside the Air Force. In a speech to the Air Force Association's national symposium meeting in Los Angeles in November 2001, Ryan's successor as chief of staff, Gen. John Jumper, dispensed with the term *aerospace* and revived the language of air and space:

> [The term *aerospace*] fails to give the proper respect to the culture and to the physical differences that abide between the physical environment of air and the physical environment of space. We need to make sure we respect those differences. I will talk about air and space. I will respect the fact that space is its own culture, that space has its own principles that have to be respected.[4]

Ascertaining how much Air Force strategic intent reflects the views put forth by the space commission is inherently difficult at this point. Nonetheless, the space commission clearly represents a case of externally centered corrective visioning. Such a case deserves some examination here, in recognition of the fact that the U.S. governmental system offers wide structural opportunities for effective criticism and even revision of strategic thinking and intent.

The Space Commission Story

As mentioned above, Senator Robert Smith succeeded in directing the space commission to consider the feasibility and advisability of creating a Space Force. In fulfilling its mandate, the commission needed to decide whether the Air Force was willing and able to play the role of the nation's lead service in this domain. If the commission were to recommend against such a dramatic reorganization, its members could expect to face tough questioning from Senator Smith, whose skepticism about the Air Force was not a closely guarded secret. Some commission members came to the task with doubts of their own. Their suspicions were triggered by the Air Force's apparent departure from the line taken in *Global Engagement*. The perception that the institution was revising its strategic intent was based on statements made by Chief of Staff Ryan, according to one commission member:

Look at Mike Ryan's early statements, which were all played back to him in the space commission. "The idea of space moving so fast is all hokum. Space at this time is only support. It's only going to be support for some time." That's what he said. You can find that quote somewhere in his early [Congressional] testimony. That was so fundamentally different from *Global Engagement* that it represented a sea change.

The concept of aerospace integration was interpreted as saying that the Air Force's space mission was primarily to support air operations. The space commission, however, "was not too captured by the idea of aerospace integration," in the words of an Air Force general who followed the commission's deliberations. Emphasis on this concept was seen as evidence that the Air Force was positioning itself as a space-enhanced Air Force rather than as the nation's Space and Air Force. Apparently, the chief's first encounter with the commission in the summer of 2000 did little to strengthen the case that the Air Force could be entrusted with the nation's increasingly important space missions. On that occasion, General Ryan put forward the Air Force's strategic vision, which included the focus on aerospace integration. The presentation culminated in a plea for greatly expanding the Air Force's budget so that the costs of modernizing and operating the nation's aerospace force would be adequately covered while also funding additional space missions. The commission found the presentation unsatisfying. One commissioner recalled the reaction:

> The senior leadership talked to us in the first pitch about the inability to afford space, because of the terrible problems with aviation recapitalization—the F-22 and so forth. Which is true, by the way; there's no question about it. But this was not the right pitch to give the space commission. That created such a furor that [we sent a message back to the Air Force saying], "You better figure out a better pitch than that, because you're confirming all the suspicions."

The commission eventually set about devising recommendations that would demand and enable the Air Force to function as the military service responsible for the domain of "national security space," while making it more feasible to establish a space force at a later time. Much effort went into understanding why the Air Force was unwilling to take institutional ownership of this increasingly well-defined area of national security policy and operations. One informed suspicion was that the Air Force's senior leaders typically viewed space missions as unfunded mandates, analogous to ones Washington imposes on the states. The inside view is that the Air Force's program and funding responsibilities in space have been dictated by outside actors, centered in the Office of the Secretary of Defense and the acquisition community. A typical effect is that programs strongly favored by the Air Force receive less funding than they otherwise would. This decades-old pattern has meant that the Air Force as an institution feels little ownership of the national security space domain, despite the fact that more than 80 percent of defense spending in this area flows through the Air Force's budget. In the words of one senior officer in the space community,

> Everybody else was making decisions about what we were going to go build and do. . . . The defense civilian leadership says we need this space stuff. They tell the Space and Missile Systems Center to go do it—and then the corporate Air Force has to pay the bills. So there is a terrible fracture line that has been going on since 1960.

The space commission set out to recommend ways to resolve the unfunded mandate problem by giving the Air Force department more formal influence over Defense Department decisions about what the service was going to build and do for military space. However, the commission also operated under the informed suspicion that the space community within the Air Force was institutionally too weak to exercise substantial influence over the department's own positions. An indication of the problem was that the vast preponderance of four-star generals had deep aviation experience but shallow space experience. The situation was perceived as similar among the other ranks of general officers. Much attention therefore came to be focused on the interrelated issues of culture and personnel. The commission devoted considerable effort to an empirical study of career progression and staffing patterns. They found that the situation was becoming worse rather than better under the concept of aerospace integration. The revealed pattern was that aviators were gaining experience in space, but space guys did not transfer into aviation. Providing aviators with opportunities to become acquainted with the space side of the Air Force further limited the career progression of officers within the smaller space community. Space competence was judged to suffer. Moorman explained the finding as follows:

> Many members of the space commission were not enamored with the Air Force's stewardship. It was not necessarily strictly about stewardship from a budgetary point of view. Rather, it seemed to me it was

also about the stewardship of the people—about career development of a space cadre and creating an environment where space could grow and prosper.

The commission, in the end, took the view that the Air Force needed to develop a critical mass and common culture of space professionals. In its report, the commissioners stated, "The Defense Department must create a stronger military space culture, through focused career development, education, and training, within which the space leaders for the future can be developed. This has an impact on each of the services but is most critical within the Air Force." The rationale was not only to develop space competence, but also to create conditions whereby the Air Force, as an institution, would be as keen to advocate missions and programs in the national security space field as in that of military aviation.

While the commission spotlighted the issue, however, only a few of its recommendations directly addressed it. One such recommendation was to do away with the practice of assigning the Commander of Air Force Space Command the additional role of Commander of the North American Air Defense Command (NORAD). This practice meant that many of those general officers who had grown up in the space community were ineligible to head Air Force Space Command, because the NORAD commander is required to be a rated pilot. The commission's thinking was that at least one head of a major command should be from the space community. Still, the emphasis was less on institutional tinkering than on cajoling the Air Force to undertake the sustained managerial efforts needed to cultivate Air Force leaders who understood and identified with the national security space field. This message struck a chord with at least one space-oriented general officer in Air Force headquarters:

> The commissioners felt that at the end of the day this is really about how to build a body of human capital that has the culture to deal with space as a medium and with its implications for national security. And so they were very, very emphatic about this idea . . . to develop a critical mass and common culture of space professionals.

The incentive to comply with this cajoling was much more political than mechanical. The commission suggested that while a space force remained a second-best option, it could well become advisable in the future. The trigger would presumably be a resurgence of the view that the Air Force as an institution was too tied to aviation to be a good steward of the military role in national security space policy and operations. This message was picked up clearly within the Air Force community. For instance, a feature article on the commission in the journal of the Air Force Association leads off as follows:

> The recommendations of a blue-ribbon panel on military space, if implemented, could cause the Air Force to revisit its initiative to merge air and space operations into a seamless aerospace continuum, set the stage for creation of a "Space Corps" within the Air Force in this decade, and possibly lead to the formation of an independent space service in the not-too-distant future.[5]

By leaving the door open to a future space force, the space commission sought to exert sustained pressure on Air Force strategic intent and its implementation in relation to national security space. The pressure was felt immediately within the corridors of Air Force headquarters, where, according to one respondent, "almost overnight we went from [considering] this an interesting academic exercise to [seeing] profound consequences for the Air Force," not least because the chairman of the commission was now the secretary of defense.

The perception of profound consequences derived primarily from the organizational recommendations to give the Air Force more responsibility and authority for national security space. The commission specifically recommended, for instance, that the Defense Department formally designate the Air Force as its executive agent for space. In the interest of giving this new status weight and longevity, the commission suggested that the executive agent responsibility be written into Title X, the basic law governing the Air Force. A second specific recommendation was to designate the under secretary of the Air Force as both the director of the National Reconnaissance Office and the Air Force acquisition executive for space. The same official was also to be delegated the so-called milestone decision authority for all defense space programs. A third specific recommendation was to move the Space and Missile Systems Center out from under the Air Force Materiel Command and to place it within Air Force Space Command.

The Air Force decided not to contest any of the major points and recommendations in the space commission report. Attention focused on developing plans to put it into effect. The ease with which the plans were developed reflected the fact that many of the issues had already been extensively debated in the course of preparing a series of volumes of the Aerospace Integration Plan. Those debates had not been concluded by December 2000, when the space commission's report was being readied for release and Rumsfeld was tapped to be defense secretary. In the words of Roger De Kok, who had led the work on aerospace integration planning, "My perception is that the space commission decided the outcome of some organizational issues, some cultural issues, and some personnel issues that the Air Force was unable to come to grips with prior to the space commission." By the time the secretary of defense registered his formal response to the space commission report in May 2001, the Air Force was ready to execute. In the event, Rumsfeld welcomed the report that his commission had written. "The commission has presented a well-thought-through, independent, and objective assessment. It identified the importance of outer space and space activities to the security and well-being of the United States, our allies, and friends," he said in the preface of his response to the Armed Services Committees. Most of the specific commission recommendations were endorsed.

Potential Impact and Effectiveness

The space commission can be seen as having produced two kinds of potential effects that are relevant to this book, apart from its impact on how the Air Force's senior leaders, including Chief of Staff John Jumper, talk about the issue of air and space. One kind of effect is to raise the status of human resource and organizational issues on the Air Force's strategic planning agenda. During the Fogleman round of strategic visioning, the Long-Range Planning Board of Directors discussed these issues at length, reflecting Tom Moorman's strong interest in the subject. Under General Ryan, human resource and organizational issues received intense attention as the Air Force fashioned a remedy to the problem of retaining pilots and career airmen—namely, the Air Expeditionary Force, an organizational construct developed in 1998–99. It was not until the space commission came onto the scene, however, that the human resource and organizational issues of greatest interest to the Air Force's space community truly reached the strategic planning agenda. Although these issues were broached in Lawrence Farrell's watershed briefing on air and space at the winter 1998 Corona conference, they did not receive immediate follow-up attention; as we have seen, the Aerospace Integration Task Force became consumed with debates over the theory and doctrine of aerospace power. The linkage between strategic visioning and strategic human resource and organizational planning grew stronger because of the space commission. Indeed, the space commission may be seen to have contributed directly to performing the Air Force's strategic human resource and organizational planning function. This interpretation suggests that externally based formal processes, sponsored by overseers, have the potential to strengthen linkages between strategic visioning and other strategic planning and policy management functions, including human resource and organizational planning.

A second kind of potential effect involves the Air Force's future strategic intent. The space commission's influence can be seen to operate through a strategic visioning event's process context factors, including the altered organizational constitution. The Air Force is now designated as the Defense Department's executive agent for space, following a directive issued by the secretary. As a result, the collective senior military leadership in the Air Force may come to identify strongly with the department's appointed role as steward for the national security space domain. Identification with this stewardship role could easily influence deliberations leading to a revised strategic vision. Another channel of influence operating through the Air Force's constitution involves the selection of individuals for senior leadership positions. Separating the roles of the commander of Air Force Space Command and the commander of NORAD, for instance, will raise the likelihood that the space community will be represented at the four-star level. Patterns of accession to top-level positions will undoubtedly affect who sits on the Corona council when the Air Force vision is revisited. Overall, the potential impact is to establish a cultural and institutional foundation, within the Air Force, for the *Global Engagement* vision's line on air and space.

The space commission could also influence future Air Force strategic visions through its impact on the defense policy subsystem, a second type of process context factor. The effect may have been to consolidate national security space as a conceptual and institutional domain. If so, the outcome is a culmination of a decade-long process that began when the National Reconnaissance Office emerged from its shroud of secrecy and began to operate in support of military operations in addition to providing strategic intelligence to the president and other central decisionmakers, as discussed in chapter 2. This effect would be felt among policymakers, such as members of the Congressional Armed Services Committees, the National Security Council, and the Joint Chiefs of Staff. If national security policymaking becomes increasingly organized around this new policy domain, the Air Force will face stronger organizational incentives to formulate a strategic vision that speaks to these issues to the satisfaction of its overseers. Another of the space commission's potential effects on the defense policy subsystem is to have kept alive the alternative of establishing a separate space force. The Commission's ultimate view was that, at the time, building up the Air

Force's role as steward of the national security space domain was a better option than that setting up a Space Force. However, they suggested that the space force option might someday become first-best. By lending their prestige to this suggestion, the space commission may have influenced the policy stream and hence the dynamic defense policy subsystem.

If it is true that the space commission has influenced factors that can be expected to condition strategic visioning in the future, the question arises as to why it was effective. One reason is that its chairman was sworn in as the secretary of defense ten days after the commission's report was submitted to Congress and made public. In John Kingdon's terms, it is hard to imagine a clearer example of the political stream coming together with the problem and policy streams. Still, other sources of the commission's effectiveness can be detected under close analysis. These relate to this chapter's main analytic interest, which is how process design features and process context factors influence the effectiveness of formal processes for corrective visioning. We therefore conclude this section on the space commission by addressing this issue using the framework introduced in chapter 5.

The space commission's main process design features include its statutory mandate. This mandate was clearly formulated, yet bounded. It posed more than one clear question, including whether it is feasible and advisable to set up a separate space force. Beyond this, the legislation limited the commission's brief to organization and management issues, allowing the members to steer clear of potentially more contentious budgetary issues. A second feature was its time frame. The commission was given six months to complete its work, once all members were on board. This time frame was sufficiently long for the group to become an effective team and to conduct independent study and analysis. In addition, the commission members knew they were working toward a firm deadline, which was itself set according to the rhythms of the electoral and policymaking processes. A third feature was the knowledge and credibility of the commission's members, arising from their military and civilian leadership careers. A fourth feature was the commission's work process. The commission met for thirty-two twelve-hour days. Since Rumsfeld doled out writing assignments, the members had to do their own study and take ownership of the analysis presented to the group. In an effort to reach a unanimous opinion, the commissioners dedicated substantial blocks of time to reviewing drafts written by its members and to reaching consensus through discussion.

In enumerating these process design features, we are struck by similarities between the space commission and the Air Force's Long-Range Planning

Board of Directors, as it operated during the Fogleman round. The members of the board of directors, including nine three-star generals, brought both knowledge and credibility to their task. Their efforts extended well over six months, allowing its members to form an effective work group. Studies and analysis relating to the specific issues under consideration were supplied. Some members were so closely involved in writing the Corona issues papers that they felt a sense of authorship. Discussion time was relatively plentiful. These similarities, together with underlying theories of individual performance and group behavior, suggest that both the space commission and the board of directors may have hit upon smart practices that are equally applicable to first-time strategic visioning and to corrective visioning.

The effectiveness of the space commission also depended on process context factors. Apart from events surrounding the 2000 presidential election, these factors include the defense policy subsystem. This context in motion included changes in the perception of space's role in national security, which accelerated throughout the 1990s. It also included the activism of elected officials such as Senator Robert Smith, who gave voice to a view that the role of steward of national security space had to be performed by a military service—if not the Air Force, then a space force. Smith's influence depended on the structure of the U.S. governmental system, which, more than most parliamentary systems, gives rise to potent power centers in the legislature, as well as in the broader authorizing environment of the Air Force. A reasonable conclusion is that the effectiveness of the space commission depended on such factors, which we subsume under the term *defense policy subsystem*, together with its process design features.

The Air Force Futures Games Case

This final case study examines a stable practice by which the Air Force's Strategic Planning Directorate has assisted the service's senior leadership in what we call corrective visioning. This practice has been exhibited in a series of Aerospace Future Capabilities War Games. Led by the Future Operational Concepts Division within the Strategic Planning Directorate, each futures game is a year's effort culminating in an experiential simulation of an international conflict between the United States (called Blue) and a figurative opponent (dubbed Red). The war game is set twenty years in the future. Each futures game is meant to spur and assist strategic thinking about whether the Air Force will possess the capabilities it needs to perform satisfactorily in future policy and technological environments. This generic public management question is given precise meaning in the process of designing each futures game.

Each futures game investigates a particular formulation of this question by tapping the knowledge, expertise, and military judgment of diverse communities in and around the Air Force. These communities include technologists, operational war fighters, logisticians, political-military analysts, and national security policymakers. The pooled knowledge and analysis is brought together in the game design and its supporting models. When the war game is finally conducted, more than 250 individuals participate in a simulated military confrontation between Red and Blue. They live and work within the same residential conference center for more than a week. The war game is then analyzed and assessed in a process requiring several weeks or even months, and the results are brought directly to the attention of the chief of staff and his deputy chiefs at Air Force headquarters in a formal briefing dubbed the futures game hotwash.

The futures game story is analytically interesting from several standpoints. First, this process has become a stable practice, in that a similar process methodology has been followed annually since 1998. While conceived in the Fogleman period, the practice came into its own under Gen. Michael Ryan, and it has outlived a second leadership succession, to Gen. John Jumper. This durability suggests that some attempts by strategic planning staffs to pursue innovative process methodologies can evolve into relatively stable practices. The status of a practice would be harder to claim for other process methodologies we have examined, including the Long-Range Planning Board of Directors' preparations for Corona visioning conferences. How a practice becomes established is a question posed by this case study.

Second, the futures games reflect the momentum of long-range strategic planning in the Air Force. We raised the issue of momentum in our earlier discussion of the Aerospace Integration Task Force and in our analysis of the Ryan-Peters round in chapter 4. What gives rise to, and sustains, momentum in strategic planning is an important practical, as well as scientific, question—perhaps even more significant than the related issue of institutionalizing long-range planning within an organization.[6]

Third, this case illustrates how a strategic planning process can become a vehicle for thrusting uncomfortable—even threatening—issues onto the formal agenda of an organization's top authority figures. The specific issue in this case is whether trends in the military capabilities of potential opponents will eventually bankrupt the Air Force's principal strategy for employing air power. Interest in analyzing threats posed by potential opponents' strategies to deny sanctuary to American forces, including Air Force combat aircraft and their ground crews, was ignited in the early 1990s by defense intellectuals, including the legendary Andrew Marshall of the Pentagon's Net Assessment unit, and by the Navy. This so-called anti-access issue was skirted during the Corona issues process before being acknowledged first by Gen. Michael Ryan and later by the Air Force senior leadership as a whole. The futures games contributed markedly to the acknowledgment and analysis of the unnerving possibility that standard Air Force operations, involving forward deployment of combat aircraft, would become extremely risky and perhaps even ineffective. As this concern had not preoccupied the principals involved in formulating the *Global Engagement* vision in the Fogleman period, the futures games case study provides insight into how formal processes, intertwined with the initiative of strategic planners, can enable an organization to scrutinize its own strategic thinking.

Origins of the Air Force Futures Games

The Aerospace Future Capabilities War Games were an outgrowth of Ronald Fogleman's tenure as chief. As part of the Corona issues process, participants began to achieve clarity about the institution's core competencies and its future operating environments, but Fogleman also wanted to understand what forces the Air Force as a whole should possess some twenty-five years in the future. In military parlance, he wanted to analyze future force structures. Fogleman tasked a number of units to develop what he called alternative Air Forces. In principle, an alternative Air Force was to be affordable, technically feasible, and operationally balanced across all Air Force missions. Some of Fogleman's tasking was parceled out to the Special Assistant to the Chief for Long-Range Planning (AF/LR), the small Staff group that worked directly for the chief and operated somewhat like an internal think tank.

AF/LR's response was to obtain ideas from industry, laboratory, and university sources about future technologies with operational relevance to the U.S. Air Force. These ideas were then evaluated by a hundred Air Force experts, who used a modified version of the well-known Delphi method to assign numerical scores to each of the contemplated technologies on the basis of their perceived performance in each of ten defined future operating environments. As this project proceeded, some in the long-range planning unit remained skeptical of its analytic merits. One skeptic was Jim Engle, a scientist and transport pilot by background, who moved into AF/LR after serving as Fogleman's executive officer. The colonel's skepticism about the soundness of the numerical scores grew into outright alarm once the Delphi study came to fruition:

> The problem was that these numbers became more "real" than they were originally intended to be. Senior leaders suddenly found themselves being able to advocate changes in programmatic spending—increases and cutbacks—based on the analysis of the impact of particular technologies on Air Force capabilities in future operating environments. The problem was that what appeared to be a hard quantitative evaluation was in fact a very soft evaluation based on subjective testimonials, which just happened to be presented numerically.

Meanwhile, in late 1996, about the time the Corona issues process reached its culmination, the Air Force was invited to take part in a war game to support the U.S. Army's own strategic visioning efforts. Ordinary war games involve preparing and running a simulated international crisis and ensuing hot war. They depict situations that could occur within five to ten years. The Army's novel futures game, by contrast, depicted a situation posited twenty years in the future. The key objective was not to evaluate how a crisis was managed or a war prosecuted, but rather to examine the operational capability of a future Army force structure. AF/LR sent Engle to participate.

Engle found the format of the Army's futures game appealing. "It was a big event where they brought a lot of expertise together and worked up to a solid analytical underpinning." In this latter respect, the futures game compared favorably in his eyes to the Air Force's modified Delphi studies. Engle was also impressed with the futures game's reception by the Army's senior leadership. The whole process compared favorably with the Air Force's approach: "It demonstrated to me that if the game were well formulated, it was a powerful construct to derive insights about alternative future forces and to communicate them to senior decisionmakers." War gaming was not regularly practiced by the Air Force, however; the service that had made the most sustained use of the methodology was the Navy.

The Army's futures game was played in the spring of 1997, by which time AF/LR had been extinguished and its functions and personnel reconstituted as the Strategic Planning Directorate under the XP. The new AF/XPX directorate, like AF/LR, was headed by David McIlvoy, a two-star general, and his civilian deputy, Clark Murdock. Engle was transferred, as well, and assigned as chief of the Future Operational Concepts Division. This modestly sized division's agenda included carrying out Fogleman's mandate of institutionalizing long-range planning, just like the other divisions within the directorate. Since it was not consumed with translating Corona directive statements into a written long-range plan, as were other parts of the directorate at the time, Engle's division had time to keep the alternative Air Forces project alive. Following completion of the Army's futures game, Engle persuaded his superiors of this process methodology's merits as an analytically sound and user-friendly vehicle for examining the capabilities of alternative Air Forces. Once McIlvoy and Murdock managed to spring the needed funds (about $1.5 million) from the budget controllers, Engle's division hired the same firms and individuals that had supported the Army's futures game. Thus began a year of effort, working up to the May 1998 game and the official hotwash review with the chief and his deputies.

Designing the Game Construct

The basic design of the 1998 futures game was to identify three different future Blue force structures and ask which one would do better against the same militarily capable opponent, Red. One Blue force structure was essentially a base case in which the Air Force in 2020 consisted of equipment and technology that was already fielded or would be fielded once its long-term spending plan, known as the Air Force Program Projection, was implemented. A second augmented Blue force structure included equipment and technology that could conceivably be fielded by 2020, including extended range aircraft and unmanned aerial vehicles (UAVs). A third Blue force structure was described as a space force. This force structure included technologies that some imagined might be available in the 2020 time frame, including munitions that would be delivered from platforms orbiting around the earth. The three alternative force structures were designed so that, in principle, they were all technically feasible in the 2020 time frame and affordable given an extrapolation of current defense spending levels.

The scenario, which was common to all three alternative air forces, assumed that the opponent, Red, would possess weaponry with sufficient range and precision to strike U.S. forces based within 1,200 miles of its coast. This situation involved considerably more danger for equipment and personnel operating at forward bases than was actually the case in 1998. This aspect of the game design reflected strategic planners' desire to draw the Air Force senior leadership into discussing the potentially huge implications of foreseeable technological and geopolitical trends.

Outside the Air Force, attention focused on trends of decreased costs and improved capabilities of missiles possessed by potential opponents. In the early 1990s, Andrew Marshall, the long-serving director of net assessment in the Office of the Secretary of Defense, began to argue that opponents could potentially build up tactical missile forces, including cruise missiles, to the point of threatening U.S. forces if they were deployed anywhere near territory the opponents controlled. In the ensuing debate among defense analysts about anti-access asymmetric strategies, the U.S. Navy began to assert that aircraft carriers would be even more important in the future, because they were mobile whereas the Air Force was tethered to fixed locations.

Although the Air Force as a whole took little notice of this brewing debate about anti-access, asymmetric strategies, AF/LR decided to give it some serious thought. In November 1995, director David McIlvoy, a bomber pilot and operational planner by background, commissioned a study to describe an opponent that could establish and maintain an exclusionary zone. The central questions were threefold. What kind of weapon systems would the opponent have? How would it have to array them? What would be the scale of the exclusionary zone? The study took over a year to complete. When it was over, the strategic planners in AF/LR were convinced that the anti-access issue was of primordial importance and that the Air Force might be advised to shift resources into long-range strike platforms, like its current B-52 bombers, and cut back on shorter-range platforms, like its current F-16 fighters. However, the task of communicating this message to the Air Force senior leadership, most of whom had spent their careers building the fighter-heavy tactical Air Force, was daunting. After a few forays in 1996–97, Engle concluded that the Air Force's senior leadership was engaged in "active denial" of the prospect that forward-deployed short-range aircraft could become sitting ducks in a future theater of war: "There was not pervasive acceptance by the senior leadership in the Air Force that it was necessary to reduce the risk faced by our assets and people inside a potential enemy threat environment. They were still stuck on the paradigm of sanctuary. They were implicitly thinking, 'Wherever we go, we're okay.'"

The 1998 futures game became the strategic planners' vehicle of choice for bringing the defense analysts' debate into the mainstream of Air Force strategic thinking and planning. This abiding interest was reflected in the details of the game's scenario. Accordingly, the opponent was assumed to possess the military capability necessary to deny U.S. forces access to a zone extending

1,200 miles from its coast. This assumption fit with classified and open source estimates that by 2020 a near-peer competitor would be able to build an exclusionary zone of roughly 1,500 miles beyond its borders.

Drawing on AF/LR's earlier study, the game designers identified the force structure, equipment, and technology that Red would have to possess in order to impose a 1,200-mile exclusionary zone. Once this step was completed, attention turned to whether it was realistic to assume that Red would acquire such capabilities. Rod McDaniels and Ron St. Martin, consultants working for Science Applications Incorporated (SAIC), were brought in to perform the validation exercise. McDaniels, a former secretary of the National Security Council, contacted several former presidential national security advisers from both Republican and Democratic administrations, including John Poindexter, Jonathan Howe, Bud McFarland, and Anthony Lake. They individually scrutinized the economic and military assumptions on which the constructed opponent was based. Lake, who had recently stepped down as President Clinton's national security adviser, became very engaged in the project. As Engle later recalled, "Lake took the 'bad guy' away and studied him for about two weeks, and then we got together. He had a lot of comments to make." Not long after, the strategic planners arranged for Lake to meet with General Ryan to review the game's design, including its specific assumptions about the opponent. As a result of the meeting with the former presidential aide, the chief approved the game design.

Meanwhile, the game designers were busy constructing the alternative Air Forces whose capabilities would be assessed in the war game. As mentioned earlier, the alternative Air Force had to be affordable and technically feasible. Once they had preliminary formulations, the strategic planners brought together representatives of functional areas across the Air Force, including operations and science and technology, in a series of more than twenty workshops and seminars. These meetings were often scenes of heated debate. Ron McDaniels had to exhibit the facilitation skills he had honed as secretary at the National Security Council: in Engle's words, McDaniels's job there had been "to facilitate consensus at a table that was fundamentally not interested in consensus." When agreement on alternative Air Forces failed to materialize, the game directors asserted their prerogative to recommend a particular game design to their superiors. The division also committed itself to reviewing key assumptions on a periodic basis and modifying them in light of newly available information.

The result of this process was a model of three alternative Air Forces. The Baseline Force was extrapolated from the Air Force Programming Projection, as mentioned above. The Extended Range Force included UAVs, extended-range strike aircraft, hypersonic missiles, and long-range cruise missiles. The Space-Heavy Air Force included augmented space-based radar, hypervelocity rods from space, and space platforms capable of launching air vehicles carrying precision weapons to strike mobile and fixed terrestrial targets. The game was designed to compare the performance of the Baseline Force, the Extended Range Force, and the Space-Heavy Air Force against the opponent in an operational scenario. The scenario began with Red invading the Russian Far East in order to gain control over oil under the Siberian tundra. Japan felt threatened by Red's move, since Siberia had become a major source of its imported petroleum, which was transported by underwater pipeline across the Sea of Japan. According to the scenario, the government of Japan then asked the U.S., as its military ally, to intervene. The stage was thus set for a war between Red and Blue and, specifically, for the engagement of each of Blue's alternative Air Forces against Red.

THE 1998 FUTURES GAME AND ITS OUTCOME. The actual play of the first Aerospace Future Capabilities War Game began on May 18, 1998, and concluded five days later. Three different games were played, one for each alternative Air Force. The results of the game with the Baseline Force were consistent with the hypothesis that Red would be able to cause significant losses to Blue's bases, aircraft, and personnel situated within the 1,200-mile exclusionary zone. Blue's ability to generate offensive sorties against Red was highly curtailed owing to the effectiveness of Red's medium-range ballistic and cruise missiles against Blue's forward bases. Blue failed to evict Red from the disputed territory by the time the war game drew to a close. According to the role players in the game, Red had accomplished its objectives and believed itself the victor. Blue continued to fight and believed that with the introduction of U.S. ground troops, victory was a matter of time.

The results of the game with the Extended Range Force were consistent with the hypothesis that this alternative Air Force would perform much better than the Baseline Force in an anti-access operational environment. When Blue initiated its offensive operations, it succeeded in destroying not only all of Red's command-and-control assets, but also many of its ballistic and cruise missile launchers. Still, Red managed to hit Blue air bases within the exclusionary zone. In a sign of escalation, Red attacked with ballistic and cruise missiles carrying chemical weapons, causing massive civilian casualties in the areas surrounding Blue's forward air bases. Because of the Extended Range Force's so-called standoff warfare capabilities, however, damage to these bases did not greatly impair Blue's offensive airpower. The role players in the game came to a common assessment that Blue won the military battle against Red.

The game involving the Space-Heavy Air Force confirmed some hypotheses and produced some worrisome surprises. This alternative Air Force performed better than the Baseline Force in military terms. In particular, it managed to eliminate the exclusionary zone within two days of fighting. The surprises emerged when those playing Red revealed their perceptions of the situation as it had unfolded. Red explained that Blue's attack was so devastating that it feared complete destruction of its homeland. This perception caused Red to escalate the conflict—specifically, to launch a nuclear attack on Blue ground forces massing in the theater. This outcome revealed that conventional warfare, conducted from space, might actually pose a risk of a nuclear conflagration.

The game designers took several months to analyze and assess the game and to settle on recommendations that the Strategic Planning Directorate and the XP would put forward. Finally, in September 1998, Engle delivered a briefing about the game results to the chief and other senior leaders on the Air Staff.

In summing up the comparative analysis of the Baseline Force and the Extended Range Force, the strategic planners recommended that the Air Force address the future anti-access world—for instance, by planning to develop forces capable of attacking targets deep within an opponent's territory during the early stages of an air campaign, using munitions delivered from platforms situated outside the exclusionary zone (but not from space). In a phrase, the briefing recommended that the Air Force plan to develop standoff warfare capabilities. "There was a broad debate within the senior staff right then and there," according to Engle. "That's when the issue of anti-access asymmetric strategies and the application of standoff warfare concepts to address them first gained acknowledgment formally by the senior leadership." The chief did not, however, endorse the concept of standoff warfare, although he gave the strategic planners a green light to continue to pursue the anti-access issue and to analyze future operational concepts involving standoff warfare.

BACK TO THE DRAWING BOARD. The Strategic Planning Directorate decided that the format of a futures game worked very well. They were pleased that the issues swirling around defense analytical circles had been acknowledged by the chief. In September 1998, the Strategic Planning Directorate decided to propose a second futures game. In thinking about the design of the follow-on game, they focused on criticisms of how the Extended Range Force was modeled. The model was admittedly crude. In the 1998 game, the commander of this Blue force had benefited from knowing a great deal about the location of Red's mobile targets, even though the model did not specify how this information would be obtained. Accordingly, the strategic planners decided that the 1999 Aerospace Future Capabilities War Game should compare the effectiveness of the Baseline Force with an alternative Air Force whose command-and-control systems were described in some detail. Such detail would allow for an analysis of information flows in the battlespace—for example, flows from airborne or space-based sensors, on one end, through commanders and finally to combat aircraft or smart munitions, on the other.

At a meeting in October 1998, General Ryan was presented with a number of optional designs for the second futures game. Among the scenario options were situations occurring in the Middle East, South Asia, or the Russian Far East in 2020. The strategic planners recommended using the same scenario as that on which the 1998 futures game had been based. The data from the model built for that game could then be reused, and insights from the two games would be more comparable. The chief formally approved using the Russian Far East scenario again. He also approved the outline of the game's experimental design. The overall objective was to assess an alternative Air Force possessing and using target-quality, deep-look intelligence, surveillance, and reconnaissance (ISR) capabilities, when facing an opponent like one in the model in 2020. The performance of this alternative was to be compared with the same Baseline Force studied in the first game. With the objective, the experimental design, and the scenario approved by the chief, the Air Force strategic planners and the contractors set off to prepare the 1999 futures game.

ELICITING KNOWLEDGE FOR THE 1999 FUTURES GAME. A key analytical task for the second futures game was to build an adequate model of the alternative force's so-called information architecture. At the outset, almost all of the knowledge needed to perform this analytical task resided outside the Air Force's strategic planning community. Potential sources of knowledge included industry, the Air Force's Space and Missile Center and Electronic Systems Center, the Air Force Research Laboratory, the Air Force Space Command, the Defense Advanced Research Projects Agency (DARPA), and the National Reconnaissance Office. These organizations, along with numerous defense contractors, were invited to an initial one-day seminar workshop to identify technologies that could provide target-quality, deep-look ISR capabilities. The main thrust of this workshop was to learn what the defense industry believed would satisfy the broadly specified requirements for the future. A two-day workshop was later held to begin to develop a consensus among the Air Force participants as to what ISR technologies and capabilities the Air Force could reasonably possess by 2020. Before analysts began to develop a formal model of the second force's information architecture, a final three-day workshop was held with the aim of achieving sufficient consensus among the Air Force participants for purposes of playing, interpreting, and disseminating insights from the game.

The process of developing the game included eighteen workshops altogether, conducted between November 1998 and March 1999. As it turned out, the most valuable knowledge and analysis was provided by representatives of the National Reconnaissance Office (NRO). Such participation by the NRO would have been unthinkable several years earlier, when its very existence was top secret. The participation of some components, however, including Air Force Space Command, was intermittent. It took direct communication from the chief's office to improve Air Force participation in the workshops.

The main purpose of some of the later workshops was to involve those who would play the game in its development. A related purpose was to familiarize the players with the theorizing and analysis on which the game had been built. For example, the retired three-star generals cast as commanders of the future force had not previously studied the theory of standoff warfare, and they were not knowledgeable on how information useful for the deep look into the opponent's territory would be generated and presented. The final series of workshops was essentially conducted to train players to play their part in the process of testing the effectiveness of the two different forces against the same opponent.

Playing the 1999 Futures Game

The second futures game was played at the Bolger Executive Leadership Center in Potomac, Maryland, in June 1999. Two games were played in parallel, with one war between Red and the Baseline Force and the other between Red and the Blue force with target-quality, deep-look ISR capability. The whole process lasted more than a week. The participants included retired admiral David Jeremiah, a former vice chairman of the Joint Chiefs of Staff, who played the role of national command authority (that is, the apex of the decisionmaking structure with the president at the top). The commander of the Baseline Force was Gen. Gene Santarelli, while the commander of the enhanced "deep-look" force was Gen. Sandy Sharpe. These recently retired senior officers had served in war fighting command positions during their Air Force careers.

The results of the game were dramatically clear. The force structure with advanced space-based ISR capabilities pushed back the exclusionary zone within the early stages of the air campaign, whereas the Baseline Force was unsuccessful in doing so. In the last in a series of formal, videotaped discussions, the commander of the Baseline Force told his fellow participants, "My general perception of our ISR architecture is that it was inadequate, given the task that I had, because I knew in my heart that there were things going on out there that I couldn't see and that Red was going to surprise me." His comments were the mirror image of those made by the commander of the enhanced force:

> Our augmented force's distinction was that we could look deep and we could look early, which [meant] we had a pretty clear understanding of the disposition of all the forces arrayed in that theater. And we could see where the ground forces were. As a matter of fact, we could see that they had intended to use bridging equipment rather than use the bridges we knew about. We knew exactly where they were going to cross the river.

The strategic planners spent the next several weeks assessing the game and preparing their scheduled hotwash session with the chief. In terms of its potential impact, the upcoming meeting with the chief, in July 1999, was favorably timed. General Ryan along with Secretary Peters had already launched an official revisiting of the Air Force's strategic vision, with the culminating event slated for the fall 1999 Corona conference. Yet many matters were still open for discussion and potential resolution, owing to the problems with the Long-Range Planning Board of Directors, as described in chapter 4.

Preparing the Briefing Session on the 1999 Game

A main argument that the strategic planners wanted to make in their briefing was that the incumbent *Global Engagement* vision was incomplete in that it did not acknowledge the anticipated threat posed by the diffusion of tactical ballistic and cruise missiles. While the existing vision enshrined its core competencies, including information superiority, it was not specific enough about the capabilities and grand operational concepts the Air Force would need to be effective in a foreseeable anti-access world. An implication of the futures game, they wanted to argue, was that target-quality, deep-look ISR capabilities would be essential to the Air Force's effectiveness in the event the United States came to face an opponent able to deny sanctuary to short-range combat aircraft. The main thought they wanted to communicate to the chief, as described by Engle, was that "as we revisit our vision, we should not miss the opportunity to couple it to standoff warfare. This would require some adjustment in our thinking about the mix of our future force capabilities."

In preparing the briefing, the strategic planners contemplated two inherent difficulties in delivering their message. One was that the results were based on a simulation loaded with assumptions about a very distant future. "When you think twenty years into the future," Engle noted, "it is very difficult to convince anybody that what you are talking about is real." The fact that the chief had approved the game design worked in favor of his giving credence to the results, but the futures game's persuasiveness depended on inducing a willing suspension of disbelief. A second inherent difficulty was that the 1999 game, like the previous one, revived the uncomfortable question of whether the Air Force's heavy investment in short-range combat aircraft was optimal if the foreseen anti-access world were actually to materialize. Even though Ryan had given the green light to explore the issue, it was not clear how receptive he would be to hearing what the strategic planners now thought about it. This uncertainty was of particular concern to Colonel Engle, who was slated to perform the role of briefer during the upcoming hotwash.

In anticipation of these difficulties, the strategic planners decided to choose their language carefully. For instance, they studiously avoided using the term *conclusion* to describe a belief influenced by the game, because it implied that the information coming out of the game was more definitive than could be asserted on the basis of a simulation exercise, even one as sophisticated as the second futures game. The strategic planners instead opted for the more tentative, disarming term, *insight*. Insights could be derived from a war game, while conclusions, in their view, could not. The briefing was also meant to be modest in its recommendations. They would not call for immediate, irreversible decisions, which might be resisted by the other senior leaders who would be seated in the briefing room. Instead, the presentation would call for further analysis of specific issues, as well as for reconsidering the Air Force's strategic vision in light of the insights gained from the game and other work done in strategic planning.

Beyond tailoring the language and recommendations to suit the situation, the strategic planners repeated a tactic they had used in the lead-up to the

1998 futures game. As mentioned above, Ryan was introduced to the first game's design by Anthony Lake, the sitting president's just-departed national security adviser, rather than by the chief's subordinates. Consistent with this approach, the strategic planners invited to the briefing session retireed Admiral David Jeremiah, the former vice chairman of the Joint Chiefs of Staff who played the role of the national command authority, along with the commanders of the two Blue forces, retired Air Force generals Santarelli and Sharpe.

The briefer was to emphasize that the 1999 game built on the 1998 game in ways the chief had sanctioned. The prepared text clearly stated this condition:

> The 1998 and 1999 games suggest a strong relationship between attacking targets from long distances and the need for high-quality, rapidly deliverable information about that intended target. During the 1998 game we were unsure how to obtain this information and how to get it to the right instrument that would attack deep targets. Chief, you directed that we study this and develop an operational concept that would enable this capability. In the last year we completed the conceptual work, and we tested it in this year's game.

The briefing was intended to focus the chief's attention on game insights, as well as on related perspectives and issues. One insight was that the force with continuous deep-look capabilities achieved a greatly improved early reduction of the exclusionary zone. Another game insight was that stand-off forces could be tasked to achieve early battlefield effects. Based on these insights, the strategic planners wanted to argue that senior leaders should think of ISR and standoff warfare as closely related issues. The decision to pursue the latter would require investing in the kinds of ISR assets that made up Blue's augmented force. They wished to argue that the relationship between ISR and standoff warfare ought to be discussed in the upcoming fall 1999 Corona conference.

As a means of persuasion, the planners decided to make full use of the video tape recordings of the assessment sessions held during the game. For instance, after setting forth the insights mentioned above, the briefer would say: "And here is how the commander of the Baseline Force assessed its performance." A video clip of General Santarelli would then appear on the screen, capturing his immediate assessment of the issue as presented during the game. The same presentation technique was applied to comments by General Sharpe, the commander of the augmented force, including the statement quoted earlier.[7]

The briefing was meant to culminate in a call to revisit the vision. The prepared argument put the main points sharply. "First, our vision seems to lack adequate reference to the need for global vigilance. Second, there is a synergy between what we see, how we use this information to command and control forces, and the types of weapons we employ against targets. Third, if we don't address these insights we could well find our future capabilities inadequate to meet the demand of our national security requirements."

The Impact

The briefing session unfolded favorably, from the standpoint of the strategic planners. On viewing the video clips, Ryan turned to Santarelli and Sharpe and invited them to elaborate. A dialogue between the chief and these former war fighters ensued. This exchange among peers eventually gave way to the rest of the prepared briefing, including the recommendations. Overall, the chief acknowledged the insights and approved the recommendations, setting the stage for revisiting the Air Force strategic vision with the aim of raising the profile of the anti-access issue and expressing the urgency of making investments in intelligence, surveillance, and reconnaissance capabilities.

The *Global Vigilance, Reach, and Power* vision appears to have been influenced by the futures games. According to Engle, "They made anti-access/standoff warfare an issue for the fall 1999 Corona and pushed it over the hump from an interesting point of debate to a policy commitment by the Air Force." The games also directly influenced Lt. Gen. Roger De Kok, who as the deputy chief of staff for plans and programs was responsible for staffing the fall 1999 Corona conference after the board of directors faltered:

> It was very important to include the phrase *global vigilance* in the vision. Vigilance itself included manned platforms, UAVs, satellites, and ICBMs [intercontinental ballistic missiles]. I believe that the importance of vigilance would not have been as universally recognized had it not been for the 1999 futures game. The concept of look early, look deep became a watchword that came out of the game. It started to remind people that although the Air Force sometimes lamented the amount of resources that were going into ISR platforms, they are incredibly important to the Air Force's own agenda of being able to strike early and strike deep.

The recognition among the senior leaders assembled at the fall 1999 Corona conference of the importance of vigilance was further reflected in the

Vision Force. As discussed in chapter 4, the Corona participants were presented with an array of options that characterized future force structures. They chose option 4b. One aspect of this option was to call for heavy investment in intelligence, surveillance, and reconnaissance capabilities, including space-based radar—one of the components of the augmented force that played against Red in the 1999 Aerospace Future Capabilities War Game.

Analyzing the Futures Games Case

As mentioned at the outset of the section, we regard this case as analytically interesting for understanding corrective visioning as a process. The futures games were arguably effective in this regard. They worked as a vehicle for gaining recognition of the anti-access issue, and they helped senior leaders and others visualize an ISR-heavy alternative Air Force. An added effect was to convince the chief that the Air Force risked a mismatch between its capabilities and the policy environment in the future. What accounts for the effectiveness of the futures games?

Our framework for answering this question, as before, is to consider the conjunction of process design features and process context factors. Because this case was presented in detail, we discuss several key process design features only briefly. One feature was adherence to the Fogleman doctrine of backcasting from the future. The futures game attempted to develop foresight into how the U.S. Air Force would contribute to achieving national security objectives in the long-run future. Technological and geopolitical trends and discontinuities were considered in developing foresight. A second feature was to gear the process to influencing the strategic thinking and agenda of one individual, the chief of staff. As such, the process of generating divergent strategic thinking was different in character from that of formulating Air Force strategic intent, which is geared toward obtaining buy-in from the entire senior leadership. The process relied on the chief to acknowledge the force of the argument and to amplify and communicate it to the wider senior leadership community.

A third process design feature was to focus attention on a limited range of important but not wholly imponderable questions. The strategic planners also held themselves accountable for producing insights about these questions. A fourth design feature was to offset the Strategic Planning Directorate's limited expertise by drawing other parts of the Air Force and a broader organizational community into a large-scale, structured process for developing foresight and visualizing alternative Air Forces. A fifth design feature was to create an environment in which it was natural for individuals, including respected outside figures, to evaluate the risks of continuing with current plans. The playing of the game, over the course of a week during which all were confined to the same conference site, offered such an environment.

A sixth process design feature was to practice spiral development of strategic thinking. The principle of user involvement was put into operation in gaining the chief's approval of the game design, initially through the meeting with Anthony Lake and later through a standard staff meeting. The principle of rapid prototyping was in evidence when the design of the 1998 game was kept streamlined, earlier work on the opponent was recycled, and models of the enhanced forces' information architecture were left incomplete. Another illustration of rapid prototyping is that within weeks after completing the first cycle of futures games, the strategic planners set off to remedy the specific modeling limitations that had been a focus of dissatisfaction during the hotwash session. Finally, attention was lavished on preparing briefing sessions with the chief, with a view to effective communication and persuasion.

Process context factors also contributed to the effectiveness of the futures games. The defense policy subsystem was the original source of the idea that the spread of tactical ballistic and cruise missiles could lead to the United States facing opponents using anti-access, asymmetric strategies. This policy subsystem is also highly competitive, thus inviting the Navy's allegation that the Air Force would be comparatively disadvantaged in an anti-access world. Air Force strategic planners wished to devise an intelligent and effective counter. Bureau constitution was a second factor. The responsibility for strategic thinking about the broad, long-run issues contemplated in the futures game ultimately rests with the chief of staff. The fact that the long-range strategic planning function had been formally institutionalized, with the creation of the Strategic Planning Directorate, provided a structure within which the futures game could be repeatedly conducted. The establishment of the Future Operational Concepts Division, specifically, provided a context in which the job of a small number of individuals was to think radically about the big questions that, in their view, should be reflected in Air Force strategic intent.

In some ways, cultural bias worked to the advantage of the futures games. The Air Force's hierarchist culture bias calls for taking expertise seriously, including the technical knowledge embedded in war game constructs, the military judgment embodied in the experienced officers who played force commanders, and the acquired wisdom of former national security advisers. The same cultural bias also worked to the futures games' advantage after the chief had bought into the insights they yielded. Once the chief believed the incumbent vision was incomplete, then the equivocality surrounding these highly abstract matters was dramatically curtailed.

Finally, we mention the effects of the installed base of strategic thinking. In a way, this body of belief should be considered a limitation that the futures game was intended to overcome. On the other hand, the fact that the incumbent vision was full of content, albeit incomplete, made the task some-what easier. The specific insights and perspective produced by the game were easy to communicate, at least to an audience that had been attentive to the Corona issues process and its written products: the *Global Engagement* vision and the long-range plan.

This analysis of the effectiveness of the Air Force futures games suggests two further points. First, its process design features have much in common with techniques of knowledge management and knowledge creation in complex organizations.[8] This literature offers some theoretical and behavioral research frameworks for gaining insight into how process design features, like those enumerated above, contribute to the effectiveness of a corrective visioning effort. Second, such effectiveness, at least in government, depends strongly on the fit between selected process design features and such process context factors as the policy subsystem, organizational constitution, cultural bias, and the installed base of strategic thinking.

The futures games effort was effective, as well, in the special sense of get-ting an unwelcome issue on the senior leadership's strategic planning agenda—in this case, asymmetric, anti-access strategies. This aspect of the case cannot be explained exclusively by such factors as the subtleties of the process design, the incentives of the policy subsystem, and the institution-alization of the long-range planning function within the bureau constitution. Two additional factors are readily apparent. One was the occupational cul-ture of the professional military. Contemplating potential threats posed by technological and geopolitical change is part of that occupational culture. Another factor is the will of the strategic planners to see the issue through, together with enough stability in the strategic planning team to allow for continuity of effort over no less than a five-year period. Such stability is not necessarily typical of military organizations in the United States.

The fact that the futures games occurred and experienced some success is related to the momentum of strategic planning in the Air Force. What are the sources of that momentum? This case seems consistent with our analy-sis of the Aerospace Integration Task Force. The answer lies in processes influenced by a mixture of a favorable context in motion, individual will and ingenuity, and a few essential mechanisms, including psychological buy-in and intellectual competition within and between organizations. Understanding the sources and limits of such momentum is an important area for research on public management, generally, and the preparing-for-the-future approach, specifically.

Lessons from the Air Force's Efforts to Overcome Incrementalism: Toward Revitalized Governance

This chapter takes on two objectives. First, it seeks to distill the most important findings from our description and analysis of the Air Force's efforts to discern its future opportunities and challenges and align its core institutional commitments to an agreed vision. Second, the chapter extracts from the Air Force experience lessons for other public service organizations attempting to revitalize their missions and commitments. The task of addressing the second goal requires that we examine relatively weighty systemic issues. Inevitably, these hinge on the question of whether lessons from the Air Force might point the way to a revitalization of governance—granting immediately that most of our account and analysis has focused on what took place internally in a single public service organization, albeit a huge one.

Many readers have stayed with us because, for one reason or other, they wanted to know the Air Force's story. They presumably concluded, perhaps even before cracking open the book, that the Air Force case deserves close analysis in its own right, with little or no reference to its applicability to other departments. Many readers in this category require little introduction to the meanings of the potentially bewildering acronyms that serve as the lingua franca of national security buffs. Indeed, they likely have developed strong personal views about the feasibility of what the Air Force has been attempting since 1994 and the degree of success that it has achieved.

Notwithstanding our interest in contributing to dialogue among national security aficionados, this book has tried to expand the case to include lessons for other government organizations. We did not embark on this dimension of the enterprise without a high degree of confidence that what we would learn about the Air Force's experience would convey broadly to other public service departments and agencies. That is, we expected the Air Force case to provide an instance of smart practice with respect to an organization's positioning itself to deal creatively and resourcefully with opportunities and challenges far into the future.

Indeed, in chapter 1 we offered tentative observations about the wider applicability of the case. First, the Air Force experience merits attention because it serves as an example of an organization seizing the initiative in the face of an epochal shift in its long-term viability. Second, leadership and culture played crucial roles. This means that advocates and students of similar approaches in other departments and agencies must assess the aptitude for visioning within the team at the top, its cohesiveness, and its ability to carry the day internally through the various sectors and levels of their organization.

Third, the Air Force seems to have learned over the course of the Fogleman and Ryan-Peters rounds how to modulate direct appeals to stakeholders and subtle maneuvers around them to effect what we term *guided incrementalism*. The immense investment in strategic visioning and planning has thus imbued the Air Force with a clearer image of how it might capitalize on the opportunities and face the challenges of the long-range future. Equally important, the effort has vested the service with a wealth of experience in how best to press its case in the Washington labyrinth. The Air Force plied its course largely through trial and error. If an agency chose to emulate the Air Force's guided incrementalism, does the case present an illustration of how best to proceed?

The Air Force has shifted ground considerably in its aspirations surrounding the connectivity of strategic visioning and programmatic commitments since 1994. In the early phase, planners—much neglected over the years—began to assert themselves, and they sounded like they wanted to achieve a one-to-one fit between their visions for the future and each program. In other words, they spoke as if they hoped to achieve comprehensive programmatic rationality in reference to the Air Force's long-term strategic vision. During the Ryan-Peters round, key players stepped back from language depicting root and branch connections between plans and programs. They began to stress the need to commit resources more discriminately, focusing on the pivotal resource battles. Tracking the consequences of funding decisions for future critical capabilities became the watchword of planners.

To date, we can say only that the Air Force has improved its game to the extent of demonstrating a capacity for guided incrementalism. It has not been able to pick all of the battles in which it spends political capital on resource claims, and it has not always won once it engaged its institutional assets. However, by improving the calculations that inform its positioning for the future, it has moved iteratively in a direction discernibly different from the course it would have pursued under unmitigated incrementalism. This does not imply that the Air Force has abandoned a more robust linkage between planning and programming. Indeed, as the administration faces the unsustainability of its fiscal framework and Defense Secretary Donald H. Rumsfeld revisits transformational issues, a premium on a closer fit might soon emerge not just among the Air Force leaders, but more generally in the Pentagon, as well.

We thus find that the Air Force has achieved guided incrementalism and has developed the mature strategic visioning ethos necessary to go beyond it. It has developed the ability to specify with exceptional clarity the capabilities it believes it should provide the nation twenty to twenty-five years in the future. It has attempted to bring this vision to bear on resource commitments by scanning programming issues with a view to identifying forks in the road for making investments in a timely fashion. Still, the Air Force has not achieved perfection in focusing on and resolving issues at the most opportune moment. It is better placed than in the mid-1990s, but it often misses opportunities to act decisively. Moreover, failures stem as often from the intractability of stakeholders as from recalcitrance in the Air Force itself.

Taking the Lessons to a Wider Audience

In many respects, the Air Force frequently arrived at an art of the possible in pursuing strategic planning through approaches that varied significantly according to changes in leadership, the institutional leverage of key players, and circumstances in its political environment. This suggests that how an agency modulates the observance of the rubrics it follows in visioning and planning might prove very important to eventual success in implementation. This consideration shifts our emphasis in distilling broadly applicable smart practices. Rather than examining whether the Air Force executed certain protocols in a timely fashion—so as to advance the requisite connectivity for the strategic visioning to achieve success—we might more profitably concentrate on the leverage points at which players must modulate potential approaches in response to specific circumstances.

Chapter 5 laid the groundwork for such a consideration in its treatment of the elements of policy entrepreneurship. With respect to a serious practice of preparing for the future, individual leaders and their institutions must perceive the need for deft positioning for opportunities. We employed this term to capture the degree to which strategic visioning and the institutional consequences that might flow from it require impeccable timing in the engagement of key planning assets. These include the aptitude on the part of leaders to inspire others to discard any elements of the status quo that impede evolutionary adaptation, the ability of the institution over time to devise and refine cogent arguments for connecting the strategic vision and resource commitments, and investments in capabilities that, even if nascent, can work a demonstration effect that convinces insiders and observers alike of the practicability and utility of innovative approaches to the fulfillment of the organization's mission.

It is useful at this point to introduce four key leverage points for connecting the various elements of preparing for the future (see figure 9-1). First, as a craft, strategic visioning entails the attainment of policy foresight and decisions regarding strategic intent. Leverage point one, therefore, states that a vision that has not led to new strategic intent will work little organizational effect, whereas a revised strategy not firmly rooted in foresight will prove to be visionary only if its progenitors encounter a stroke of dumb luck. Second, strategic planning and policy management must come together so that they attain a high degree of reciprocity. Two leverage points assert themselves here. The strategic vision must link with both medium-term policy and expenditure planning (leverage point two) and human resources and organizational planning (leverage point three). Otherwise, the strategic vision stands little chance of affecting the organization's strategic planning and policy management. Finally, leverage point four proves the locus for whether strategic planning and policy management actually position an organization favorably in its preparation for the future. It denotes the crucial nature of implementation—whether the organization actually followed through on its strategic visioning and planning to position itself optimally for the future.

Focusing on these leverage points gives some guidance to those crafting initiatives similar to the Air Force's in their own organizations. Before examining the leverage points with this objective in mind, however, we must treat a daunting overarching reality. Many people, even if they admire what the Air Force has done, will conclude that what the service attempted would not work in their own situation owing to the intractability of most organi-

Figure 9-1. *Preparing for the Future: Functional Hierarchy Representation*

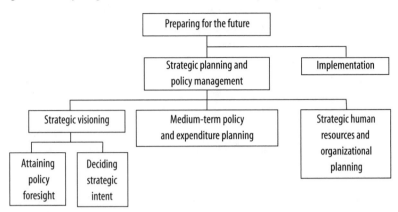

zations and the recalcitrance of their stakeholders. In other words, they will say, "Why bother?"

Revitalizing the Role of Public Service in Government

We would not be having this discussion in the golden era of public service in the United States. In the middle of the past century, the upper levels of the federal bureaucracy were characterized by a high degree of expertise, executive competence, and dedication to identifying and pursuing the national interest. Senior officials played their political roles exceedingly well and were highly skilled at the executive-bureaucratic gamesmanship necessary to present their assessments of policy options and press their views of the optimal directions in which to proceed.[1] Indeed, some highly regarded students of the constitutional role of senior bureaucrats even began to argue that the merit system made the bureaucracy more democratically representative of the populace than did the system of elected political leadership and their appointees.[2] This, it was believed, added to the legitimacy of permanent officials' roles.

A relentless process of erosion has made this exalted view of public service a thing of the past. The standing of the federal bureaucracy has faced assaults from both liberals and conservatives opposed to allowing officials a high degree of autonomy in pursuing executive-bureaucratic gamesmanship. Such autonomy, many believed, laid the groundwork for officials countering authoritative political direction either overtly or covertly. Both ideological camps found especially worrying the perceived tendency for officials to garner sufficient resources through logrolling to secure and build institutional citadels.[3] These entities, critics of the time argued, became more bent on self-perpetuation and aggrandizement than on discerning and responding to the public interest or adapting institutionally so as to address current and impending societal goals. The entire rationale behind the mid-twentieth century view that a certain degree of political autonomy in public service was legitimate seemed to have evaporated in a matter of years. Beginning with Richard Nixon and proceeding to George W. Bush (with the possible exception of George Bush Sr.), successive presidents made bashing the bureaucracy a staple of their electoral pitches as candidates.

The darkest periods in this era of hostility toward the roles of bureaucracy have coincided with radical efforts to cut back the size of the federal government. Economic downturns, especially in the 1970s, provided some justification for efforts to roll back government. However, the Reagan administration, like the George W. Bush administration, pursued fiscal policies that generated ballooning deficits, which greatly constricted possibilities for programmatic adaptation and expansion in departments and agencies. Significantly, the Air Force and the other services did not have to contend with the age of stringency until the end of the cold war. At the outset of this period, the Air Force's institutional response was not entirely one of hunkering down in an attempt to preserve what it could of its citadel. Instead, it accepted that it would have to divest itself of programs in order to make investments toward addressing impending, but not widely perceived demands. It further recognized that it would have to formulate much better arguments for moving funds from programs with strong political support to those that were more valuable from the standpoint of national security.

The public administration literature increasingly advocates a return to similar inventiveness in coping with fiscal stringency and countering the constricted view of bureaucratic autonomy. This trend might partially owe to a shift in the former condition during Bill Clinton's second term, when deficits became ever-expanding surpluses. The focus for discourse over budget issues thus briefly changed from a politics of constraint to one of choice. However, the change in thinking among key students of public administration also acknowledges that efforts to constrict bureaucrats' autonomy have produced an undesirable side effect: namely, the stifling of initiative and creativity.

We noted in chapter 6 that economic conditions and skepticism about the public spiritedness of career bureaucrats have led to an emphasis on the standards of fiscal and responsive competence in efforts to resolve both policy and administrative issues. This reached the point by the 1980s that long-range strategic issues often received little or no weight in debates between players in the executive-bureaucratic complex. As a consequence, decision-makers now run the risk of routinely settling on suboptimal policies as they seek to identify and pursue solutions to many of the greatest challenges faced by the nation.

Students of public service organizations often register alarm about this trend. For instance, we dwelt at length in chapter 1 on Martha Derthick's exhaustive work on the Social Security Administration (SSA), which pointed up the potential effectiveness of agencies positioning themselves for opportunities.[4] Derthick revisited the SSA in the late 1980s. She found an agency that had lost its capacity to keep ahead of the curve regarding adaptation of policy and administration to shifting requirements.[5] The combination of fiscal stringency and the proliferation of specific mandates from political authorities had produced a dangerous gap between what is demanded of the agency and the resources it receives. According to Derthick, the inattention of policymakers to administration exacerbated this condition. Similarly, William T. Gormley Jr., in a 1989 book on approaches to guiding the bureaucracy, notes the deleterious effects of a "rash of bureaucracy-bashing reforms."[6] Gormley registers the fear that the nation has "shifted our expectations of the bureaucracy from problem solving to compliance."

Prescriptions for what to do about the overencumbering of bureaucracy range from resignation to exhortations for politicians to reconcile their differences more coherently and consistently before further burdening bureaucrats. In the former camp, Martha Feldman, in her book *Order without Design*, concedes matters to incremental approaches when she reckons that "positive social action can occur without being consciously coordinated or organized."[7] Joel D. Aberbach and Bert A. Rockman, on the other hand, cite politicians as culprits who must change their ways by loosening constraints on bureaucracy and specifying "realistic, noncontradictory goals for agencies."[8] Perhaps most significantly, a relative newcomer to the discussion—one whose recent book won two prestigious prizes—strongly repudiates the constrictive views of bureaucratic autonomy that emerged in the 1980s. The author, Daniel P. Carpenter, maintains that, historically, creative public service has emerged only when "agency leaders assembled coalitions . . . by building a socially grounded esteem for the activities of their organization," thereby acquiring political autonomy.[9] Carpenter calls for multiplicity in agencies' ties with others in the policy arena. This would allow them to broker interests rather than simply refracting them.

A body of thought is thus emerging around the view that political authorities must guide officials more coherently. By extension, they must also provide bureaucrats with the resources necessary to accomplish stated objectives. More fundamentally, political authorities must provide an atmosphere in which officials might function more autonomously. This would facilitate public servants' contributing creatively both to policymaking and administration.

An important question arises from such proposals. To what degree can we ascribe legitimacy to senior officials working more assertively within the boundaries of their latitude to operate with political autonomy? This book describes an instance in which military officers, most notably General Fogleman and General Ryan, decided to assume explicit responsibility for crafting the future of their service. Broadly speaking, however, scholars cannot simply praise such efforts in the hope that it will incite entrepreneurial leaders to act more courageously and organizations to work more coherently. We have to look closely at the feasibility of a return to greater political autonomy in U.S. public service.

A recent work by Donald F. Kettl underscores the necessity of this sort of reflection.[10] Kettl argues that even if we could return to the public service paradigm that prevailed in the golden era, the complexity of governance has far exceeded the capacities of the previous approaches. In the middle of the last century, officials based their leverage in structures and mandates, but stakeholders still began to construe the leverage of career officials in the policy arena as undemocratic. The potential for such guardedness has risen exponentially with the growth in the complexity of government. To Kettl, this stems from the fact that often, "the real task of administration is coordination—weaving together separate programs into a sensible policy."[11] Kettl sees coordinative processes as rivaling or even supplanting defined agency mandates as the loci for the allocation of societal values in various policy sectors.[12] Officials exert leverage less from expertise and strong links with client groups than from their acumen about how to get things done. While this might appear to support a return to the political autonomy of officials, Kettl warns that we have yet to devise a highly developed theory of how such roles for officials would fit within our constitutional framework.

This caveat notwithstanding, some scholars make considerable advances toward specifying the type of theoretical justifications that could connect the realities of current decisionmaking and administrative processes with efforts to revitalize permanent officials' contribution to governance. Carpenter asserts that during the latter part of the nineteenth century, when bureaucracy came of age in the United States, officials went beyond leverage gained through expertise. What counted most, Carpenter argues, was the official's credibility as an advocate for the public good.[13] Carpenter highlights the importance of the "moral politics" of the era in legitimizing advocacy of this sort on the part of officials.

Similarly, Mark H. Moore stresses the need for officials to develop a sense of themselves as independent moral actors.[14] Employing strikingly normative language, Moore asserts that officials are "duty bound to have and present ideas of public value" and "even have the right and responsibility to nominate new ideas for consideration as circumstances change."[15] The notion that senior public servants shoulder a responsibility to read the signs of the times and advocate on the basis of their interpretation of existing or impending circumstances certainly strikes a chord with the Air Force experience. Indeed, this observation comports with our presupposition that strategic competence is a special, although not necessarily exclusive, characteristic of a highly qualified and strongly dedicated senior public service. Eugene Bardach perhaps captures this characteristic best when he exhorts officials to develop craftmanship thinking, which he defines as creativity combined with public spiritedness.[16]

How do we move from such theoretical justifications to praxis? While we might encourage some agencies to emulate the approach employed by the Air Force since 1994, we cannot recommend that all agencies do so. Our concerns stem from the literature and the analysis of process context factors in earlier chapters. Martha Derthick, for instance, highlights that attempts to introduce innovations comprehensively throughout the public service tend to increase administrative risks.[17] Paul Light similarly cautions against comprehensive initiatives because they frequently collect praise seekers who have no real intention of going beyond lip service to an ideal. In Light's terms, the initiatives become hollow monuments.[18]

We thus argue for emulation largely through self-selection on the part of agencies. This should occur on the basis of a hard-nosed examination by an organization's leaders of their aptitude for an effort such as that pursued by the Air Force. Top political and career executives must decide whether such an exercise holds true potential for releasing and rechanneling inventiveness and creativity or whether it is likely to prove just another futile effort to herd cats. Broadly, recent literature provides increasingly robust guidance for such discernments. Light, for instance, stresses the importance of the degree of professionalization within an agency work force—a standard under which the Air Force would score very high indeed.[19] Carpenter connects the issue of professionalism to leverage in the effort to attain a substantial degree of political autonomy and suggests that leaders will probably encounter difficulties if they have not "acquired lasting esteem and durable links to social, political, and economic organizations . . . that rival or surpass those of politicians."[20]

Finally, Sandford Borins and Daniel P. Carpenter separately identify what we call the apex issue as highly relevant to the latitude that career officials might enjoy in pursuing relatively free advocacy for a new organizational vision and associated resource commitments.[21] If organizations have relatively few layers of political appointees between the department or agency head and the top permanent officials, then they seem more likely to engage in creative efforts to revamp themselves.

The rest of this chapter examines the Air Force's experience with respect to each of the leverage points discussed above. It spotlights lessons that are applicable to other government organizations considering an investment in strategic visioning comparable to that made by the Air Force. The leverage point approach helps us keep our focus on the key difficulties with connectivity between the various elements of preparing for the future. It also posits a dynamic whereby connectivity does not always have to occur with equal intensity through the elements of the process to achieve success. As discussed in the preceding section, personalities, institutional factors, and demonstration effects can invite modulation of emphases when opportunities and challenges present themselves at specific stages in the process.

Linking Policy Foresight and Strategic Intent

In launching a prolonged period of intense strategic visioning, the Air Force attempted two things. First, it tried to expand its strategic horizons beyond the previous time frame of planners—the ten years or so that it takes to modernize an existing system or platform. By so doing, it challenged the leadership to leap beyond projecting the status quo onto the medium-term future and to contemplate the types of opportunities and challenges that it would face in twenty-five or thirty years. Second, the Air Force subscribed to the view that planning should attain an effective voice. Rigorous backcasting would provide the link between the policy foresight emerging from visioning and commitments that fundamentally altered the Air Force's strategic intent.

Fogleman: Stretching Horizons

General Fogleman's grasp of what the Air Force might look like as far out as 2025 clearly exceeded the ken of most, if not all, his colleagues. Fogleman expressly eschewed a prophetic intervention, however. He believed that by bringing his colleagues through a process of realization similar to the one he had undergone, he could lure them into backcasting on their own.[22] This would allow them to grasp for themselves the gap between desired future capabilities and requirements and the trajectory of the status quo with only incremental changes in budget commitments and technology. Fogleman thus emphatically acknowledged the importance of connectivity between the achievement of policy foresight about the long-range future and transformation of an organization's formalized strategic intent.

Fogleman took several steps to strengthen the linkage between policy foresight and the Air Force's strategic intent. Most of these centered on preparation for the fall 1996 Corona meeting of the Air Force's four-star generals, who would delineate the core competencies that the service sought to achieve by 2025. Critically, he assigned his vice chief, Gen. Thomas Moorman, the task of coordinating issue development for the Corona meeting through a committee of three-star generals that included the vice commanders of each of the Air Force's major commands. Moorman, a non-pilot, had served much of his career working on programs operating from space. He thus embodied the heightened role that Fogleman anticipated for space.

Eugene Bardach writes cogently about the utility of committees such as the board of directors for facilitating policy development on the basis of consensus. He makes the point that such coordinative structures cannot be simply deployed in a formulaic way.[23] Nonetheless, his characterization of the roles of such machinery as "reconciling worldviews and professional ideologies" serves as an apt description of General Moorman's contribution. That is, Moorman functioned not just as a ringmaster, but also as a seminar director. He thus helped build a consensus that served as the foundation for strategic visioning.

The Fogleman round displays several mechanisms for linking policy foresight and commitments to strategic intent that are worth emulating. The first key element perhaps presents a tall order for the leaders of any organization. Fogleman brought to the job sufficient policy insight to occupy Air Force efforts at revising strategic intent well beyond the three years that he served as chief. He also enjoyed exceptional standing among his colleagues, and he considered himself unencumbered by a mandate from his four-star colleagues because his nomination had emerged when the consensus choice for chief of staff had failed to carry the day politically. Few leaders bring to the apex of organizations the combination of a strong focus on the opportunities and challenges presented in the long-range future, impeccable standing among other members of the leadership, and a decided sense of freedom in defining the central objectives of their term.

The fact that Fogleman did not take his situation for granted provides a sense of proportion about his exceptional attributes. Fogleman took great pains to engage the force of his personality selectively. Here, organizations can readily adapt elements of his approach to their own circumstances. Indeed, some of these factors carried over to the Ryan-Peters period, when force of personality played substantially less of a role. Fogleman built a bridge to the future when he assigned General Moorman the responsibility for preparing for the fall 1996 Corona conference. The leader who can partner creatively in this way reveals that he can both share the spotlight with others and subject his vision for the future to intense scrutiny from someone coming at policy foresight from a substantially different perspective.

Both Fogleman and Moorman paid keen attention to the need, first, to socialize the Air Force four- and three-star cadres in the area of long-range visioning and, second, to plant the seeds for diffuse ownership of radical changes in strategic intent through collective deliberation and tasking responsibility for issue preparation both vertically and horizontally throughout the Air Force. An organization that lacks a leader as interested in the long-range future and as dynamic as Fogleman could compensate by giving even stronger emphasis to building bridges between intraorganizational cultures, stimulating unconventional thinking about the future, and raising the potential for buy-in through dynamics that encourage wide participation both in visioning and reconfiguring strategic intent.

Despite Fogleman's pervasive influence during the first round, institutional and environmental factors played significant roles, as well. With respect to institutional factors, the Air Force's migration to a more explicit incorporation of space as a central component of its mission served up both challenges and opportunities. The main challenge lay in the fact that giving a higher profile to space would open the possibility of competition between two shooting commands, Air Combat Command and Air Force Space Command, albeit in the relatively distant future. Even so, a heightened profile for the Space Command presented opportunities, as well. Fogleman brought his colleagues to a realization that the Air Force had to use or lose its accumulated prerogatives toward operating and coordinating a very high proportion of space-based communications and surveillance applications for the entire U.S. military. Fogleman believed that pressures toward placing weapon systems on space-based platforms would inevitably compel the Air

Force to either embrace space as a locus of mainstream operations or yield it to a new service. The adaptations that he envisioned included a highly significant institutional component.

Thus, looking at the Air Force institutionally, the emergence of an increased role for space might have undermined the cohesiveness of the service as it attempted strategic visioning. This, in turn, could have weakened the case for adaptation advanced by the Air Force internally and externally. To the contrary, the need to grapple with a major challenge to the status quo forced the players to abandon the old lexicon for a new one that would have space and air dovetailing each other through each of the envisioned core competencies. We do not mean to imply that the players immediately began to shunt resources around in a manner that followed declared strategic intent. However, the contours for cogent argumentation had emerged, and these would frame discourse for years to come.

The emergence of such institutional issues and how the Air Force leadership addressed them might prove instructive to those attempting to engender strategic visioning in other organizations. Departments and agencies frequently face both internal and external pressures that threaten the business lines that hold the greatest sway institutionally. Given a choice, leaders within such organizations will tend to continue their pattern of pivoting from one dominant business line. For instance, budget department people usually do not like giving a high profile to those who concentrate on management policy, and officials focusing on health policy might wish that they operated out of a Department of Health rather than a Department of Health and Human Services. Narrowly construed departments, especially emergent ones, can also face daunting obstacles. For instance, the mandates of more narrowly specialized agencies can encounter perennial attacks from those who believe the organization functions as an advocate of narrow interests or a needless addition of bureaucratic veto points. The departments of Education and Energy frequently have faced such criticisms since created under President Jimmy Carter. Even those in an emergent business within an organization might find it prudent to stay within a wider institutional umbrella. This requires, however, that those in the previously dominant line significantly adjust their view of the umbrella organization's key missions.

Regarding environmental factors, one of the obvious elements was external pressure from those seeking either a separate space service or, at least, a significant shooting role for the Space Command within the framework of the Air Force. Another involved the Air Force's delicate task of inching the national security community toward a revised view of the service's capabilities for halting aggression from a hostile force. The concept of parallel warfare introduced the idea that air attacks might well cause an enemy to stop aggression before substantial engagement of U.S. ground forces.

Based on these factors, we conclude that leaders might find it easier to initiate strategic visioning in organizations facing environmental crossroads similar to those encountered by the Air Force in the 1990s than in organizations experiencing relative equilibrium. Had the Air Force scenario unfolded without the benefit of Fogleman's determination and foresight or his ability to partner and engage as he led his service through strategic visioning, then the environmental issues pressing in on the Air Force might have had to be much more severe to trigger a thoroughgoing process.

We recognize that such a proposition would not appeal to the likes of General Fogleman, as it suggests that only a crisis can bring about the concentration of minds required to carry off rigorous strategic visioning. However, the Air Force experience under Fogleman is evidence that both individuals and institutions can display the anticipatory qualities of policy entrepreneurship at critical turning points that have not risen to a crisis level. Savvy officials—and by extension, institutions—motivated to discern and pursue the long-term public interest will read the signs of the times much earlier than those outside an organization and devise ways of addressing mounting issues before they mushroom to crisis proportions.

Ryan and Peters: Searching for a Workable Connection between Foresight and Intent

With regard to the Ryan-Peters round, we have stressed that the chief and the secretary worked together more closely than had General Fogleman and Secretary Widnall. Neither General Ryan nor Secretary Peters held strong convictions about the need for visioning far into the future, but events began to push them irrevocably in that direction in 1998 (with Peters serving in an acting capacity at the time). First, the core competencies articulated by the 1996 vision statement, *Global Engagement,* had constituencies that did not shrink from reminding stakeholders of the investments necessary to bring critical elements of that document to fruition. The Air Force could not back away from the vision without prompting a backlash, especially in the space community. Second, the Air Force began to feel deeply the strains associated with its failing to substantially alter force structure while engaging in a never-ending succession of brushfires around the world. General Ryan's championing of an Expeditionary Aerospace Force captured the centrality of this challenge. The core questions operating behind this proposition stemmed from myriad unresolved issues connected with parallel warfare and the future feasibility of forward basing. Third, the nation was gearing up for the 2000 presidential election and a new administration, and the Air Force was also facing the 2001 Quadrennial Defense Review (QDR).

Ryan and Peters's decision to recommit to strategic visioning thus stemmed more from necessity than from a hunger for another round of attaining policy foresight. Nonetheless, their opting for a further iteration reflects two factors that might prevail in other organizations, especially if they have previously invested in strategic visioning. First, an intense period of strategic visioning—particularly one involving a high degree of collegial discernment and commitment—establishes institutional expectations and routines that take on lives of their own. Second, as the organization faces new opportunities and challenges, a significant number of key players will employ the prior strategic visioning exercise as a benchmark not just for deciding strategic intent, but also for revising it.

How then did the institutional issues unfold in the second round? From the outset, players in the Ryan-Peters round recognized that they had to rework *Global Engagement*, but they struggled with how extensively to revise it. The wind-up continued through 1998. Discussions centered on the obvious lack of connectivity between the 1996 vision and the Air Force's actual trajectory with regard to programmatic commitments. A Herculean effort focused on developing Thrust Area Transformation Plans in an attempt to bring a dynamic principle to the pursuit of what many viewed as static core competencies. Ryan and Peters had assigned to the board of directors the task of steering the thrust area process. However, the board of directors had become too large and eclectic to function as a Moorman-style forum for developing consensus among the major commands. Furthermore, its staff support and some of its members believed that it should have played a more significant role in linking strategic intent and programmatic commitments, though it lacked a mandate to do so.

In November 1998, the tensions led to an aborted board of directors meeting and the abandonment of the Thrust Area Transformation Plans. Faced with this impasse, Ryan and Peters took a still more dramatic step. They decided to vest the Corona council with the task of revising the 1996 vision. The board of directors would confine its deliberations to preparation for a fall 1999 Corona conference that would lay the groundwork for the 2001 Quadrennial Defense Review. In this respect, the action-forcing dimension of the QDR—the necessity for the Air Force to formulate a cogent argument—overrode concerns about the connectivity of the vision and pro-gramming.

Significantly, Ryan and Peters continued to take different views of strate-gic visioning even as it was associated with preparation for the QDR. Ryan was beginning to step up to long-range issues that he knew would emerge through the process; Peters believed that an exercise yielding cogent argu-ments for negotiations on the Program Objective Memorandum (POM) for 2002 would provide a potent demonstration of the need for a reallocation of resources in the buildup to the QDR. In any case, the two men took exceptional pains to collaborate, working together in long sessions in the secretary's office.

We call this an apex relationship. Peters and Ryan each stood at the apex of their cadres—respectively, the top political appointee assigned to the Department of the Air Force and the senior career Air Force officer operat-ing in the Pentagon. Because they were both committed to collaboration, the usually highly divergent approaches of the political appointee and the career official converged in a manner not common in U.S. agencies. Their efforts to work cooperatively gave focus to the connections between the two cul-tures beyond the individual contacts and deals made deep into the department's organizational chart. Ryan's position proved critical here because his standing as the commander of the entire Air Force gave his interventions on behalf of the service great legitimacy. Peters also chose, even while serving as secretary in an acting capacity, to involve himself critically in the management of the Air Force as a service and not simply as a depart-ment. Peters's and Ryan's independent decisions to leverage the legitimacy with which their apex positions imbued them proved decisive for the second round of strategic planning.

This type of arrangement finds many parallels in executive-bureaucratic arenas that, unlike those usually found in the United States, channel rela-tions between the political leadership and career officials hierarchically. In the United Kingdom, for instance, the top political appointee of a depart-ment relates to the person standing at the pinnacle of the public service career in a fashion similar to that found in the U.S. Department of the Air Force. In the U.S. federal government, however, large departments over-whelmingly feature a structure in which the top career officials report to political appointees who are not at the top level of the hierarchy, but rather work several levels below the secretary. This undermines the effectiveness of career officials, since their advice does not always reach the highest lev-els of the hierarchy. To be sure, even appointees and officials operating within the much more disciplined political and bureaucratic cadres of relatively hierarchical systems such as Great Britain's learn how to circumvent the normal chain of command. In the United Kingdom, however, principals of the two cadres can bring a great deal of coherence to any policy process once they decide to work collaboratively. Precisely this dynamic asserted itself in the Ryan-Peters relationship. Its operation meant that the second round addressed opportunities and challenges relatively cogently. That is, the process yielded results with respect to both altering the 1996 vision document and aligning the strategic visioning exercise more closely with program resourcing.

In citing the apex quality of the Ryan-Peters round and probing its significance, we can hardly argue that U.S. departments and agencies be reconfigured so that political appointees and career officials working most closely together embody the pinnacles of their respective cadres. Notwithstanding the immense appeal of arguments for removing the layers of political appointees in departments and agencies, we have to accept that the modal relationships will remain ones in which the top career positions begin relatively far down in hierarchies.[24] Thus, several career officials with the same rank in the public service compete for the attention of individual political appointees who themselves occupy positions four or five levels down in departmental or agency hierarchies (that is, assistant secretaries and deputy assistant secretaries).

We asked Patrick Wolf, who examined 170 studies of innovative efforts in federal agencies spanning 1890 to the mid-1990s, if he could identify apex agencies among his cases.[25] He identified twenty-four studies of reform within apex agencies. These included organizations such as the Forest Service, the Census Bureau, Centers for Disease Control, the Federal Bureau of Investigation, and the Bureau of the Budget (now the Office of Management and Budget), although many agencies on his list have since migrated partially or entirely out of the apex category as a result of the relentless accretion of political appointees in organization hierarchies. Wolf observed that apex agencies seem to share an important characteristic: they tend to focus on specialized and relatively technical activities that might prompt political principals to interact with a single go-between who can interpret the agency's activities and needs in a coherent way.[26]

The Air Force clearly manifests such characteristics. As for nonapex agencies, substantial benefits might accrue if political appointees at the top of departmental and agency hierarchies encouraged their colleagues lower down to assume more open stances toward the leading career officials reporting to them and thereby foster a capacity to partner in substantial efforts to bring about institutional transformation. The top political appointees could mandate subordinate appointees to expand their horizons beyond the exigencies of the immediate partisan agenda to encompass canvassing future opportunities and challenges. In other words, the benefits stemming from the sort of synergetic dynamic that Secretary Peters and General Ryan struck need not be confined to apex relationships.

With regard to the institutional factors that were important in the Ryan-Peters round, we note again that the board of directors did not function very effectively. This owed in part to the size of the board and its inclusive membership, as well as to the issues it addressed or, perhaps more accurately, chose not to consider. The specter of major resource consequences affected the board of directors much more strongly during the Ryan-Peters round than in Fogleman's process. Major command board members now realized how much their commands would have to sacrifice to put the service on track toward the future. Furthermore, it had become clear by 1998 that the board of directors did not hold sway in the programming arena. That field continued to be dominated by the Air Staff, under the aegis of the vice chief and the Air Force Council consisting of the Pentagon-based three-star generals.

The shortcomings of the board of directors led the Air Staff to assume much of the critical responsibility of preparing for the fall 1999 Corona conference. From 1997, planning and programming both operated under two-star generals reporting to the same three-star deputy chief of staff, in the Strategic Planning Directorate. The demise of the Thrust Area Transformation Plans provoked the Strategic Planning Directorate to devise an approach to linking strategic intent with programmatic commitments that ultimately led to the delineation of fork-in-the-road decisions. The more realistic aspirations associated with this approach prompted the division to concentrate on critical capabilities that the Air Force sought to obtain within twenty years. This tack allowed it to present cogent arguments at the Corona conference about the staging of resource commitments necessary to achieve its vision within the desired time frame.

Two institutional lessons present themselves through the experience with the board of directors and the Strategic Planning Directorate. The first of these concerns the contrast between enshrining a strategic vision and actually realigning resources to implement the requisite programming. Organizations can devolve such activity to their constituent elements. That is, the central management might assign various business units general targets and a finite bucket of resources with which to achieve these goals. This system thus would allow the units a high degree of discretion over how they fulfill their contribution to the organization's mission, so long as they stay within their fiscal ceiling. Such an approach would have proven difficult for the Air Force during the period in which the Ryan-Peters round unfolded. This owed largely to the unresolved issues concerning the future roles of the Air Combat and Space commands and the mounting unfunded requirements associated not only with modernizing Air Mobility, but also with transforming its capabilities to reflect the concept of an Expeditionary Aerospace Force.

Organizations similarly lacking clarity in arraying priorities and allotting responsibility for them to constituent units find two avenues for resolving conflicts over resourcing. They can make the decisions centrally and give highly specific guidance to the business units, or they can employ a deliberative process that allows the internal stakeholders to grasp collectively the importance of the reallocation of resources in order to begin servicing long-term goals. The experience of the Air Force during the Ryan-Peters round suggests the difficulty of pursuing either course if major unresolved issues remain concerning an organization's vision. Such organizations likely will have to return to the principals for further reconciliation of issues. This suggests that successive rounds play important roles not because the organization is bereft of a vision, but because it will have to revisit unresolved issues that continue to be nettlesome. In other words, additional rounds, while revealing that key matters have eluded settlement, confirm the organization's continued commitment to visioning.

The second institutional lesson emanates from our observations about the role of the Strategic Planning Directorate. This Staff operation worked effectively at closing the gap between what the Corona council required for its fall 1999 meeting to be successful and the rather meager performance of the board of directors in preparing issues for the four-star generals. However, it frequently antagonized the major commands along the way. We noted in chapter 6 that Staff operations generally can function similarly well in one-time circumstances, but they usually cannot compensate consistently for the underperformance of collective bodies with formalized roles. This pertains especially if the latter exist to legitimize a consultative process by involving business units as well as the headquarters leadership in developing issues. Only truly organic processes that effectively identify the agenda and available options for the principals will hold any hope of reliably functioning with sufficient authority to contribute to the reconciliation of differences.

Finally, changes in the policy environment were a significant factor in the Ryan-Peters round, along with the leadership issues associated with the chief's and secretary's styles and the institutional issues emanating from the spotty performance of the board of directors and the vigorous efforts of the Strategic Planning Directorate. First, the Clinton administration pursued an effort to halt Serbian aggression in Kosovo that relied largely on airpower and achieved considerable success. The episode drove home General Link's arguments about the future role of airpower in halting aggression to an extent that even made some members of the Air Force leadership nervous. They believed that the episode might give the nation a false sense of confidence and deepen further the other services' resentments.

Second, concerns about the eventual emergence of a peer competitor (putatively, China) with the capacity for proscribing forward basing and air and naval operations within an extended exclusionary zone began to gain much wider currency in the public forum. This issue and its associated challenges had already emerged and received considerable assessment in the Air Force's futures games in 1998. In fall 1999, such fears motivated warnings from the Bush campaign that the United States faced potential challenges that called for truly transformational approaches to future programs. These would require that the United States not use cold war programs as stepping-stones to the future, but rather leapfrog beyond the technology preordained by incremental adaptation. Taken together, apparent success in Kosovo and transformational rhetoric emboldened the Air Force to think big about its future.

As described in chapter 8, the investment in the 1998 and 1999 futures games and the attention accorded their results by General Ryan brought two important facts to the fore. First, the potential for an opponent to deploy anti-access capabilities to the point of imposing extended exclusionary zones posed very serious challenges to the Air Force's future capacity to pursue combat with forward-based short-range aircraft. Second, only with deep intelligence, surveillance, and reconnaissance, most notably from space-based radar, could the Air Force halt aggression without very substantial losses of personnel and equipment. The Kosovo experience was saying, "General Link was right; the Air Force rules." The findings from the futures games, however, said, "Maybe none of the services will prevail if a peer competitor gains advanced anti-access capabilities." The Strategic Planning Directorate worked assiduously in the buildup to the fall 1999 Corona conference to bring these results to bear on efforts to revise the 1996 vision document.

The futures games thus provide an insight with substantial potential for application to other organizations. The distant future is a moving target. Deciding strategic intent in the present should not lead to the enshrinement of that intent to the degree that an organization ignores counterindications when previously inconceivable scenarios present themselves. That is, it should continue to strenuously pursue policy foresight. Gaming provides a first step toward this objective. As chapter 8 demonstrates, however, it requires considerable resources and the support of the senior leadership both at headquarters and within the organization's business units.

Linking Strategic Visioning with Policy and Expenditure Planning and Human Resources and Organizational Planning

The preceding section probed the need for connectivity between attaining policy foresight and deciding strategic intent. Three components must similarly be linked in any effort to move the strategic visioning process to the level of strategic planning and policy management. That is, connections have to develop between strategic visioning, medium-term policy and expenditure planning, and strategic human resources and organizational planning. The first element, of course, will become a dead letter unless it begins to translate significantly into new or substantially altered program commitments and resource allocations. With time, it must also become embodied substantially in human resource commitments and organizational frameworks. We now briefly examine the evidence of follow-through along these two lines.

Chapter 6 examined extensively the connections between the strategic visioning exercises and medium-term policy and expenditure planning. It identified substantial adaptations on two levels. First, the visioning rounds appreciably stretched the Air Force leadership's view of planning away from mapping the present into the future. Immediately after the first round, this shift of emphasis took the shape of a naive quest to reorient the Air Force toward preparation for requirements in the distant future. Between this phase and the decision to pursue a second round, planners had adopted a more practical mixed-scanning approach that led in time to the identification of fork-in-the-road issues. This meant marshalling and pressing cogent argumentation in support of specific resource decisions that would prove crucial to putting the Air Force on track toward achieving its most important desired capabilities. At a fork in the road, the Air Force would forfeit opportunities if it did not commit sufficient resources to pursue a critical capability.

Second, the relationship between planners and programmers tightened dramatically. Skeptics will undoubtedly point out that that does not necessarily mean much, given the previous state of affairs. Since the Fogleman round, however, programmers found themselves contending with plans and thus with planners through numerous protocols that intruded on business as usual. These included the 1996 and 1999 Corona conferences and the preparatory work done for them by the board of directors, as well as the 1997 Long-Range Plan, the 1997 and 2001 Quadrennial Defense Reviews, the Annual Planning and Programming Guidance, and each year's Air Force Planning Projection.

Efforts to improve the connectivity between planning and programming included placing the two disciplines under one deputy chief of staff, as well as corporate management initiatives such as the Air Force headquarters 2002 initiative and the Air Force Resource Allocation Process (AFRAP). The Air Force also began to address the most serious source of disjunction between the two disciplines—namely, the lack of a mechanism for allocating resources according to how they will advance strategic corporate commitments and integrating the priorities of the Air Staff and the major commands. However, some new approaches offer the prospect of substantial progress even with regard to these problems. Since 2001, major command commanders have briefed their medium-term program objectives directly to the Air Force Council, with the secretary and the chief present. Moreover, the Staff now extends greater discretion to the major commands in determining how they will meet requirements.

What can we glean from the Air Force's experience that might instruct other government organizations about linking strategic visioning and resourcing? The process whereby a government organization's corporate plans and priorities affect the allocation of resources remains a largely unknown field of inquiry. That is, usually only insiders and a few keen, well-placed observers can hazard observations about how, if at all, strategic commitments translate into programmatic resources in complex bureaucratic organizations. Nonetheless, some generic points might prove applicable elsewhere in the public service.

First, with respect to leadership, the apex nature of the relationship between Secretary Peters and General Ryan seems to have played a role. While still serving as undersecretary, Secretary Peters involved himself both in the board of directors, which oversaw planning activities, and the council, which controlled the programming process. He did not want to relinquish this involvement when he took over as acting secretary, but rather maintained a strong interest in the activities of both bodies.

During his tenure as secretary, Peters displayed a preference for working collaboratively with General Ryan on key exercises. The practice whereby the major command commanders briefed their program objectives before the secretary and the chief built on this emphasis on teamwork between the two officials. It emerged partly because of the apex factor and partly because of the way the secretary's management approach dovetailed with the chief's relatively flexible manner. The two men also turned their different perspectives on the relationship between planning and budgeting into a virtue. Ryan responded increasingly to institutional pressure for heightened involvement in planning, while Peters primarily sought backing for his struggles for resources. However, both men were sufficiently pragmatic to exploit potential synergies.

In addition to the leadership factors that furthered efforts to link strategic visioning and medium-term policy and expenditure planning, some institutional developments worked effects, as well. It became increasingly clear to the Air Force leaders that many tensions stemmed from the division of authority. Whereas the Staff controlled the final imprimatur on corporate manifestations of planning and programming, the major commands actually dominated the generation of resource requests. Critically, their bids often bore the backing of powerful external stakeholders, thereby crosspressuring the Staff politically.

The establishment of direct briefing of program objectives to the secretary and the chief responded to deepening concerns about this division and its attendant pressures. As Maj. Gen. Daniel Hogan—the officer responsible for the AFRAP project—noted in his interview with us, the fact that major corporations used similar powwows to hash out key resource issues helped convince players that the Air Force might profitably adopt a similar approach. In addition, major commands spontaneously began to integrate their efforts. They now have gone through several years of interacting in the major planning exercises and efforts to bring the results of these to bear on programming. Their bureaucratic structures for planning and programming mirror those in the Pentagon. It became second nature for major commands to increasingly coordinate with one another before putting forward submissions to the Air Staff.

Such developments seem to point to the importance of allowing institutions to adapt gradually to the circumstances introduced by an intense period of strategic visioning. It takes time for the leadership, in both head-quarters and the operational divisions, to diagnose how best to realign structures to accommodate the fruits of more substantial investments in preparation throughout the organization for the long-range future. Along the way, participants will learn that neither headquarters nor particular business centers control the franchise when it comes to reconciling strategic visions and programmatic commitments. Just as the development of strategic intent requires collective support, so does the crafting of programmatic commitments that will further its fulfillment.

Environmental factors have quickened the Air Force's migration toward a better integration of planning and programming. Exuberance associated with the expectation that a Republican administration would substantially increase resources for the Pentagon, together with the hope that the Air Force would press its case for a disproportionate share of the additional funds, lulled the service into complacency at the time of the 1999 Corona conference. The relatively meager offerings at the outset of the Bush admin-istration seemed, on the other hand, to warrant considerable disillusionment. In the aftermath of September 11, however, the Air Force received fairly strong signals that it stood to gain the most from so-called transformational investments, although the administration failed to pursue this avenue as aggressively as expected. The Air Force did benefit not just from the demonstration effect of the programs it deployed in Afghanistan, but also from a higher degree of coherence in its argumentation. The degree to which players have made the connection between the latter and the importance of institutional efforts to integrate planning and programming remains to be seen. However, a strong sense has developed among the lead-ership that the investment in planning has paid off.

The ups and downs and ins and outs of environmental factors seem to reflect our argument that much of the task of connecting visioning and resourcing involves deft positioning for opportunities. Organizations must learn two things as they try to bring the fruits of forward planning to bear on the development of programs and the allocation of funds to implement them. First, only rarely will external conditions sustain a comprehensive effort. Organizations must therefore invest substantially in the process of winnowing their wish lists so as to identify issues whose resolution are most likely to further their most important long-term objectives. Second, even after completing this task, organizations must give a great deal of attention to timing. Kingdon's surfer metaphor helps here. It really does not matter to the weather and the tides that the surfer has decided to spend his Sunday morning riding waves at the beach. Similarly, the policy arena bloodlessly serves up auspicious or inauspicious circumstances for an organization's intention to assign greater resources to a particular business line. To be sure, the organization can, by advancing the topicality of issues, stimulate the policy agenda in a way that the surfer cannot influence the weather and the tides. It cannot, however, turn relatively calm waves into thundering surf.

It takes a different type of discipline for a public service entity to bring its strategic vision to bear on its human resources commitments and organizational planning. This applies even when the department or agency attempts the big-bang approach by undertaking a radical reconfiguration of personnel and units. The skill sets and cultural approaches required to make such a restructuring work might prove as elusive as they had under the previous dispensation.

Rather than making dramatic moves, the Air Force took cautious significant steps in the human resources and organizational realms. Lodging planning and programming under the same deputy chief of staff prompted major commands to follow suit by similarly brigading planning and programming. The heightened institutional profile for and support of planning allowed key veterans of the board of directors and the Corona deliberations over the 1996 vision to continue to pursue their agendas. As discussed in chapter 8, the Space Command focused its planning and programming investments on probing the parameters of Fogleman's view that many functions performed in air would ultimately migrate to space. Other commands used more integrative approaches to planning and programming to bring their issues to the fore. For instance, the Materiel Command astutely leveraged the Expeditionary Aerospace Force (EAF) concept to dig deep roots for the agile combat support core competency enshrined in the vision document. Air Mobility persistently and successfully pressed the view that fulfilling the EAF approach would require a great deal more investment in transports and tankers than anticipated by those mesmerized by the tug of war between the Air Combat and Space commands.

The Space Command received a higher profile in the Staff through the assignment of an undersecretary-level political appointee to oversee the sector. In addition, a number of previously top-secret space activities—including many that the highly secretive National Reconnaissance Office performs—came into public view for the first time. The Air Force began requiring newly minted officers to undergo intensive training in aerospace concepts. This innovation sought to break down the cultural divide between the space community and other segments of the service. A newly constituted unit within the Air Combat Command called C4ISR (that is, command, control, communications, computers, intelligence, surveillance, and reconnaissance) for the first time coordinated activities at the crossroads between air and space operations and support. The Air Force plays a substantial ringmaster role in the C4ISR field not only for itself, but for other services, as well. The new unit thus sought to become a center of advocacy both for internal integration and for the Air Force's responsibilities in the "purple" realm of interservice coordination.

These various attempts to accommodate space more fully through human resources policy and organizational structures failed to placate those who considered the Air Force lethargic in its response to the opportunities and challenges in the sector. Some believed that General Ryan did not help matters. To some, he seemed to have toned down General Fogleman's rhetoric so that it would pose less of an internal threat to those with a vested interest in keeping air combat as the core business of the Air Force. He sometimes challenged the entire concept emerging from the 1996 vision whereby the Air Force would consider those working through space-based mediums operators rather than simply support.

Congress finally intervened, under the leadership of then New Hampshire Senator Bob Smith, by inserting a provision in the Fiscal Year 2000 Defense Authorization Act mandating a Commission to Assess United States National Security Space Management and Operations. This brought to the fore many of the issues that the Air Force had put on the back burner in the post-Fogleman period. The fact that the current defense secretary, Donald Rumsfeld, had chaired the commission until just before it filed its report meant that its findings would receive close attention in the Office of the Secretary of Defense. This wrinkle could obscure the fact that General Fogleman and his vice chief, General Moorman, both served on the commission, which distinguished itself for the length and intensity of its deliberations. That the commission could engage reformist members of the Air Force elite speaks volumes about a cultural transformation that more traditional members of the air combat community might have missed. The commission made clear its belief that space had to draw on a strong segmental culture in order to rise to future challenges and opportunities. The report remained agnostic about whether this culture would operate as a unit within the Air Force or as a separate service. However, it laid a clear "use it or lose it" gauntlet at the feet of those thinking they could finesse the issue by giving lip service to reciprocal concepts like aerospace integration while continuing to view space as support for air combat.

Reformers in other organizations might extract from the Air Force experience the lesson that they can expect ebbs and flows in the degree to which an organization's leadership will reflect cultural trends within departments and agencies. Fogleman and Moorman emerged, respectively, from the air combat and space communities, and they forged a potent alliance in the proselytization of the service toward a more expansive view of the future role of space. The Ryan-Peters regime ran much more on a partnership between the chief and the secretary than one between the chief and successive vice chiefs. In addition, the emergent space culture could no longer claim a four-star champion who could convey and address their concerns with the opportunities and challenges of future space operations. An organization that makes a grand gesture to build bridges between a dominant and emergent business line should be careful to devise convincing alternate approaches when changes in the personalities at the top put an end to the accommodative arrangement.

Both Ryan and Peters became absorbed with the disjunction between the bold horizons of the 1996 vision and the day-to-day stresses of maintaining the tempo of operations and managing internal and external competition for resources. Thus the Air Force lost time in instituting the types of human resources and organizational changes that would convince outsiders that it took seriously the cultural and institutional obstacles to forging even a relatively conventional integrationist view of the future role of space. Departments and agencies would profit from setting a schedule for human resources and organizational moves aimed at achieving gradual progress, so that long-term adaptations in culture and structures will remain on track independent of changes in leadership. Otherwise, both internal and external stakeholders might conclude that the organization had not taken its strategic vision seriously.

The role of the overseer stands as a reminder to those in departments and agencies preparing for the future to pay close attention to shifts in the policy environment. Such shifts can give renewed impetus to the culture developing around a challenger to the dominant business line within an organization. Much of the Air Force leadership backslid into complacency, thinking it could finesse the space community by repositioning it within the integrative framework of aerospace. However, overseers intervened at a timely point by mandating a congressional commission to analyze the future of military space.

Linking Strategic Planning and Policy Management to Implementation

This leverage point often proves the most difficult to navigate in the process of preparing for the future. The Air Force accomplished a relatively high degree of linkage in this area. Successes range from the formidable and visible achievements associated with unmanned aerial vehicles (UAVs) to the gradual progress toward development of space-based radar. Chapter 7 examined the case of UAVs in detail. It identified factors such as General Fogleman's attraction to the technology; the keen interest of the Department of Defense's top leadership; the listing of UAVs under the core competency "Information Superiority" in the 1996 vision document; the Air Combat Command's acceptance of the potential of UAVs, notwithstanding the obvious threats to its pilot-dominated culture; spiral development featuring rapid prototyping and user feedback; and availability for iteratively more difficult combat use. As a whole, these factors go far in explaining how UAVs ascended so rapidly as a favored technology. At the core of the process, however, we find the combined working of two factors: the Air Force's adapting an important segment of strategic intent in response to perceived opportunities and challenges and a receptive policy environment crucial to the achievement of success.

From the standpoint of organizations seeking to emulate such a process, we return again to the importance of departments and agencies positioning themselves for opportunities. Our list of key leverage points in the process of preparing for the future simply identifies some of the crucial areas in which an organization would hope to achieve a high degree of connectivity. Actually linking up the elements of the process, however, relies very much on the ebb and flow of events. A key prescription that emerges from this treatment, therefore, is that implementation requires concentration. Players must map the crucial steps from strategic intent to implementation. They must provide for feedback so that the policy foresight behind the intent shifts the sights as the target moves. Above all, they have to continually position for opportunities. Only this way can they make a move when bottlenecks clear at the various leverage points.

Over to Policy Entrepreneurship

An old Irish expression often deployed when a stranger asks for directions goes something like this: "I can tell you how to get there, but if I were you I wouldn't start from here." That strikes us as a polite way of saying, "You haven't positioned yourself correctly to readily get where you want to go." The tortuous path from policy foresight to implementation requires attentiveness at all leverage points to optimal positioning in anticipation of opportunities and challenges. This chapter found a highly instructive resonance from the mounting literature pointing to the legitimacy of career officials negotiating such pathways entrepreneurially. It distilled from the Air Force experience insights about smart practices for organizations setting out on a similarly ambitious transformational itinerary.

The literature calls for more effective leveraging of public spiritedness among career officials. The Air Force experience provides an abundance of insights into the possible parameters for a revitalization of permanent public servants' contributions to governance. We hope that the book will prompt political appointees and career officials in other government organizations to plot collaboratively and to adroitly follow similar paths. Otherwise, both cadres will most certainly continue to pursue the achievement of evolutionary success from the wrong places. That is, they will find themselves regularly positioned in pathways that will require heroic efforts to compensate for poor foresight and insufficient dexterity at critical decisional turning points. Notwithstanding the constraints that should exist in officials' exercise of political autonomy, the Air Force case illustrates how the nation can greatly benefit from a much more concerted and robust engagement of permanent public servants in policy entrepreneurship.

Notes

Chapter 1

1. For an analysis of the various dimensions of a technological capability, see Dorothy Leonard-Barton, *Wellsprings of Knowledge: Building and Sustaining the Sources of Innovation* (Harvard Business School Press, 1995).

2. For a discussion of this core technological capability by a popular writer, see Tom Clancy, *Fighter Wing: A Guided Tour of an Air Force Combat Wing* (New York: Berkeley Books, 1995).

3. Nancy Roberts and Pamela King, *Transforming Public Policy* (San Francisco: Jossey-Bass, 1996).

4. David Osborne and Ted Gaebler, *Reinventing Government: How the Entrepreneurial Spirit Is Transforming the Public Sector* (Reading, Mass.: Addison-Wesley, 1992). The book falls within the tradition of works on innovation in the private sector, most obviously Thomas J. Peters and Robert H. Waterman, *In Search of Excellence* (New York: Warner, 1982).

5. Al Gore, *Creating a Government That Works Better and Costs Less* (New York: Plume, 1993); and Donald Kettl, *Reinventing Government? Appraising the National Performance Review* (Brookings, 1994).

6. Joel D. Aberbach and Bert A. Rockman, *In the Web of Politics: Three Decades of the U.S. Federal Executive* (Brookings, 2000), pp. 156–60.

7. John W. Kingdon, *Agendas, Alternatives, and Public Policies*, 2d ed. (HarperCollins, 1995), p. 122.

8. Except as otherwise noted, quotations from Air Force personnel are based on interviews we conducted for this project from 1998 to 2001. See methodological appendix for details.

9. Theda Skocpol, *Social Policy in the United States: Future Possibilities in Historical Perspective* (Princeton University Press, 1995), p. 303.

10. Martha Derthick, *Policymaking for Social Security* (Brookings, 1979), p. 22.

11. See, for instance, Laurence E. Lynn Jr. and David deF. Whitman, *The President as Policymaker: Jimmy Carter and Welfare Reform* (Temple University Press, 1981), pp. 48–49. The authors ascribe excessive specificity to the Department of Health, Education and Welfare team's contribution to Jimmy Carter's attempt to reform welfare.

12. In this regard, it is interesting that Skocpol gives virtually no play to the role of career officials in the Department of Health and Human Services in the development of President Bill Clinton's Health Care reform effort. See Theda Skocpol, *Boomerang: Clinton's Health Security Effort and the Turn against Government in U.S. Politics* (New York: Norton, 1996).

13. Colin Campbell, *Governments under Stress: Political Executives and Key Bureaucrats in Washington, London and Ottawa* (University of Toronto Press, 1983), pp. 9–10; and Bert A. Rockman, *The Leadership Question: The Presidency and the American System* (New York: Praeger, 1984), p. 85.

14. Kingdon, p. 181.

15. Skocpol, p. 163.

16. Henry Mintzberg, *The Rise and Fall of Strategic Planning* (Prentice-Hall, 1994).

17. Hugh Heclo, *A Government of Strangers* (Brookings, 1977).

18. Aberbach and Rockman, pp. 117–18, 170.

19. Ibid., p. 17.

20. Ibid., p. 20.

21. On polyarchy, see Robert A. Dahl, *Polyarchy: Participation and Opposition* (Yale University Press, 1971). On incremental change, see Charles E. Lindblom, *The Intelligence of Democracy: Decision Making through Mutual Adjustment* (New York: Free Press, 1965).

22. Mancur Olson, *The Rise and Decline of Nations: Economic Growth, Stagflation and Social Rigidities* (Yale University Press, 1982).

23. Colin Campbell, *The U.S. Presidency in Crisis: A Comparative Perspective* (Oxford University Press, 1998), pp. 39–41, with a special debt to James MacGregor Burns, *The Deadlock of Democracy: Four-Party Politics in America* (New York: Free Press, 1963).

24. See, for instance, Mark H. Moore, *Creating Public Value: Strategic Management in Government* (Harvard University Press, 1995).

25. This was a conclusion of the X-Team that reviewed long-range planning processes and products in May 1997; the team included a noted management consultant (Mr. Allan Kennedy) with long experience working with major private sector enterprises in the United States and overseas.

26. Eugene Bardach, *Getting Agencies to Work Together: The Practice and Theory of Managerial Craftsmanship* (Brookings, 1998).

27. R. Kent Weaver and Bert A. Rockman, eds., *Do Institutions Matter? Government Capabilities in the United States and Abroad* (Brookings, 1993), p. 452. See also Allen Schick, "Governments versus Budget Deficits," in Weaver and Rockman, eds., *Do Institutions Matter?* p. 228.

28. Martha S. Feldman, *Order without Design: Information Production and Policy Making* (Stanford University Press, 1989), p. 94.

29. Kingdon, pp. 16–18.

30. Colin Campbell and George J. Szablowski, *The Superbureaucrats: Structure and Behaviour in Central Agencies* (Toronto: Macmillan, 1979), pp. 65–66; Colin Campbell and Graham K. Wilson, *The End of Whitehall: Death of a Paradigm?* (Oxford: Blackwell, 1995), p. 199; and Colin Campbell and John Halligan, *Political Leadership in an Age of Constraint: Bureaucratic Politics under Hawke and Keating* (Sydney: Allen & Unwin, 1992), p. 38.

31. Campbell and Wilson, *The End of Whitehall,* pp. 126–29; Campbell and Halligan, *Political Leadership in an Age of Constraint,* pp. 158–59; Peter Aucoin, *The New Public Management: Canada in Comparative Perspective* (Montreal: Institute for Research on Public Policy, 1995), pp. 129, 186; and Jonathan Boston and Jane Pallot, "Linking Strategy and Performance: Developments in the New Zealand Public Sector," *Journal of Policy Analysis and Management,* vol. 16 (Summer 1997), p. 392.

32. Paul Light, *Tides of Reform: Making Government Work, 1945–1995* (Yale University Press, 1997), p. 19.

33. Michael Barzelay, *The New Public Management: Improving Research and Policy Dialogue* (University of California Press, 2001).

34. Peter Aucoin, "Administrative Reform in Public Management: Paradigms, Principles, Paradoxes and Pendulums," *Governance,* vol. 3 (April 1990), pp. 125–26.

35. United States General Accounting Office (GAO), "Performance Budgeting: Past Initiatives Offer Insights for GPRA," report prepared for Congressional Committees (March 1997), p. 3.

36. Ibid., pp. 5, 7.

37. Aaron Wildavsky, "Rescuing Policy Analysis from PPBS," *Public Administration Review,* vol. 29 (March/April 1969), pp. 190–92.

38. Sandford Borins, *Innovation with Integrity: How Local Heroes Are Transforming American Government* (Georgetown University Press, 1998), p. 38. He borrows the term *skunkworks* from Peters and Waterman.

39. Ibid., p. 52.

40. Borins borrows the concept of groping from Robert Behn, "Managing by Groping Along," *Journal of Policy Analysis and Management,* vol. 7 (Fall 1988), pp. 643–63.

41. Borins, *Innovation with Integrity,* pp. 57, 64. In making his point about organizations requiring large capital investments, Borins cites Olivia Golden, "Innovation in Public Sector Human Service Programs: The Implications of Innovation by 'Groping Along,'" *Journal of Policy Analysis and Management,* vol. 9 (Spring 1990), pp. 219–48.

42. Federal Benchmarking Consortium (FBC), "Serving the American Public: Best Practices in Customer-Driven Strategic Planning," Study Report (February 1997), p. 175.

43. Ibid., pp. 169–71.

44. Ibid., p. 165.

45. Ibid., p. 175.

46. Borins, *Innovation with Integrity,* p. 49.

47. Ibid., p. 47.

48. FBC, "Serving the American Public," p. 164.

49. Campbell and Wilson, *The End of Whitehall,* p. 126.

50. FBC, "Serving the American Public," p. 167.

51. Ibid., p. 164.

52. Borins, *Innovation with Integrity,* pp. 97–102.

53. Ibid., p. 102.

54. FBC, "Serving the American Public," pp. 160, 166.

55. GAO, "Performance Budgeting: Past Initiatives Offer Insights for GPRA," p. 11.

56. Patrick J. Wolf, "Why Must We Reinvent the Federal Government? Putting Historical Development Claims to the Test," *Journal of Public Administration Research and Theory,* vol. 7 (July 1997), p. 377.

57. Daniel P. Carpenter, *The Forging of Bureaucratic Autonomy: Reputations, Networks and Policy Innovation in Executive Agencies, 1862–1928* (Princeton University Press, 2001).

Chapter 2

1. Except as otherwise noted, quotations of Air Force personnel are based on interviews we conducted for this project from 1998 to 2001. See methodological appendix for details.

2. Walter J. Boyne, *Beyond the Wild Blue: A History of the U.S. Air Force* (St. Martins, 1997), p. 284.

3. For in-depth background on the period leading up to the Gulf War, see Richard Herrmann, "Coercive Diplomacy and the Crisis over Kuwait, 1990–1991," in Alexander L. George and William E. Simons, eds., *The Limits of Coercive Diplomacy* (Boulder, Colo.: Westview Press, 1994), pp. 229–64.

4. John A. Warden, III, *The Air Campaign: Planning for Combat* (Washington: National Defense University Press, 1988).

5. For a full historical rendering of this episode, see Benjamin S. Lambeth, *The Transformation of American Air Power* (Cornell University Press, 2000), chap. 4.

6. Michael O'Hanlon, *How to Be a Cheap Hawk* (Brookings, 1998), p. 57.

7. Boyne, *Beyond the Wild Blue,* p. 39.

8. It is significant that the collapse of this hitherto stable alliance occurred in the same period in which the functions of the disestablished Tactical Air Command and Strategic Air Command were combined in the newly established Air Combat Command. This huge restructuring, launched in 1992, eliminated at the major command level the organizational basis for the tactical-conventional versus strategic-nuclear split within the Air Force. Given that this split prompted the formation of close ties between the Army and the tactical Air Force, the birth of Air Combat Command called into question a good deal of the rationale for these ties.

9. A well-written popular account of these developments is Ben R. Rich and Leo Janos, *Skunkworks* (Boston: Little, Brown, 1994).

10. For a full treatment of these developments, see Lambeth, *The Transformation of American Air Power,* chaps. 5, 7, and 8.

Chapter 3

1. Except as otherwise noted, quotations of Air Force personnel are based on interviews we conducted for this project from 1998 to 2001. See methodological appendix for details.

2. This point was mentioned not only in our interview with Fogleman, but also in a recently published interview with the former chief conducted by a former Air Force historian. See Richard H. Kohn, "The Early Retirement of Gen. Ronald R. Fogleman, Chief of Staff, United States Air Force," *Aerospace Power Journal,* vol. 15, no. 1 (Spring 2001) (www.airpower.maxwell.af.mil/airchronicles/apj/apj01/spr01).

3. Walter J. Boyne, *Beyond the Wild Blue: A History of the U.S. Air Force* (St. Martins, 1997), p. 314.

4. Kohn, "The Early Retirement of Gen. Ronald R. Fogleman," p. 4.

5. Bruce W. Tuckman, "Developmental Sequences in Small Groups." *Psychological Bulletin,* vol. 63, no. 6 (1965): pp. 384–99.

6. Kohn, "The Early Retirement of Gen. Ronald R. Fogleman," p. 4.

7. On the circumstances leading to Fogleman's retirement in September 1997, see Kohn, "The Early Retirement of Gen. Ronald R. Fogleman."

Chapter 4

1. Except as otherwise noted, quotations of Air Force personnel are based on interviews we conducted for this project from 1998 to 2001. See methodological appendix for details.

2. Alan L. Gropman, "Air Force Planning and the Technological Development of Planning Process in the Post–World War Air Force—the First Decade (1945–1955)," in Harry R. Borowski, ed., *Military Planning in the Twentieth Century* (Washington: Office of Air Force History, 1984).

3. Thom Shanker, "Incentives Added for Pilots of Remote Predator Planes," *New York Times*, October 17, 2002, p. A18.

4. Federal Benchmarking Consortium (FBC), "Serving the American Public: Best Practices in Customer-Driven Strategic Planning," Study Report (February 1997), p. 164.

5. Amitai Etzioni, *The Active Society: A Theory of Societal and Political Processes* (New York: Free Press, 1968).

6. Etzioni, *The Active Society,* p. 283. William T. Gormley Jr., in his treatment of the rise of policy analysis in the U.S. government, associates this with the search for programmatic rationality and characterizes many of the key reform approaches as inspired by mixed scanning. He notes about the effects of the innovations, "Budgetmaking today is not entirely rational, but it's more rational than it used to be—no small achievement." See *Taming the Bureaucracy: Muscles, Prayers, and Other Strategies* (Princeton University Press, 1989), pp. 159, 170–71. Paul Light uses the term *liberation management* to describe such initiatives, including the more recent Government Performance and Results Act (GPRA); he notes they have stressed "strategic planning . . . particularly as it related to budget reform." See *The Tides of Reform: Making Government Work, 1945–1995* (Yale University Press), p. 39.

7. Secretariats designed to support strategic planning on the part of principals cannot consistently be relied on to close the gap if principals and, in this case, their deputies fail to develop coherent views of issues and the options for their resolution. See Colin Campbell, *Governments under Stress: Political Executives and Key Bureaucrats in Washington, London and Ottawa* (University of Toronto Press, 1983), pp. 342–43; and Colin Campbell, "Juggling Inputs, Outputs and Outcomes in the Search for Policy Competence: Recent Experience in Australia," *Governance*, vol. 14 (April 2001), p. 259.

Chapter 5

1. This fundamental claim mirrors that set forth in Gary Hamel and C. K. Prahalad, *Competing for the Future* (Harvard Business School Press, 1995).

2. This interpretation of strategic intent is heavily influenced by Mark H. Moore, *Creating Public Value: Strategic Management in Government* (Harvard University Press, 1995). However, Moore's discussion of strategic management in government is not as centrally concerned with managerial action keyed to a time frame of a decade or more.

3. Attached to this definition is a proviso that the policy argument would satisfy appropriate standards of policy and organizational analysis. For a discussion of craft norms of policy analysis, which is also relevant to organizational analysis, see Giandomenico Majone, *Evidence, Argument, and Persuasion in the Policy Process* (Yale University Press, 1989).

4. Eugene Bardach, *Getting Agencies to Work Together: The Practice and Theory of Managerial Craftsmanship* (Brookings, 1998).

5. "A small win is a concrete, complete, implemented outcome of moderate importance. By itself, one small win may seem unimportant. A series of wins at small but significant tasks, however, reveals a pattern that may attract allies, deter opponents, and lower resistance to subsequent proposals." Karl E. Weick, *Making Sense of the Organization* (Oxford: Blackwell, 2001), p. 431.

6. Drawing on experimental psychological research, Weick argues that public knowledge of an effort is a crucial committing condition.

7. Organizational constitution is a public administration concept that refers mainly to structural properties of the organization, as well as to customary practices of governance. Organizational cultural bias refers specifically to cultural theory; see Christopher Hood, *The Art of the State: Culture, Rhetoric, and Public Management* (Oxford: Clarendon, 1998). Installed base of strategic thinking is taken from Hamel and Prahalad, *Competing for the Future*. The policy subsystem is a political science concept, explained especially well in Frank R. Baumgartner and Bryan D. Jones, *Agendas and Instability in American Politics* (University of Chicago Press, 1994).

8. The infelicitous terms *groupness* and *gridness* come from cultural theory as developed by anthropologist Mary Douglas. She argues that the variability of an individual's involvement in social life can be adequately captured by two dimensions of sociality: group and grid. Groupness refers to the extent of an individual's incorporation into bounded units. The greater the incorporation, the more individual choice is subject to group determination. Gridness denotes the degree to which an individual's life is circumscribed by externally imposed prescriptions. The more binding and extensive the scope of the prescriptions, the less of life that is open to individual negotiation. See Michael Thompson, Richard Ellis, and Aaron Wildavsky, *Cultural Theory* (Boulder, Colo.: Westview Press, 1990), p. 5. See also Hood, *The Art of the State*.

9. The term *coordinate authority* is borrowed from Charles E. Lindblom, *Politics and Markets* (Basic Books, 1977). The term *strategic apex* is taken from Henry Mintzberg, *Designing Effective Organizations: Structures in Fives* (Englewood Cliffs, N.J.: Prentice-Hall, 1983).

10. The definitions are taken from Oliver Williamson, *Markets and Hierarchies* (New York: Free Press, 1976).

11. The notion of rules attaching to roles is presented in James G. March, *A Primer on Decision-making* (New York: Free Press, 1994).

12. This factor is closely related to the perspective on organizations fully elaborated in James G. March, *The Pursuit of Organizational Intelligence* (Oxford: Blackwell, 1999).

13. Albert Breton, *Competitive Government* (Cambridge University Press, 1998).

14. This list combines items drawn from such works as Hamel and Prahalad, *Competing for the Future;* Jacquelyn K. Davis and Michael J. Sweeney, *Strategic Paradigms 2025: U.S. Security Planning for a New Era* (Dulles, Va.: Brassey's, 1999); John W. Kingdon, *Agendas, Alternatives, and Public Policies,* 2d ed. (HarperCollins, 1995).

15. This kind of explanatory argument is typical of case-oriented research, where the aim is to understand the outcome of historical experiences or events. It is distinct from a statistical argument, which tries to explain the variance in dependent variables. See Charles C. Ragin, *The Comparative Method: Beyond Quantitative and Qualitative Strategies* (University of California Press, 1987).

16. These reports are available at http://www.whitehouse.gov/nsc/nss.pdf; http://www.dtic.mil/jcs/nms/.

17. Agile combat support and information superiority were conceptually more innovative. The core competency of rapid global mobility was not conceptually novel, but it had recently grown in importance with the end of the cold war and the reemergence of the Air Force as largely a garrison, expeditionary force, as against one primarily deployed in or near prospective theaters of war. This core competency was, in effect, stressed in the Rice-McPeak strategic vision, *Global Reach—Global Power.*

18. On this aspect of scientific management, see Mintzberg, *Designing Effective Organizations*; Gary Miller, *Managerial Dilemmas* (Cambridge University Press, 1992); Mauro Guillén, *Models of Management* (University of Chicago Press, 1993).

19. The idea of variants within hierarchism, as well as within other culture biases, is elaborately developed in Hood, *The Art of the State.*

20. This comparison may be somewhat misleading, insofar as the process of revisiting the vision was preceded by projects—such as the Aerospace Integration Task Force—that sought to refine and indeed challenge the *Global Engagement* vision. The revisiting effort was specifically oriented to consolidating these earlier projects. One of the reasons for the extended duration of the Fogleman-era Corona issues process was that similar projects ran parallel with it, rather than preceded it. A good example is the Alternative Air Forces studies. The comparison is not misleading insofar as the board of directors had a longer time to gel as a group before having to perform.

21. In the hierarchist culture of the Air Force (owing, in particular, to high gridness), it is appropriate for the highest officeholders to give much credence to the advice of the functional staffs with jurisdiction and expertise relevant to the subject at hand.

22. The political stream, taken from Kingdon, *Agendas, Alternatives, and Public Policies,* is part of a different model of policymaking than the policy subsystem, taken from Baumgartner and Jones, *Agendas and Instability in American Politics.* The latter puts more emphasis on the structural properties of policy subsystems than on factors, like the political and policy stream, that we regard as context in motion. Here, however, we relax this restriction and bring these contextual factors into the framework, under the heading "policy subsystem."

23. If we were to expand this list marginally, we would be inclined to list the organization's system of professional development. We are convinced, after many dozens of interviews, that the level of preparation of the individuals involved in strategic visioning contributed to the quality of the product. A distinguishing characteristic of the military services is their system for developing people, including those who are eventually selected for top positions.

Chapter 6

1. William W. Kaufmann, "The McNamara Strategy," in Alan A. Altshuler, ed., *The Politics of the Federal Bureaucracy* (Dodd, Mead and Company, 1968).

2. Kaufmann, "The McNamara Strategy," pp. 185–6.

3. Aaron Wildavsky, "Rescuing Policy Analysis from PPBS," *Public Administration Review,* vol. 29 (March–April 1969), pp. 189–202.

4. Wildavsky, "Rescuing Policy Analysis from PPBS," pp. 190–1.

5. Kaufmann, "The McNamara Strategy," p. 188.

6. William A. Niskanen, *Structural Reform of the Budget Process* (Washington: American Enterprise Institute, 1973), pp. 17–19, 55–57.

7. Richard Rose and B. Guy Peters, *Can Government Go Bankrupt?* (Basic Books, 1978).

8. Aaron Wildavsky, "From Chaos Comes Opportunity: The Movement toward Spending Limits in American and Canadian Budgeting," *Canadian Public Administration Review,* vol. 26 (Summer 1983), p. 181.

9. Paul Craig Roberts, *The Supply-Side Revolution: An Insider's Account of Policymaking in Washington* (Harvard University Press, 1984); and David Stockman, *The Triumph of Politics: How the Reagan Revolution Failed* (Harper & Row, 1986).

10. Colin Campbell, *Managing the Presidency: Carter, Reagan and the Search for Executive Harmony* (University of Pittsburgh Press, 1986), p. 156.

11. See James Dao, "Bush Sees Big Rise in Military Budget for Next Five Years," *New York Times,* February 2, 2002, p. A1; Bradley Graham, "Bush to Propose Sustained Rises in Military Spending," *Washington Post,* February 3, 2002, p. A6; Vernon Loeb, "New Weapons Systems Are Budget Winners," *Washington Post,* February 8, 2002, p. A29.

12. Thomas E. Ricks, "Joint Chiefs Aim Big Budget Request at Next President," *Washington Post,* June 5, 2000, pp. A1, A5.

13. Thomas E. Ricks, "Report: Pentagon Underfunded," *Washington Post*, September 15, 2000, p. A25.

14. See, for instance, Jerry Lewis and Jack Murtha, "Why the F-22 Fighter Plan Doesn't Fly," *Washington Post*, August 2, 1999, p. A19; Michael E. O'Hanlon, "The Plane Truth: Fewer F-22s Mean a Stronger National Defense," Policy Brief 53 (Brookings, September 1999).

15. Michael O'Hanlon, "The Hole in the Bush Defense Plan," *Washington Post*, November 5, 1999, p. A33.

16. Thomas E. Ricks, "Pentagon Study May Bring Big Shake-Up," *Washington Post*, February 9, 2001, pp. A1, A12.

17. Bradley Graham and Juliet Eilperin, "Air Force Tries to Save F-22 Jet," *Washington Post*, July 22, 1999, pp. A3, A8: Bradley Graham, "Navy Chief Promotes Missile Defense Role," *Washington Post*, February 28, 2000, pp. A1, A5; and F. Whitten Peters, "Are We Ready to Lose the Next Air War?" *New York Times*, July 24, 1999, p. A29.

18. Thomas E. Ricks, "For Pentagon, Asia Moving to Forefront," *Washington Post*, May 26, 2000, pp. A1, A28.

19. Greg Schneider, "Defense Industry Sees Gap in Both Candidates' Plans," *Washington Post*, October 19, 2000, p. A9.

20 .Thomas E. Ricks, "Space Is Playing Field for Newest War Game," *Washington Post*, January 29, 2001, pp. A1, A4.

21. Walter Pincus, "From Missile Defense to a Space Arms Race?" *Washington Post*, December 30, 2000, p. A2.

22. Joel D. Aberbach, Robert A. Putnam, and Bert A. Rockman, *Bureaucrats and Politicians in Western Democracies* (Harvard University Press, 1981); Colin Campbell, "The Political Roles of Senior Government Officials in Advanced Democracies," *British Journal of Political Science*, vol. 18 (April 1988); and Joel D. Aberbach and Bert A. Rockman, *In the Web of Politics: Three Decades of the U.S. Federal Executive* (Brookings, 2000).

23. Graham Scott, Peter Bushnell, and Nikitin Sallee, "Reform of the Core Public Service: The New Zealand Experience," *Governance*, vol. 3 (April 1989).

24. Jonathan Boston and Jane Pallot, "Linking Strategy and Performance: Developments in New Zealand," *Journal of Policy Analysis and Management*, vol. 16 (Summer 1997), p. 382.

25. Boston and Pallot, "Linking Strategy and Performance," p. 389.

26. Allen Schick, *The Spirit of Reform: Managing the New Zealand State Sector in a Time of Change*, report prepared for the State Services Commission and the Treasury (Wellington, New Zealand, 1996), pp. 3–4.

27. Schick, *The Spirit of Reform*, p. 43.

28. Colin Campbell, "Juggling Inputs, Outputs and Outcomes in the Search for Policy Competence: Recent Experience in Australia," *Governance*, vol. 14 (April 2001).

29. See, for instance, Aaron Wildavsky, *The Politics of the Budgetary Process*, 2d ed. (Boston: Little, Brown, 1974), pp. 207–08.

30. Headquarters U.S. Air Force, "AFRAP [Air Force Resource Allocation Process] Status Report" (United States Air Force, May 26, 2000).

31. AFCS Process Recce Team Report, "Air Force Corporate Structure," presentation to the secretary and the chief of staff of the Air Force, January 18, 2000.

32. Except as otherwise noted, quotations of Air Force personnel are based on interviews we conducted for this project from 1998 to 2001. See methodological appendix for details.

33. Vernon Loeb, "In the Air Force, Age and Upkeep Taking Off," *Washington Post*, August 12, 2001, p. A5.

34. Michael E. O'Hanlon, *Defense Policy Choices for the Bush Administration, 2001–05* (Brookings, 2001), p. 100.

35. Thomas Ricks, "Rumsfeld Mulls Two Options: Status Quo or 10% Military Cut," *Washington Post*, August 9, 2001, p. A4.

36. Thomas Ricks, "Review Fractures Pentagon," *Washington Post*, July 14, 2001, p. A1.

37. James Glanz, "Cast of Star Wars Makes Comeback in Bush Plan," *New York Times*, July 22, 2001, p. 6; Vernon Loeb, "Air Force Turns 747 into Holster for Giant Laser to Drill Missiles," *Washington Post*, July 22, 2001.

38. James Dao, "Much Maligned B-1 Bomber Proves Hard to Kill," *New York Times*, August 1, 2001, p. A1.

39. See, for instance, Thomas E. Ricks, "Bull's-Eye War: Pinpoint Bombing Shifts Role of GI Joe," *Washington Post*, December 12, 2001, pp. A1, A29; Eric Schmitt and James Dao, "Use of Pinpoint Air Power Comes of Age in New War," *New York Times*, December 24, 2001, pp. A1, B3.

40. See Dao, "Bush Sees Big Rise in Military Budget for Next Five Years;" Graham, "Bush to Propose Sustained Rises in Military Spending."

41. United States Air Force, *Strategic Plan*, vol. III (2000), p. 6.

42. Vernon Loeb, "Pentagon Says Homeland Defense Is Top Priority," *Washington Post*, October 12, 2001, p. A23.

43. Colin Campbell and John Halligan, *Political Leadership in an Age of Constraint: The Australian Experience* (University of Pittsburgh Press, 1992), pp. 147–49; Colin Campbell and Graham Wilson, *The End of Whitehall: Death of a Paradigm?* (Oxford: Blackwell, 1995), pp. 235–41.

Chapter 7

1. A UAV is defined as a self-propelled aircraft that sustains flight through aerodynamic lift. It is designed to be returned and reused, and it does not have a human on board. A UAV is nonlethal; its typical mission is to provide reconnaissance and surveillance.

2. A highly readable discussion of this system and its evolution is Linda Shiner, "Predator: First Watch," *Smithsonian Air and Space Magazine* (April–May 2001) (www.airandspacemagazine.com/asm/Mag/Index/2001/AM/prfw.html [March 2003]).

3. Dorothy Leonard-Barton, *Wellsprings of Knowledge* (Harvard Business School Press, 1995), pp. 91–110.

4. This section draws heavily on Thomas P. Ehrhard, "Unmanned Aerial Vehicles: A Comparative Study of Weapon System Innovation," Ph.D. dissertation, Johns Hopkins University, School of Advanced International Studies, June 2000. We are very grateful to Lieutenant Colonel Ehrhard for allowing us to make extensive use of his unpublished doctoral thesis.

5. The development of unmanned aerial drones for intelligence gathering purposes dates back to 1960, after a U-2 was shot down and its pilot, Francis Gary Powers, captured. In Vietnam, a total of 3,435 operational reconnaissance UAV sorties were flown between 1964 and 1975. See Richard M. Clark, "Uninhabited Combat Aerial Vehicles: Airpower by the People, for the People, but Not with the People," School of Advanced Airpower Studies, Maxwell Air Force Base, Alabama, June 1999, pp. 18–19.

6. Ehrhard argues that the budget slashing after the Cold War amounted to an abdication of tactical reconnaissance by all services, observing that "the services pointed to the National Reconnaissance Office (NRO) to pick up the slack using national assets, a task that the NRO was ill-prepared or configured to accomplish." (Ehrhard, "Unmanned Aerial Vehicles," p. 513.)

7. These issues came back to life after the Gulf War. Reflecting on Army, Navy, and Marine use of the Pioneer UAV in that conflict, the Department of Defense's final report on Desert Storm concluded that UAVs proved excellent at providing an immediately responsive intelligence collection capability. Issue momentum was enhanced in 1993 with the major Department of Defense study on tactical airborne reconnaissance and with the decision to set up the Defense Airborne Reconnaissance Office to manage defense programs related to this mission area. The issues' careers were possibly further advanced with the 1995 publication of a comprehensive study of air power in the Gulf War, which concluded that tactical airborne reconnaissance was deficient and characterized the hope that satellite systems could compensate for the shortfall as misplaced. (Quoted in Ehrhard, "Unmanned Aerial Vehicles," p. 505.)

8. They also saw UAVs in the same light as an earlier breakthrough innovation in airpower: during the Clinton administration, Perry had been midwife to the birth of the F-117 stealth fighter, which was revolutionary in being able to apply precision airpower with impunity. For historical background, see Ben R. Rich and Leo Janos, *Skunkworks* (Boston: Little, Brown, 1994). The authors describe Perry as the Carter administration's czar of research and development and godfather of the stealth fighter program (p. 302). Ehrhard argues that Perry, Deutsch, Lynn, and others

believed that the services had to be by-passed to achieve weapon systems innovation. More specifically, they believed that "the services' parochial blinders, hidebound nature, and appetite for gold plating left them unable to produce effective, cheap UAVs in a rapid fashion." Ehrhard, "Unmanned Aerial Vehicles," p. 504.

9. In an interview for this book, Ehrhard said that Fogleman made statements to the effect that "I am going to put my best pilots involved with Predator because if this system fails, it's not going to be because of my pilots." At the time, in the fall of 1995, the Army's Hunter UAV program was faltering, in part because of a string of three crashes attributable to human error. Ehrhard, "Unmanned Aerial Vehicles," p. 527.

10. The Army Chief of Staff ceded the medium-altitude UAV, Predator, in exchange for Air Force assurances that it would be responsive to Army battlefield reconnaissance requirements. Ehrhard, "Unmanned Aerial Vehicles," p. 546.

11. Except as otherwise noted, quotations of Air Force personnel are based on interviews we conducted for this project from 1998 to 2001. See methodological appendix for details.

12. The Corona issues process, as noted earlier, was designed to culminate in the fall of 1996, which would allow the Air Force to disseminate an updated strategic vision in the immediate run-up to the Quadrennial Defense Review, expected to start in early 1997.

13. As discussed in earlier chapters, the principle of buy-in of the strategic visioning process was meant to achieve shared understanding and collective endorsement of a particular body of strategic thinking, so that the Air Force's overall pattern of decisionmaking and policy entrepreneurship would display significant continuity despite the rotation of general officers through high-level positions and, especially, the turnover in chiefs every four (or fewer) years.

14. The use of GPS solved the perennial problem of achieving locational accuracy, which was a downfall of UAV programs in the 1980s, as discussed earlier.

15. Steve Aftergood, "RQ-1 Predator MAE UAV, FAS Intelligence Resource Program" (www.fas.org/irp/program/collect/predator.htm [October 22, 2001]), p. 3.

16. Shiner, "Predator: First Watch," p. 2. The radar builds a cumulative topological map of the ground that looks like a grainy black-and-white photograph.

17. Hansen was an employee with MITRE Corporation, a partner institution of the Electronic Systems Command (ESC). The quote is taken from "Experimentation: A Fast Way to Field New Technology," *MITRE Matters*, November 2000 (www.mitre.org/news/matters/11-00/mm_11-00_2.shtml [March 2003]).

18. Ibid.

19. Leonard-Barton, *Wellsprings of Knowledge,* pp. 111–34.

20. By November 1998, Predator had accumulated 10,400 hours of flying time ("Predator," *UAV Forum,* www.uavforum.com/vehicles/production/predator.htm). However, the program was criticized by the Defense Department's Directorate of Operational Test and Evaluation in its annual report to Congress for 1997. The

report stated that "for the first four months of the Joint Endeavor deployment, less than half of the tasked missions were completed as scheduled. Weather was the cause of low mission completion rates (wind, precipitation, icing, poor visibility). For the operational targets that were exploited, image quality in general fell short of the system design goals, but was considered usable by the warfighter." (Quoted on the webpage of the Air Force's Eleventh Expeditionary Reconnaissance Squadron, www.fas.org.irp/agency/usaf/usafe/16_af/16aew/406eabg/.../index.htm).

21. Shiner, "Predator: First Watch," p. 3.

22. Roxana Tiron, "Despite Doubts, Air Force Stands by Predator," *National Defense Magazine* (www.nationaldefensemagazine.org/article.cfm?ID=681), p. 2.

23. Shiner, "Predator: First Watch."

24. As an indication, the Air Force headquarters issued a formal policy statement, or instruction, promoting spiral development in 2000, based on a draft written by the Air Force's Electronic Systems Command located outside Boston. See Air Force Instruction 63-123: Evolutionary Acquisition for C2 Systems (April 1, 2000).

25. For a cautious assessment of spiral development, see Wayne M. Johnson and Carl O. Johnson, "The Promise and Perils of Spiral Acquisition: A Practical Approach to Evolutionary Acquisition," *Acquisition Review Quarterly,* vol. 9, no. 3 (Summer 2002), pages 175–88 (also available at www.dau.mil/pubs/arq/2002arq/JohnsonSM2.pdf [March 2003]).

Chapter 8

1. Except as otherwise noted, quotations of Air Force personnel are based on interviews we conducted for this project from 1998 to 2001. See methodological appendix for details.

2. At the time of the interview, Jumper was commander of Air Combat Command.

3. In the words of one respondent who espoused this perspective, "For the [space-based radar] system to work, you need to have lots of satellites up there. We're talking about twenty-five or thirty satellites. Once you have this capability, the military and deterrent effect for global operation is just enormous. . . . From the perspective of broader national security interests, the ability to leave in any adversary's mind the idea that anytime, anywhere, we can be watching what they're doing—and that we can act at great ranges and with great precision—puts teeth into the notion of conventional deterrence."

4. Amy Butler, "Jumper Said to Appease Space Community with 'Air and Space' Rhetoric," *Inside the Air Force,* March 8, 2002.

5. John A. Tirpak, "The Space Commission Reports," *Air Force Magazine,* vol. 4, no. 3 (March 2001) (http://www.afa.magazine/March2001/0301space.html).

6. The analytical importance of momentum to the analysis of practices in government is underscored in Eugene Bardach, *Getting Agencies to Work Together*

(Brookings, 1998). We also associate this perspective with Albert O. Hirschman; see, for instance, *The Strategy of Economic Development* (Yale University Press, 1958), and Albert O. Hirschman and Charles E. Lindblom, "Economic Development, R&D, and Policy-Making: Some Converging Views," in Albert O. Hirschman, ed., *A Bias for Hope* (Yale University Press, 1970).

7. The briefing has been reenacted for educational purposes, as part of a teaching case study. The CD and teaching case are available through the Center for the Analysis and Regulation of Risk at the London School of Economics and Political Science.

8. John Sparrow, *Knowledge in Organizations: Access to Thinking at Work* (London: Sage, 1998); and Ikujiro Nonaka and Hirotaka Takeuchi, *The Knowledge-Creating Company* (Oxford University Press, 1995).

Chapter 9

1. Joel D. Aberbach, Robert A. Putnam, and Bert A. Rockman, *Bureaucrats and Politicians in Western Democracies* (Harvard University Press, 1981), pp. 8–9.

2. Norton E. Long, "Bureaucracy and Constitutionalism," *American Political Science Review*, vol. 46 (September 1952), pp. 808–18.

3. Herbert Kaufman would represent the former camp; see "Administrative Decentralization and Political Power," *Public Administration Review*, vol. 29 (January–February 1969), pp. 4–5. Matthew Holden posed the latter scenario; see "Imperialism in Bureaucracy," *American Political Science Review*, vol. 60 (December 1966), p. 944.

4. Martha Derthick, *Policymaking for Social Security* (Brookings, 1978).

5. Martha Derthick, *Agency under Stress: The Social Security Administration in American Government* (Brookings, 1990), pp. 213–16.

6. William T. Gormley Jr., *Taming the Bureaucracy: Muscles, Prayers, and Other Strategies* (Brookings, 1989), p. 224.

7. Martha S. Feldman, *Order without Design: Information Production and Policy Making* (Stanford University Press, 1989), p. 141.

8. Joel D. Aberbach and Bert A. Rockman, *In the Web of Politics: Three Decades of the U.S. Federal Executive* (Brookings, 2000), p. 187.

9. Daniel P. Carpenter, *The Forging of Bureaucratic Autonomy: Reputations, Networks, and Policy Innovation in Executive Agencies, 1862–1928* (Princeton University Press, 2001), p. 363.

10. Donald F. Kettl, *The Transformation of Governance: Public Administration for Twenty-First Century America* (Johns Hopkins University Press, 2002).

11. Kettl, *The Transformation of Governance*, p. 166.

12. Kettl, *The Transformation of Governance*, p. 168.

13. Carpenter, *The Forging of Bureaucratic Autonomy*, pp. 353, 364.

14. Mark H. Moore, *Creating Public Value: Strategic Management in Government* (Harvard University Press, 1995), p. 294.

15. Moore, *Creating Public Value*, p. 301.

16. Eugene Bardach, *Getting Agencies to Work Together: The Practice and Theory of Managerial Craftsmanship* (Brookings, 1998), p. 321.

17. Derthick, *Agency under Stress*, p. 222.

18. Paul C. Light, *Tides of Reform: Making Government Work, 1945–1995* (Yale University Press, 1997), pp. 219 and 235.

19. Light, *Tides of Reform*, p. 221.

20. Carpenter, *The Forging of Bureaucratic Autonomy*, p. 354.

21. Sandford Borins, *Innovating with Integrity: How Local Heroes Are Transforming American Government* (Georgetown University Press, 1998), pp. 290–91; Carpenter, *The Forging of Bureaucratic Autonomy*, pp. 365–66.

22. Beryl A. Radin, citing former Navy Secretary Richard Danzig, strongly advocates organizational discernment as against personal prophecy, in setting a strategic vision. See Radin, *The Accountable Juggler: The Art of Leadership in a Federal Agency* (Washington: CQ Press, 2002), pp. 129–30; and Richard Danzig, Secretary of the Navy, Webb Lecture, presented at the National Academy of Public Administration, Washington, November 17, 2000.

23. Bardach, *Getting Agencies to Work Together*, pp. 306, 308.

24. Paul C. Light, *Thickening Government: Federal Hierarchy and the Diffusion of Accountability* (Brookings, 1995).

25. Patrick Wolf, "Why Must We Reinvent the Federal Government? Putting Historical Development Claims to the Test," *Journal of Public Administration Research and Theory*, vol. 7 (July, 1997), pp. 353–88.

26. Personal communication with Patrick Wolf, February 20, 2002.

Methodological Appendix

$\mathbf{A}$s noted in the preface, the Strategic Planning Directorate of the Air Force Staff funded the research for this book. Throughout the project, the deputy director of that office—initially Dr. Clark Murdock and later Mr. James B. Engle—served as our primary point of contact, offering guidance on how to proceed and assisting us in gaining access to potential respondents. We attempted in the course of the study to conduct interviews with all parties who contributed significantly to strategic planning itself and to the process of connecting strategic planning to the Air Force's assessment of its present and future programmatic commitments. This required that we interview officials not only in the Pentagon, but also in the major commands.

We tended to concentrate our interviews at the higher executive levels both in the Air Force and in the Department of the Air Force. Our sessions with serving officers included eight interviews with generals, twelve with lieutenant generals, seven with major generals, four with brigadier generals, thirteen with colonels, four with lieutenant colonels, and one with a major. We had three interviews with retired generals and one with a retired major general. In addition, we had six sessions with political appointees occupying positions that require Senate confirmation, twenty with members of the Senior Executive Service, and ten with consultants. We had more than one session with some of our respondents, and several of our meetings included individuals reporting to the principal respondent. We taped all of our interviews and then had them transcribed. Even sessions at the highest levels usually lasted about an hour, and many at lower levels stretched to or even exceeded two hours.

In addition to formal interviews with individuals, we benefited from extensive briefing sessions each time we visited a major command. These meetings included a wide range of officers—normally ranking from major to colonel—working not only in the planning and programming fields, but also in acquisitions and requirements. Usually, the top civilian officials in these areas would attend as well. In all commands, we were given the opportunity to discuss the course of our research with majors and lieutenant colonels who shared their thoughts on how efforts toward integrating planning and programming were playing out in practice. These sessions usually occurred over lunch, so they were not taped. However, the issues raised by the lower-ranking officers often provided grist for interviews with their superiors and generally informed our research.

Because the Air Force decided in the midst of the project to conduct another iteration of strategic planning, our interviews themselves went through two phases. The first involved ascertaining how the Fogleman round had unfolded and what the Air Force had accomplished from the associated exercises. The interview protocol for this stage is provided below. After the second iteration, we found it necessary to return to many respondents or interview new individuals because of the roles they were playing in the second round. This appendix thus also provides an example of the questions asked in these sessions, in which we focused on respondents' views of how the second round was unfolding.

Protocol for the First Round of Interviews

The protocol presented here was used as the guideline for our initial interviews with both military and civilian participants in the strategic visioning process. It represents more of a check list of the issues we addressed with respondents than a precise order of our questions in each session.

Respondent Information

Note: Information should be obtained for multiple positions if applicable.

Name: _____   Tenure in post: _____

Titles: _____   Service: _____

Ranks: _____   Branch of government: _____

Units: _____

Preliminary Remarks

Thank you very much for seeing us. As you know we are conducting a study of the Air Force's corporate strategic planning process over the past several years. We believe that the results of this research will serve two purposes. First, they will help provide a record of the strategic planning process, its consequences, and its legacy. Second, they will offer insights to those attempting to advance strategic planning either in other governmental organizations or in nongovernmental concerns.

For the sake of accuracy and the efficient use of your time, we would like to tape record this session. Is this all right with you?

We take pride in our ability over the years to protect the identity of our respondents. In some cases, however, a matter might be sufficiently sensitive that you do not want your reflections to appear in our book in any form. In such cases please say something like "this is strictly off the record" or ask us to turn off the tape recorder.

Since we are tracking a process that has unfolded over the past several years, I wonder if you could tell us when you first became aware of the corporate strategic planning process in the U.S. Air Force?

Interview Questions

1. May I ask you a few questions about your job at that time?
    a. What was your formal title at the time?
    b. (With supplementaries fill in the information of first page of interview schedule.)
    c. What specifically were your main responsibilities at the time?
    d. How did what you do relate to the roles of others in this service (for example, the Air Force), department (for example, the Department of Defence and other services), branch (for example, the White

House), and other branches of government (for example, Congress)?

e. Would you please give us an idea of who took the lead in the matters falling within your areas—was it yourself, someone else, or a combination of these?

2. (If now in a different job.) What about your current position?
    a. Repeat questions 1. a–e with reference to the second post.

3. Turning now to the strategic planning process beginning in the mid-1990s, were there action-forcing imperatives out there in the geopolitical environment?

4. What was the role of the political leadership?

5. Did personalities play a part?

6. How about institutional factors within or outside the Air Force?

7. Was anything happening to the Air Force culture or the types of people rising to key leadership roles?

8. Where were people going for models of what to do?
    a. Elsewhere in government?
    b. The business world?
    c. Were there other influences?

9. At the core, what focused peoples' attention?
    a. Issues of survival?
    b. Maximizing resources?
    c. Technological change?
    d. New geopolitical circumstances?
    e. A new ethos about public interest?
    f. If it was a combination of the above, could you please describe the blend?

10. How did the process actually unfold?
    a. How did it run from an institutional standpoint?
    b. Who were the key players? (Individual, institutional.)

    c.   What were their roles and how effectively did they fulfill these? (Individual, institutional.)

11. Did the entire exercise function coherently?

12. What roles did formal or informal group dynamics play?

13. What was the degree of personal and institutional interface with stakeholders outside of the Air Force? (Office of the Secretary of Defense, Joint Chiefs of Staff, other services, the White House, other departments, congressional players, and so forth.)

14. What effect did this have on the process and its outcomes?

15. What were the consequences of the strategic planning process?
    a.   What were some of the more important substantive decisions?
    b.   Were they coherent?
    c.   Did they stick?
    d.   Have they actually enhanced guidance?
    e.   Have they helped the Air Force bridge to the future?
    f.   Have they helped the alignment of plans, programs, and resources?
    g.   Have they been good for the country?

16. We would like to discuss more specifically the legacy that the process itself has left. Overall how would you characterize this legacy?
    a.   Has it changed the decisional infrastructure of the Air Force?
    b.   Has it changed the decisional culture?
    c.   Is it adaptable to changes in leadership and institutional roles?
    d.   Does it mesh with developments elsewhere in the arena? In the Army, Navy, and Marines? Among other stakeholders?

17. Looking back at the time when the first outputs from the corporate strategic planning process were generated, what were your thoughts about the process's likely shelf life and how this might be extended?

18. We would now like to shift the focus from the installation of the process to the last two years or so. Please tell us whether the nature of the process has changed, and if so, how.

    a.   Has this involved the substantive issues being addressed, or the rubrics of corporate strategic planning, or a mixture of these? (Probe for explanations.)

    b.   Have there been changes in the overarching context that have provoked adjustments in planning? (Political factors, technological issues, developments between the forces.)

    c.   What, if anything, has occurred within the Air Force to prompt changes in the process? (Institutional issues, leadership, personalities, cultural factors.)

19. Would you go so far as to say that the last few years have involved more than simply refinement of the process? If so, how?

20. Would it be accurate to say that developments in the past year or two have amounted to a new and substantially different iteration in the development of corporate strategic planning? Please elaborate on your assessment.

    a.   Specifically, what changes seem to justify this analysis?

    b.   Who were the main movers and shakers behind the adjustments?

    c.   Were there any institutional factors that came to the fore here?

    d.   Did developments in the Air Force culture play a role?

21. Stepping aside, has corporate strategic planning changed "the big picture" and how the Air Force fits within this?

    a.   Is the Air Force significantly further along in creating new core competences?

    b.   Has the process improved the alignment of its competences and budget requirements?

    c.   May the same be said in relation to its management requirements?

    d.   Has the process worked significant effects in the wider defense policy arena? Have these involved changes in the dynamics of deliberations about defense issues? Have these extended to the substantive matters which have emerged in the defense community?

22. Looking at the future from your perspective,

    a.   How far out do the most difficult questions seem to cluster?

    b.   Has strategic planning helped you (and the Air Force) grapple with the issues arising in that time frame? If so, how? If not, why not?

    c.   What, if anything, would you like to see changed in the process to optimize its utility?

23. May we end with just a few questions about yourself?
    a.   Could you tell us where you received your postsecondary education?
    b.   Could you outline briefly the various stages in your career path?

Thank you very much for cooperating with our research. Would you want to recommend any other participants in the process whom we might want to visit as part of this study? (Names and positions.)

Example of a Supplementary Interview Conducted during the Ryan-Peters Round

The following questions were used as the basis for a follow-up interview during the Air Force's second round of strategic planning. The respondent in this case was a major command commander.

1.   Our project initially focused on Gen. Ronald Fogelman's efforts to improve corporate strategic planning in the Air Force. The process culminated in the 1996 vision and the 1997 Long-Range Plan. Could you trace your participation in the 1996–97 process?

2.   Of course, one of General Fogelman's main concerns was the future role of the Air Force as a service. Is it your experience that the issues of greatest salience concerning the Air Force's future were effectively defined and addressed through the 1996–97 process? Please elaborate.
    a.   In reflecting on the strengths and weaknesses of the vision and the Long-Range Plan, what factors—for instance, personal, institutional, and process—played especially important roles in shaping these outputs?

3.   We know that General Fogelman believed very strongly that his process would allow the Air Force to envision its future and then backcast to current programmatic commitments in order to make critical adjustments in the allocation of resources. Would you say that the 1997 Air Force plan actually spawned this type of backcasting?

   a.   Can you point up ways in which backcasting has subsequently
        worked effects on resource commitments in the Air Force?
   b.   In so far as the plan and/or the budgeting process have fallen short,
        is this a good or bad thing?
   c.   What types of institutional alignments would be required for back-
        casting to have a stronger effect? For instance, how well does the
        link between planning and programming work? What about the
        relations between the Air Force Staff and the major commands?

4.   With respect to the institutionalization of corporate strategic planning
     in the Air Force, is this part of the Fogelman legacy?
   a.   Would you say that the players took time out between completion
        of the plan in spring 1997 and General Ryan's decision to reignite
        the planning process in fall 1998? If so, what brought this pause
        on?
   b.   Was it a natural occurrence in view of the intensity of the vision-
        ing/planning process?
   c.   Was some momentum lost?

5.   General Fogelman placed a strong emphasis on decisional machinery in
     the 1996–97 process—that is, with his heavy reliance on the board of
     directors and the Corona council. General Ryan once again worked
     through these bodies to produce the revised vision. Did General Ryan
     use these groups roughly the same as General Fogelman or differently?
   a.   Do you believe that General Ryan sought similar or different types
        of outputs from the two groups?

6.   Could you tell us a bit about how the 1999 iteration of the planning
     process has unfolded?
   a.   Do you believe it reignited because of internal issues, preparation
        for the next Quadrennial Defense Review, or some combination of
        the two?
   b.   Some observers have noted that the 1999 process has been less
        comprehensive in scope than the previous one. If so, has this pro-
        vided a more realistic paradigm for crafting the future of the Air
        Force, or has it meant that some crucial issues have been deferred
        to another time?

    c.   We have heard that secretary and chief wanted separate things out of the fall Corona. From your perspective, was this the case? If so, did the process and results sufficiently integrate the two?

    d.   Some respondents have characterized the results of the 1999 Corona conference as historic. Do you agree with this characterization? If so, why? If not, why not?

    e.   Are the legacies of the 1996 and 1999 Coronas complementary or layered?

7.   Did the 1999 iteration move the ball in the difficult task of aligning planning and programming?

    a.   Do you believe that as a result of the 1999 process, the Air Force will substantially alter the paths its follows to the future?

    b.   Concerning the headquarters 2002 initiative, what issues might it address that have come out of the experience of corporate strategic planning since 1996?

Index

ment, 60–61; on Rice's work, 28; Ryan's working style compared, 82–83, 87–88; space commission, 183; Widnall relationship, 21–22, 84

Fogleman round: carryover value, vii, 4–5, 63–74; connectivity issues, 220–24; doctrine issues summarized, 2–3; effectiveness factors, 108–13, 115–17; originating incentives, 35–36; process framework, 102–07, 108–13. *See also* Long-Range Planning Board of Directors; Predator

Fork-in-the-road decisionmaking, 25, 149–51, 231

Future Operational Concepts Division. *See* Aerospace Future Capabilities War Games

Futures games. *See* Aerospace Future Capabilities War Games

Future Years Defense Program (FYDP), 63

General Accounting Office (GAO), 16

General Atomics Aeronautical Systems, 161

Global Engagement: 1, 3, 71, 73; and Predator development, 156; and Ryan-Peters visioning success, 99, 118–19. *See also* Corona conference *(1996);* Long-Range Planning Board of Directors (Fogleman round); Space *entries*

Global Reach–Global Power, 27–29, 42–43

Global Vigilance, Reach, and Power, 1, 178. *See also* Corona conference *(1999);* Long-Range Planning Board of Directors (Ryan round)

Goldwater-Nichols Act, 39

Gordon, John, 46

Gore, Al, 4, 92

Gormley, William T., Jr., 217

Government Performance and Results Act (GPRA), 13, 16–17

Gridness characteristic, 104, 106

Guided incrementalism: and critical capa-

bilities, 146–48; emergence, 144–46, 212–13; and fork-in-the road issues, 149–51

Gulf War, 28–32, 33, 34, 36, 68

Handy, John, 50, 59, 142, 148

Hansen, Steve, 163

Hawley, Richard, 72

Heclo, Hugh, 10

Hitch, Charles J., 122

Hogan, Daniel, 143, 233

Horner, Charles, 31, 183

Incrementalism: as accepted theory, 12; AWACS example, 42, 158; and budgets, 130–31; mixed scanning compared, 78. *See also* Guided incrementalism

Information-based warfare: as core competency, 159–60, 167–68; Fogleman's introduction to, 38–40; futures games impact, 201–02, 203–04, 205, 206–07; with space operations, 33–35, 36

Innovations in American Government Awards, 19

Installed base of strategic thinking: and AITF performance, 176–77, 181; futures games, 118–19, 209; as organizational characteristic, 105, 106; and strategic intent consensus, 110–11; and visioning effectiveness, 118–19

Intelligence, military. *See* Information-based warfare

Iraq, 28–32

ISR. *See* Information-based warfare

Jeremiah, David, 202, 205

Johnson administration, 16

Joint Strike Fighter (JSF), 65, 137

Joint Vision 2010, 51, 52

Jumper, John P.: on air and space terminology, 184; critical capability planning, 147; transformation planning, 76, 172, 179–80; on UAVs, 164